HENRY MILLER was born in Manhattan in 1891, and attended elementary and high school in Brooklyn, where his family moved when he was one. The rest of his education has been informal, acquired through wide reading and through travel. His first published book, *Tropic of Cancer*, appeared in Paris in 1934, although he had written many stories and two novels before that time. He lived in France for ten years, returning to the United States at the beginning of World War II after he had made an eight months' trip through Greece which resulted in *The Colossus of Maroussi*. In the early 1940's with the American artist, Abe Rattner, Miller made a cross-country tour of the United States which is recorded in *The Air-Conditioned Nightmare* and *Remember to Remember*. Mr. Miller settled in Big Sur, California, in 1945, but now spends much time travelling throughout Europe. In 1958 he was elected to membership in the National Institute of Arts and Letters, and in 1961 was awarded a special citation of the Prix International des Editeurs on the occasion of the publication of *Tropic of Cancer* in the United States and Italy.

## ALSO BY HENRY MILLER

# the wisdom of the heart

## HENRY MILLER

A NEW DIRECTIONS PAPERBOOK

## TO RICHARD GALEN OSBORN

originally of Bridgeport, Connecticut, who rescued
me from starvation in Paris and set my feet in the
right direction. May Heaven protect him and guide
him safely to port.

First published as ND Paperbook No. 94, 1960

# ACKNOWLEDGMENTS

"Creative Death" was first published in *Purpose*, London; "The
Wisdom of the Heart" and "Seraphita" in *The Modern Mystic*,
London; "Reflections on Writing" and "Into the Future" in *Creative Writing*, Chicago; "Raimu" and "Tribute to Blaise Cendrars"
in the *T'ien Hsia Monthly*, Shanghai; "Benno, the Wild Man from
Borneo" and "The Enormous Womb" in *The Booster*, Paris; "The
Absolute Collective" in *The Criterion*, London; "The Eye of Paris"
in *Globe*, Minneapolis; "The Cosmological Eye" in *Transition*,
Paris; "Mademoiselle Claude" in *Americans Abroad*, Paris (ed. by
Peter Neagoe); "Balzac and His Double" in *Twice a Year*, New
York.

Printed in the United States of America

New Directions Books are published for James Laughlin by
New Directions Publishing Corporation
333 Sixth Avenue, New York 10014.

THIRD PRINTING

# CONTENTS

# CREATIVE DEATH

"I DON'T WANT my Fate or Providence to treat me well. I am essentially a fighter." It was towards the end of his life that Lawrence wrote this, but at the very threshold of his career he was saying: "We have to hate our immediate predecessors to get free of their authority."

The men to whom he owed everything, the great spirits on whom he fed and nourished himself, whom he had to reject in order to assert his own power, his own vision, were they not like himself men who went to the source? Were they not all animated by that same idea which Lawrence voiced over and over again—that the sun itself will never become stale, nor the earth barren? Were they not, all of them, in their search for God, for that "clue which is missing inside men," victims of the Holy Ghost?

Who were his predecessors? To whom, time and again before ridiculing and exposing them, did he acknowledge his indebtedness? Jesus certainly, and Nietzsche, and Whitman and Dostoievski. All the poets of life, the mystics, who in denouncing civilization contributed most heavily to the lie of civilization.

Lawrence was tremendously influenced by Dostoievski. Of all his forerunners, Jesus included, it was Dostoievski whom he had most difficulty in shaking off, in surpassing, in "transcending." Lawrence had always looked upon the sun as the source of life, and the moon as the symbol of non-being. Life and Death—like a mariner he kept before him constantly these two poles. "He who gets nearer the sun," he said, "is leader, the aristocrat of aristocrats. Or, he who like Dostoievski, gets nearer the moon of our non-being." With the in-betweens he had no concern. "But the most powerful being," he concludes, "is that which moves towards the as-yet-unknown blossom!" He saw man as a seasonal phenomenon, a moon that waxes and wanes, a seed that emerges out of primal darkness to return again therein. Life brief, transitory, eternally fixed between the two poles of being and non-being. Without the clue, without the revelation no life, but being sacrificed to existence. Immortality he interpreted as this futile wish for endless existence. To him this living death was the Purgatory in which man ceaselessly struggles.

Strange as it may seem today to say, the aim of life is to live, and to live means to be aware, joyously, drunkenly, serenely, divinely aware. In this state of god-like awareness one sings; in this realm the world exists as poem. No why or wherefore, no direction, no goal, no striving, no evolving. Like the enigmatic Chinaman one is rapt by the everchanging spectacle of passing phenomena. This is the sublime, the a-moral state of the artist, he who lives only in the moment, the visionary moment of utter, far-seeing lucidity. Such clear, icy sanity that it seems like madness. By the force and power of the artist's vision the static, synthetic whole which is called the world is destroyed. The artist gives back to us a vital, singing universe, alive in all its parts.

In a way the artist is always acting against the time-destiny movement. He is always a-historical. *He accepts Time absolutely*, as Whitman says, in the sense that any way he rolls (with tail in mouth) is direction; in the sense that any moment, every moment, may be the all; for the artist there is nothing but the present, the eternal here and now, the expanding infinite moment which is flame and song. And when he succeeds in establishing this criterion of passionate experience (which is what Lawrence meant by "obeying the Holy Ghost") then, and only then, is he asserting his humanness. Then only does he live out his pattern as Man. Obedient to every urge—without distinction of morality, ethics, law, custom, etc. He opens himself to *all* influences—everything nourishes him. Everything is gravy to him, including what he does *not* understand—*particularly* what he does *not* understand.

This final reality which the artist comes to recognize in his maturity is that symbolic paradise of the womb, that "China" which the psychologists place somewhere between the conscious and the unconscious, that pre-natal security and immortality and union with nature from which he must wrest his freedom. Each time he is spiritually born he dreams of the impossible, the miraculous, dreams he can break the wheel of life and death, avoid the struggle and the drama, the pain and the suffering of life. His poem is the legend wherein he buries himself, wherein he relates of the mysteries of birth and death—*his* reality, *his* experience. He

3

buries himself in his tomb of poem in order to achieve that immortality which is denied him as a physical being.

China is a projection into the spiritual domain of his biologic condition of non-being. To be is to have mortal shape, mortal conditions, to struggle, to evolve. Paradise is, like the dream of the Buddhists, a Nirvana where there is no more personality and hence no conflict. It is the expression of man's wish to triumph over reality, over becoming. The artist's dream of the impossible, the miraculous, is simply the resultant of his inability to adapt himself to reality. He creates, therefore, a reality of his own—in the poem—a reality which is suitable to him, a reality in which he can live out his unconscious desires, wishes, dreams. The poem is the dream made flesh, in a two-fold sense: as work of art, and as life, which is a work of art. When man becomes fully conscious of his powers, his role, his destiny, he is an artist and he ceases his struggle with reality. *He becomes a traitor to the human race.* He creates war because he has become permanently out of step with the rest of humanity. He sits on the door-step of his mother's womb with his race memories and his incestuous longings and he refuses to budge. He lives out his dream of Paradise. He transmutes his real experience of life into spiritual equations. He scorns the ordinary alphabet, which yields at most only a grammar of thought, and adopts the symbol, the metaphor, the ideograph. *He writes Chinese.* He creates an impossible world out of an incomprehensible language, a lie that enchants and enslaves men. It is not that he is incapable of living. On the contrary, his zest for life is so powerful, so voracious that it forces him to kill himself over and over. He dies many times in order to live innumerable lives. In this way he wreaks his revenge upon life and works his power over men. He creates the legend of himself, the lie wherein

4

he establishes himself as hero and god, the lie wherein he triumphs over life.

Perhaps one of the chief difficulties in wrestling with the personality of a creative individual lies in the powerful obscurity in which, wittingly or unwittingly, he lodges himself. In the case of a man like Lawrence we are dealing with one who glorified the obscurity, a man who raised to the highest that source and manifestation of all life, the body. All efforts to clarify his doctrine involve a return to, and a renewed wrestling with, the eternal, fundamental problems which confronted him. He is forever bringing one back to the source, to the very heart of the cosmos, through a mystic labyrinth. His work is altogether one of symbol and metaphor. Phoenix, Crown, Rainbow, Plumed Serpent, all these symbols center about the same obsessive idea: *the resolution of two opposites in the form of a mystery.* Despite his progression from one plane of conflict to another, from one problem of life to another, the symbolic character of his work remains constant and unchanged. He is a man of one idea: *that life has a symbolic significance.* Which is to say that life and art are one.

In his choice of the Rainbow, for example, one sees how he attempted to glorify the eternal hope in man, the illusion on which his justification as artist rests. In all his symbols, the Phoenix and the Crown particularly, for they were his earliest and most potent symbols, we observe that he was but giving concrete form to his real nature, his artist being. For the artist in man is the undying symbol of the union between his warring selves. Life has to be given a meaning because of the obvious fact that it has no meaning. Something has to be created, as a healing and goading intervention, between life and death, because the conclusion that life points to is death and to that conclusive fact man instinctively and persistently shuts his eyes. The sense of mystery, which is at the

5

bottom of all art, is the amalgam of all the nameless terrors which the cruel reality of death inspires. Death then has to be defeated —or disguised, or transmogrified. *But in the attempt to defeat death man has been inevitably obliged to defeat life, for the two are inextricably related.* Life moves on to death, and to deny one is to deny the other. The stern sense of destiny which every creative individual reveals lies in this awareness of the goal, this acceptance of the goal, this moving on towards a fatality, one with the inscrutable forces that animate him and drive him on.

All history is the record of man's signal failure to thwart his destiny—the record, in other words, of the few men of destiny who, through the recognition of their symbolic role, made history. All the lies and evasions by which man has nourished himself— *civilization*, in a word—are the fruits of the creative artist. It is the creative nature of man which has refused to let him lapse back into that unconscious unity with life which characterizes the animal world from which he made his escape. As man traces the stages of his physical evolution in his embryonic life, so, when ejected from the womb, he repeats, in the course of his development from childhood to old age, the spiritual evolution of man. In the person of the *artist* the whole *historical* evolution of man is recapitulated. His work is one grand metaphor, revealing through image and symbol the whole cycle of cultural development through which man has passed from primitive to effete civilized being.

When we trace back the roots of the artist's evolution, we rediscover in his being the various incarnations, or aspects of hero which man has always represented himself to be—king, warrior, saint, magician, priest, etc. The process is a long and devious one. It is all a conquest of fear. The question why leads to the question whither and then *how*. Escape is the deepest wish. Escape from death, from the nameless terror. And the way to escape death is to escape life. This the artist has always manifested through his creations. By living into his art he adopts for his world an intermediary realm in which he is all-powerful, a world which he dominates and rules. This intermediary realm of art, this world in which he moves as hero, was made realizable only out of the deepest sense of frustration. It arises paradoxically out of lack of power, out of a sense of inability to thwart fate.

This, then, is the Rainbow—the bridge which the artist throws over the yawning gulf of reality. The radiance of the rainbow, the promise it bespeaks, is the reflection of his belief in eternal life, his belief in perpetual spring, in continuous youth, virility, power. All his failures are but the reflection of his frail human encounters with inexorable reality. The mainspring is the dynamic impact of a will that leads to destruction. Because with each *realistic* failure he falls back with greater intensity on his creative illusions. His whole art is the pathetic and heroic effort to deny his human defeat. He works out, in his art, an unreal triumph—since it is neither a triumph over life nor over death. It is a triumph over an imaginary world which he himself has created. The drama lies entirely in the realm of idea. His war with reality is a reflection of the war within himself.

Just as the individual, when he arrives at maturity, evinces his maturity by the acceptance of responsibility, so the artist, when he recognizes his real nature, *his destined role*, is obliged to accept the responsibility of leadership. He has invested himself with power and authority, and he must act accordingly. He can tolerate nothing but the dictates of his own conscience. Thus, in accepting his destiny, he accepts the responsibility of fathering his ideas. And just as the problems which each individual encounters are unique for him, and must be lived out, so the ideas which germinate in

**7**

the artist are unique and must be lived out. He is the sign of Fate itself, the very symbol of destiny. For when, by living out his dream logic, he fulfills himself through the destruction of his own ego, he is incarnating for humanity the drama of individual life which, to be tasted and experienced, must embrace dissolution. In order to accomplish his purpose, however, the artist is obliged to retire, to withdraw from life, utilizing just enough of experience to present the flavor of the *real* struggle. If he chooses to *live* he defeats his own nature. He *must* live vicariously. Thus he is enabled to play the monstrous role of living and dying innumerable times, according to the measure of his capacity for life.

In each new work he re-enacts the spectacle of the sacrifice of the god. Because behind the idea of the sacrifice is the very substantial idea of the sacrament: the person incarnating the great power is killed, in order that his body may be consumed and the magic powers redistributed. The hatred for the god is the underlying motive of the worship of the god: it is based on the primitive desire to obtain the mysterious power of the man-god. In this sense, then, the artist is always crucified—in order to be consumed, in order to be divested of the mystery, in order to be robbed of his power and magic. The need of god is this hunger for a greater life: it is one and the same as the hunger for death.

We may image man forth as a sacred tree of life and death and if, further, we also think of this tree as representing not only the individual man, but a whole people, a whole Culture, we may begin to perceive the intimate connection between the emergence of the Dionysian type of artist and the notion of the sacred body.

Pursuing the image of man as tree of life and death, we may well conceive how the life instincts, goading man on to ever greater and greater expression through his world of form and symbol, his *ideology*, cause him at last to overlook the purely human, relative, fundamental aspects of his being—his animal nature, his very human body. Man rushes up the trunk of livingness to expand in a spiritual flowering. From an insignificant microcosm, but recently separated from the animal world, he eventually spreads himself over the heavens in the form of the great *anthropos*, the mythical man of the zodiac. The very process of differentiating himself from the animal world to which he still belongs causes him to lose sight more and more of his utter humanness. It is only at the last limits of creativeness, when his form world can assume no further architectural dimensions, that he suddenly begins to realize his "limitations." It is then that fear assails him. It is then that he tastes death truly—a *foretaste*, as it were.

Now the life instincts are converted into death instincts. That which before had seemed all libido, endless urge to creation, is now seen to contain another principle—the embrace of the death instincts. Only at the full summit of creative expansion does he become truly *humanized*. Now he feels the deep roots of his being, in the earth. Rooted. The supremacy and the glory and the magnificence of the body finally asserts itself in full vigor. Only now does the body assume its *sacred* character, its true role. The trinal division of body, mind and soul becomes a unity, a holy trinity. And with it the realization that one aspect of our nature cannot be exalted above another, except at the expense of one or the other.

What we call wisdom of life here attains its apogee—when this fundamental, rooted, sacred character of the body is divined. In the topmost branches of the tree of life thought withers. The grand spiritual efflorescence, by virtue of which man had raised himself to god-like proportions so that he lost touch with reality— because he himself was reality—this great spiritual flowering of Idea is now converted into an ignorance which expresses itself as the

9

mystery of the Soma. Thought retraverses the religious trunk by which it had been supported and, digging into the very roots of being, rediscovers the enigma, the mystery of the body. Rediscovers the kinship between star, beast, ocean, man, flower, sky. Once again it is perceived that the trunk of the tree, the very column of life itself, is religious faith, the acceptance of one's tree-like nature —not a yearning for some other form of being. It is this acceptance of the laws of one's being which preserves the vital instincts of life, even in death. In the rush upward the "individual" aspect of one's being was the imperative, the only obsession. But at the summit, when the limits have been felt and perceived, there unfolds the grand perspective and one recognizes the similitude of surrounding beings, the inter-relationship of all forms and laws of being—the organic relatedness, the wholeness, the oneness of life.

And so the most creative type—the individual artist type—which had shot up highest and with the greatest variety of expression, so much so as to seem "divine," this creative type of man must now, in order to preserve the very elements of creation in him, convert the doctrine, or the obsession of individuality, into a common, collective ideology. This is the real meaning of the Master-Exemplar, of the great religious figures who have dominated human life from the beginning. At their furthest peak of blossoming they have but emphasized their common humanity, their innate, rooted, inescapable humanness. Their isolation, in the heavens of thought, is what brings about their death.

When we look at an Olympian figure like Goethe we see a gigantic human tree that declared no "goal" except to unfold its proper being, no goal except to obey the deep organic laws of nature. That is wisdom, the wisdom of a ripe mind at the height of a great Culture. It is what Nietzsche described as the fusion in one being of two divergent streams—the Apollonian dreamer type and the ecstatic Dionysian. In Goethe we have the image of man incarnate, with head in the clouds and feet deeply rooted in the soil of race, culture, history. The past, represented by the historical, cultural soil; and the present, represented by the varying conditions of weather that compose his mental climate, *both the past and the present nourished him.* He was deeply religious without the necessity of worshipping a god. He had made himself a god. In this image of a Man there is no longer any question of conflict. He neither sacrifices himself to art, nor does he sacrifice art to life. Goethe's work, which was a grand confession—"life's traces," he called it—is the poetic expression of his wisdom, and it fell from him like ripe fruit from a tree. No station was too noble for his aspirations, no detail too insignificant for his attention. His life and work assumed grandiose proportions, an architectonic amplitude and majesty, for in both his life and his work there was the same organic foundation. He is the nearest, with the exception of da Vinci, to the god-man ideal of the Greeks. In him soil and climate were at their most favorable. He had blood, race, culture, time—*everything* with him. *Everything nourished him!*

At this lofty point when Goethe appears, when man and culture are both at peak, the whole of past and future spreads out. The end is now in sight, the road henceforth is downward. After the Olympian Goethe the Dionysian race of artists sets in, the men of the "tragic age" which Nietzsche prophesied and of which he himself was a superb example. The tragic age, when all that which is forever denied us makes itself felt with nostalgic force. Once again the cult of Mystery is revived. Once again man must re-enact the mystery of the god, the god whose fertilizing death is to redeem and to purify man from guilt and sin, to free him from the wheel of birth and becoming. Sin, guilt, neurosis—they are one and the same, the fruit of the tree of knowledge. The tree of life now becomes the tree of death. But it is always the same tree. And it is from this tree of death that life must spring forth again, that life must be reborn. Which, as all the myths of the tree testify, is precisely what happens. "At the moment of the destruction of the world," says Jung, referring to Ygdrasil, the world-ash, "this tree becomes the guardian mother, the tree of death and life, one 'pregnant.'"

It is at this point in the cultural cycle of history that the "transvaluation of all values" must set in. It is the reversal of the *spiritual* values, of a whole complex of reigning ideological values. The tree of life now knows its death. The Dionysian art of ecstasies now reasserts its claims. The drama intervenes. The tragic reappears. Through madness and ecstasy the mystery of the god is enacted and the drunken revellers acquire the will to die—to die creatively. It is the conversion of that same life instinct which urged the tree of man to fullest expression. *It is to save man from the fear of death, so that he may be able to die!*

To go forward into death! Not backward into the womb. Out of the quicksands, out of the stagnant flux! This is the winter of life, and our drama is to secure a foothold so that life may go forward once again. But this foothold can only be gained on the dead bodies of those who are *willing* to die.*

* Fragment from an unfinished book: *The World of Lawrence.*

# BENNO,
## THE WILD MAN FROM BORNEO

&middot;

BENNO HAS ALWAYS reminded me of a Sandwich Islander. Not only that his hair is by turns straight and kinky, not only that he rolls his eyes in delirious wrath, not only that he is gaunt and cannibalistic, positively ferocious when his breadbasket is empty, but that he is also gentle and peaceful as a dove, calm, placid, cool as a volcanic lake. He says he was born in the heart of London, of Russian parents, but that is a myth he has invented to conceal his truly fabulous origin. Anyone who has ever skirted an archipelago knows the uncanny faculty which the islands have of appearing and disappearing. Unlike the mirages of the desert these mys-

13

terious islands do truly disappear from sight, do truly bob up from the unknown depths of the sea. Benno is very much like that. He inhabits an archipelago of his own in which there are these mysterious apparitions and disparitions. Nobody has ever explored Benno with any thoroughness. He is elusive, slippery, treacherous, volatile, uncanny. Sometimes he is a mountain peak covered with bright snow, sometimes a broad glacial lake, sometimes a volcano spouting fire and brimstone. Sometimes he rolls quietly down to the ocean front and lies there like a big white Easter egg waiting to be dipped and packed away in a softly padded basket. And sometimes he gives the impression of one who was not born of a mother's womb, but of a monster who picked his way out of a hard-boiled egg. If you examine him closely you will see that he has rudimentary claws like the mock turtle, that he has spurs like the clover cock, and if you examine very closely you will discover that, like the dodo bird, he carries a harmonica in his right tubercle.

At an early age, a very early age, he found himself living the lonely, desperate life of a river pirate on a little island off Hell Gate. Near by was an ancient whirlpool, such as Homer speaks of in the Carthaginian version of the *Odyssey*. Here he perfected himself in that culinary art which was to stand him in good stead during his uninterrupted privations. Here he acquired a knowledge of Chinese, Turkestani, Kurd and the less well-known dialects of Upper Rhodesia. Here also he learned to write in that hand which only the prophets of the desert have mastered, an illegible hand which is nevertheless intelligible to students of esoteric lore. Here too he gleaned an inkling of those strange Runic patterns which he was later to employ in his pink and orange gouaches, his linoleum fretworks, his arboreal hallucinations. Here he studied the seed and the ovum, the unicellular life of the animalculae which daily filled his lobster-pots. Here the mystery of the egg first en-grossed him—not only its shape and balance, but its logic, its ordained irreversibility. Over and over again the egg crops up, sometimes in a china blue dream, sometimes counterpointed against the tripod, sometimes chipped and nascent. Exhausted by ceaseless exploration and investigation Benno is forever returning to the source and fundament, the center of his own vital creation: *the egg.* Always it is an Easter egg, which is to say a holy egg. Always the lost racial egg, seed of pride and strength, which has perdured since the destruction of the holy temple. When there is nothing left but despair Benno curls up inside his holy egg and goes to sleep. He sleeps the long schizophrenic sleep of the winter season. It is more congenial than running about looking for sirloin steaks and chopped onions. When he gets unbearably hungry he will eat his egg, and then for a time he sleeps anywhere, often right outside the Closerie des Lilas, beside the statue erected in memory of Marshal Ney. These are the Waterloo sleeps, so to speak, when all is rain and mud—and Blücher never appears. When the sun comes out Benno appears again—alive, chipper, perky, sardonic, irritable, buzzing, questioning, dubious, querulous, suspicious, effervescent, always in blue overalls and sleeves rolled up, always a quid of tobacco in the corner of his mouth. By sundown he has made a dozen new canvases, large and small. Whereupon it is a question of space, of frames, of nails and thumb-tacks. The cobwebs are shaken down, the floor washed, the ladder removed. The bed is left stranded in the middle air, the lice make merry, the cowbells ring. Nothing to do but to stroll out to Parc Montsouris. Here, denuded of flesh and raiment, deserted by human kind, Benno studies the tom-tit and the amarillo, makes note of the weather-cocks, tests the sand and gravel which his kidneys are constantly throwing out.

With Benno it is always a feast or a famine. Either he is loading crushed rock on the Hudson or he is painting the side of a house. He is a dynamo, a gravel-crusher, a lawn-mower, an eight-day clock all in one. Now and then he lies up for repairs; the barnacles are scraped off and all seams dried and caulked. Sometimes a new poop-deck is installed. You look at his progeny and it is Easter Island by the Count Potocki de Montalk: new landmarks, new monuments, new relics, all slithering in a Camembert green light which comes up out of the bulrushes. There he is, Benno, sitting in the midst of his archipelago, and the eggs running about like mad. Only new eggs this time, with new equilibrium, all frolicking on the greensward. Benno, fat and lazy, lolls in the sun with the gravy running down his chops. He reads last year's newspapers to while away the time. He invents new dishes made of sea-weed and scallops, or failing scallops, mountain oysters. All with a dash of Worcestershire sauce and fried parsley. At such moments he loves everything that is succulent and bursting with juice. He tears the bones apart and growls like a contented wolf. He ruts.

As I say, all to conceal his fabulous origin. To conceal his monstrous birth Benno goes about smooth of tongue, sleek as a puma after the rains, talking now of this thing, now of that. Inside him there is an unholy abracadabra fermenting. Strange equations form, queer plant-like growths, fungus, toadstools, marshmallow, poison ivy, the mandrake, the eucalyptus, all forming inside him in the hollow of the entrails in a sort of wild linoleum pattern which the burin will trace when he comes out of his trance. There are at least nine different cities buried beneath his midriff; the middle one is Samarkand where he had a rendezvous once with death. Here he passed through a glazing process which left the middle layers smooth and mirror-like. Here, when he is in utter desperation, he strolls among the stalagmites and stalactites, cool as a knife and garnished with mulberry leaves. Here he sees himself ever young, the Swiss Family Robinson kill-joy, the Gloomy Gus who played by Hell Gate's shores. Here the nostalgic odors are revived, the smell of the mud-crab and the sea turtle, all the tender little delicacies of the old island life when his palate was being formed.

Like the bed louse and the amaranthus Benno makes progress in all directions at once. At twelve he was a virtuoso; at sixty he will be fresh and dandy, a bright young bantam with a red comb and featherweight gloves, to say nothing of the spurs. Circular progress, but no speed and no errors. Between enthusiasms he dips like the leviathan to snooze on the ocean floor; or, like the sea-cow, he will come up to graze along the Labrador Coast. Now and then he flies from wall to wall—with the close-clipped wings which he invents during hibernation. Occasionally he grows a coat of fast Merino wool fresh from the Oberammergau region. In his right moments he trusts nobody. He was born with the evil eye, the acetylene torch planted in the middle of his forehead. When he is restive he champs and paws at the bit; when he is full of oats he kicks up his heels; when he is angry he snorts fire. Usually he is gentle and placid, still as the Hibernian in his fen. He loves the green meadows and the high hills, the kites soaring over Soochow, the gibbet and the rack; he loves the leather-heeled coolies, the oyster pirates, the wardens of Dannemora and the patient carpenter with his adze and footrule. Trigonometry he loves also and the intricate flights of the homing pigeon, or the fortifications of the Dardanelles. He loves everything that is complicated by rule and logarithm or spiced with fiery tinctures: he loves the styptic poisons, the triple bromides, the touch of carborundum, the glaze of mercurochrome. He loves light and space as well as champagne and oysters. But best of all he loves a rumpus, because then the wild man of Borneo comes out and the sky is full of prickly heat. In anger he will bite his own tail or bray like the donkey. In anger he is apt to cut off his own fetlocks. His anger comes up out of the groin, like jets of prussic acid. It puts a clean coat of varnish over his work, his loves, his friendships. It is the heraldic emblem, the tarantula which you will find embroidered on all his nightshirts, on his socks and even his cuff-buttons. Bright, feathery anger which he wears like a plume. It becomes him like an emolument, or an emulsion.

Such is Denno, as I have always known him and found him to be. A sturdy cutlass with a Penobscot mien and the swagger-gait of a caballero. He will go far, unless he is cut down by the sword. He belongs to the inky peninsulas, the open waterways, the Culebra Cuts. Like the squid he has no known origin, stemming rather from pride and arrogance, from aqueous depths and clabby footholds. He marks off his own precincts and defends his terrain like a saber-toothed tiger. He adopts the protective coloration of the zebra and if necessary can lie in the tall grass for aeons of time. Basically he is volcanic ash, immiscible in water, incorruptible and slow to rust. He is of the old line of Pelagians, the ridge-runners who traveled over the sunken Andes to found a Mexican world. He is tough as an old turkey, but warm-hearted and inhumanly tender. A sort of wild man from Borneo with central heating, spring mattress, castors and a boomerang in his left hand.

# REFLECTIONS ON WRITING

KNUT HAMSUN once said, in response to a questionnaire, that he wrote to kill time. I think that even if he were sincere in stating it thus he was deluding himself. Writing, like life itself, is a voyage of discovery. The adventure is a metaphysical one: it is a way of approaching life indirectly, of acquiring a total rather than a partial view of the universe. The writer lives between the upper and lower worlds: he takes the path in order eventually to become that path himself.

I began in absolute chaos and darkness, in a bog or swamp of ideas and emotions and experiences. Even now I do not consider myself a writer, in the ordinary sense of the word. I am a man telling the story of his life, a process which appears more and more inexhaustible as I go on. Like the world-evolution, it is endless. It is a turning inside out, a voyaging through X dimensions, with the result that somewhere along the way one discovers that what one has to tell is not nearly so important as the telling itself. It is this quality about all art which gives it a metaphysical hue, which lifts it out of time and space and centers or integrates it to the whole cosmic process. It is this about art which is "therapeutic": significance, purposelessness, infinitude.

From the very beginning almost I was deeply aware that there is no goal. I never hope to embrace the whole, but merely to give in each separate fragment, each work, the feeling of the whole as I go on, because I am digging deeper and deeper into life, digging deeper and deeper into past and future. With the endless burrowing a certitude develops which is greater than faith or belief. I become more and more indifferent to my fate, as writer, and more and more certain of my destiny as man.

I began assiduously examining the style and technique of those whom I once admired and worshipped: Nietzsche, Dostoievski, Hamsun, even Thomas Mann, whom today I discard as being a skillful fabricator, a brick-maker, an inspired jackass or draught-horse. I imitated every style in the hope of finding the clue to the gnawing secret of how to write. Finally I came to a dead end, to a despair and desperation which few men have known, because there was no divorce between myself as writer and myself as man: to fail as a writer meant to fail as a man. And I failed. I realized that I was nothing—less than nothing—a minus quantity. It was at this point, in the midst of the dead Sargasso Sea, so to speak, that I really began to write. I began from scratch, throwing everything overboard, even those whom I most loved. Immediately I heard my own voice I was enchanted: the fact that it was a separate, distinct, unique voice sustained me. It didn't matter to me if what I wrote should be considered bad. Good and bad dropped out of my vocabulary. I jumped with two feet into the realm of aesthetics, the non-moral, non-ethical, non-utilitarian realm of art. My life itself became a work of art. I had found a voice, I was whole again. The experience was very much like what we read of in connection with the lives of Zen initiates. My huge failure was like the recapitulation of the experience of the race: I had to grow foul with knowledge, realize the futility of everything, smash everything, grow desperate, then humble, then sponge myself off the slate, as it were, in order to recover my authenticity. I had to arrive at the brink and then take a leap in the dark.

I talk now about Reality, but I know there is no getting at it, leastwise by writing. I learn less and realize more: I learn in some different, more subterranean way. I acquire more and more the gift of immediacy. I am developing the ability to perceive, apprehend, analyze, synthesize, categorize, inform, articulate—all at once. The structural element of things reveals itself more readily to my eye. I eschew all clear cut interpretations: with increasing simplification the mystery heightens. What I know tends to become more and more unstatable. I live in certitude, a certitude which is not dependent upon proofs or faith. I live completely for myself, without the least egotism or selfishness. I am living out my share of life and thus abetting the scheme of things. I further the development, the enrichment, the evolution and the devolution of the cosmos, every day in every way. I give all I have to give, voluntarily, and take as much as I can possibly ingest. I am a prince and a pirate at the same time. I am the equals sign, the spiritual counterpart of the sign Libra which was wedged into the original Zodiac by separating Virgo from Scorpio. I find that there is plenty of room in the world for everybody—great interspatial depths, great ego universes, great islands of repair, for whoever attains to individuality. On the surface, where the historical battles rage, where everything is interpreted in terms of money and power, there may be crowding, but life only begins when one drops below the surface, when one gives up the struggle, sinks and disappears from sight. Now I can as easily not write as write: there is no longer any compulsion, no longer any therapeutic aspect to it. Whatever I do is done out of sheer joy: I drop my fruits like a ripe tree. What the general reader or the critic makes of it is not my concern. I am not establishing values: I defecate and nourish. There is nothing more to it.

This condition of sublime indifference is a logical development of the egocentric life. I lived out the social problem by dying: the real problem is not one of getting on with one's neighbor or of contributing to the development of one's country, but of discovering one's destiny, of making a life in accord with the deep-centered rhythm of the cosmos. To be able to use the word cosmos boldly, to use the word soul, to deal in things "spiritual"—and to shun definitions, alibis, proofs, duties. Paradise is everywhere and every road, if one continues along it far enough, leads to it. One can only go forward by going backward and then sideways and then up and then down. There is no progress: there is perpetual movement, displacement, which is circular, spiral, endless. Every man has his own destiny: the only imperative is to follow it, to accept it, no matter where it lead him.

I haven't the slightest idea what my future books will be like, even the one immediately to follow. My charts and plans are the slenderest sort of guides: I scrap them at will, I invent, distort, deform, lie, inflate, exaggerate, confound and confuse as the mood seizes me. I obey only my own instincts and intuitions. I know nothing in advance. Often I put down things which I do not understand myself, secure in the knowledge that later they will become clear and meaningful to me. I have faith in the man who is writing, who is myself, the writer. I do not believe in words, no matter if strung together by the most skillful man: I believe in language, which is something beyond words, something which words give only an inadequate illusion of. Words do not exist separately, except in the minds of scholars, etymologists, philologists, etc. Words divorced from language are dead things, and yield no secrets. A man is revealed in his style, the language which he has created for himself. To the man who is pure at heart I believe that everything is as clear as a bell, even the most esoteric scripts. For such a man there is always mystery, but the mystery is not mysterious, it is logical, natural, ordained, and implicitly accepted. Understanding is not a piercing of the mystery, but an acceptance of it, a living blissfully with it, in it, through and by it. I would like my words to flow along in the same way that the world flows along, a serpentine movement through incalculable dimensions, axes, latitudes, climates, conditions. I accept a priori my inability to realize such an ideal. It does not bother me in the least. In the ultimate sense, the world itself is pregnant with failure, is the perfect manifestation of imperfection, of the consciousness of failure. In the realization of this, failure is itself eliminated. Like the primal spirit of the universe, like the unshakable Absolute, the One, the All, the creator, i.e., the artist, expresses himself by and through imperfection. It is the stuff of life, the very sign of livingness. One gets nearer to the heart of truth, which I suppose is the ultimate aim of the writer, in the measure that he ceases to struggle, in the measure that he abandons the will. The great writer is the very symbol of life, of the non-perfect. He moves effortlessly, giving the illusion of perfection, from some unknown center which is certainly not the brain center but which is definitely a center, a center connected with the rhythm of the whole universe and consequently as sound, solid, unshakable, as durable, defiant, anarchic, purposeless, as the universe itself. Art teaches nothing, except the significance of life. The great work must inevitably be obscure, except to the very few, to those who like the author himself are initiated into the mysteries. Communication then is secondary: it is perpetuation which is important. For this only one good reader is necessary.

If I am a revolutionary, as has been said, it is unconsciously. I am not in revolt against the world order. "I revolutionize," as Blaise Cendrars said of himself. There is a difference. I can as well live on the minus side of the fence as on the plus side. Actually I believe myself to be just above these two signs, providing a ratio between them which expresses itself plastically, non-ethically, in writing. I believe that one has to pass beyond the sphere and influence of art. Art is only a means to life, to the life more abundant. It is not in itself the life more abundant. It merely points the way, something which is overlooked not only by the public, but very often by the artist himself. In becoming an end it defeats itself. Most artists are defeating life by their very attempt to grapple with it. They have split the egg in two. All art, I firmly believe, will one day disappear. But the artist will remain, and life itself will become not "an art," but art, i.e., will definitely and for all time usurp the field. In any true sense we are certainly not yet alive. We are no longer animals, but we are certainly not yet men. Since the dawn of art every great artist has been dinning that into us, but few are they who have understood it. Once art is really accepted it will cease to be. It is only a substitute, a symbol-language, for something which can be seized directly. But for that to become possible man must become thoroughly religious, not a believer, but a prime mover, a god in fact and deed. He will become that inevitably. And of all the detours along this path

24

art is the most glorious, the most fecund, the most instructive. The artist who becomes thoroughly aware consequently ceases to be one. And the trend is towards awareness, towards that blinding consciousness in which no present form of life can possibly flourish, not even art.

To some this will sound like mystification, but it is an honest statement of my present convictions. It should be borne in mind, of course, that there is an inevitable discrepancy between the truth of the matter and what one thinks, even about himself: but it should also be borne in mind that there exists an equal discrepancy between the judgment of another and this same truth. Between subjective and objective there is no vital difference. Everything is illusive and more or less transparent. All phenomena, including man and his thoughts about himself, are nothing more than a movable, changeable alphabet. There are no solid facts to get hold of. Thus, in writing, even if my distortions and deformations be deliberate, they are not necessarily less near to the truth of things. One can be absolutely truthful and sincere even though admittedly the most outrageous liar. Fiction and invention are of the very fabric of life. The truth is no way disturbed by the violent perturbations of the spirit.

Thus, whatever effects I may obtain by technical device are never the mere results of technique, but the very accurate registering by my seismographic needle of the tumultuous, manifold, mysterious and incomprehensible experiences which I have lived through and which, in the process of writing, are lived through again, differently, perhaps even more tumultuously, more mysteriously, more incomprehensibly. The so-called core of solid fact, which forms the point of departure as well as repair, is deeply embedded in me: I could not possibly lose it, alter it, disguise it, try as I may. And yet it *is* altered, just as the face of the world is altered, with each moment that we breathe. To record it then, one must give a double illusion—one of arrestation and one of flow. It is this dual trick, so to speak, which gives the illusion of falsity: it is this lie, this fleeting, metamorphic mask, which is of the very essence of art. One anchors oneself in the flow: one adopts the lying mask in order to reveal the truth.

I have often thought that I should like one day to write a book explaining how I wrote certain passages in my books, or perhaps just one passage. I believe I could write a good-sized book on just one small paragraph selected at random from my work. A book about its inception, its genesis, its metamorphosis, its accouchement, of the time which elapsed between the birth of the idea and its recording, the time it took to write it, the thoughts I had between times while writing it, the day of the week, the state of my health, the condition of my nerves, the interruptions that occurred, those of my own volition and those which were forced upon me, the multifarious varieties of expression which occurred to me in the process of writing, the alterations, the point where I left off and in returning, completely altered the original trend, or the point where I skillfully left off, like a surgeon making the best of a bad job, intending to return and resume some time later, but never doing so, or else returning and continuing the trend unconsciously some few books later when the memory of it had completely vanished. Or I might take one passage against another, passages which the cold eye of the critic seizes on as examples of this or that, and utterly confound them, the analytical-minded critics, by demonstrating how a seemingly effortless piece of writing was achieved under great duress whereas another difficult, labyrinthian passage was written like a breeze, like a geyser erupting. Or I could show how a passage originally shaped itself when in bed, how it became transformed upon arising, and again transformed at the moment of sitting down to record it. Or I could produce my scratch pad to show how the most remote, the most artificial stimulus produced a warm, life-like human flower. I could produce certain words discovered by hazard while riffling the pages of a book, show how they set me off—but who on earth could ever guess how, in what manner, they were to set me off? All that the critics write about a work of art, even at the best, even when most sound, convincing, plausible, even when done with love, which is seldom, is as nothing compared to the actual mechanics, the real genetics of a work of art. I remember my work, not word for word, to be sure, but in some more accurate, trustworthy way; my whole work has come to resemble a terrain of which I have made a thorough, geodetic survey, not from a desk, with pen and ruler, but by touch, by getting down on all fours, on my stomach, and crawling over the ground inch by inch, and this over an endless period of time in all conditions of weather. In short, I am as close to the work now as when I was in the act of executing it—closer perhaps. The conclusion of a book was never anything more than a shift of bodily position. It might have ended in a thousand different ways. No single part of it is finished off: I could resume the narrative at any point, carry on, lay canals, tunnels, bridges, houses, factories, stud it with other inhabitants, other fauna and flora, all equally true to fact. I have no beginning and no ending, actually. Just as life begins at any moment, through an act of realization, so the work. But each beginning, whether of book, page, paragraph, sentence or phrase, marks a vital connection, and it is in the vitality, the durability, the timelessness and changelessness of the thoughts and events that I plunge anew each time. Every line and word is vitally connected with my life, my life only, be it in the form of deed, event, fact, thought, emo-

27

tion, desire, evasion, frustration, dream, revery, vagary, even the unfinished nothings which float listlessly in the brain like the snapped filaments of a spider's web. There is nothing really vague or tenuous—even the nothingnesses are sharp, tough, definite, durable. Like the spider I return again and again to the task, conscious that the web I am spinning is made of my own substance, that it will never fail me, never run dry.

In the beginning I had dreams of rivaling Dostoievski. I hoped to give to the world huge, labyrinthian soul struggles which would devastate the world. But before very far along I realized that we had evolved to a point far beyond that of Dostoievski—beyond in the sense of degeneration. With us the soul problem has disappeared, or rather presents itself in some strangely distorted chemical guise. We are dealing with crystalline elements of the dispersed and shattered soul. The modern painters express this state or condition perhaps even more forcibly than the writer: Picasso is the perfect example of what I mean. It was quite impossible for me, therefore, to think of writing novels; equally unthinkable to follow the various blind alleys represented by the various literary movements in England, France and America. I felt compelled, in all honesty, to take the disparate and dispersed elements of our life—the soul life, not the cultural life—and manipulate them through my own personal mode, using my own shattered and dispersed ego as heartlessly and recklessly as I would the flotsam and jetsam of the surrounding phenomenal world. I have never felt any antagonism for or anxiety over the anarchy represented by the prevailing forms of art; on the contrary, I have always welcomed the dissolving influences. In an age marked by dissolution, liquidation seems to me a virtue, nay a moral imperative. Not only have I never felt the least desire to conserve, bolster up or buttress anything, but I might say that I have always looked upon decay as being just as wonderful and rich an expression of life as growth.

I think I should also confess that I was driven to write because it proved to be the only outlet open to me, the only task worthy of my powers. I had honestly tried all the other roads to freedom. I was a self-willed failure in the so-called world of reality, not a failure because of lack of ability. Writing was not an "escape," a means of evading the every day reality: on the contrary, it meant a still deeper plunge into the brackish pool—a plunge to the source where the waters were constantly being renewed, where there was perpetual movement and stir. Looking back upon my career, I see myself as a person capable of undertaking almost any task, any vocation. It was the monotony and sterility of the other outlets which drove me to desperation. I demanded a realm in which I should be both master and slave at the same time: the world of art is the only such realm. I entered it without any apparent talent, a thorough novice, incapable, awkward, tongue-tied, almost paralyzed by fear and apprehensiveness. I had to lay one brick on another, set millions of words to paper before writing one real, authentic word dragged up from my own guts. The facility of speech which I possessed was a handicap; I had all the vices of the educated man. I had to learn to think, feel and see in a totally new fashion, in an uneducated way, in my own way, which is the hardest thing in the world. I had to throw myself into the current, knowing that I would probably sink. The great majority of artists are throwing themselves in with life-preservers around their necks, and more often than not it is the life-preserver which sinks them. Nobody can drown in the ocean of reality who voluntarily gives himself up to the experience. Whatever there be of progress in life comes not through adaptation but through daring, through obeying the blind urge. "No daring is fatal," said

René Crevel, a phrase which I shall never forget. The whole logic of the universe is contained in daring, i.e., in creating from the flimsiest, slenderest support. In the beginning this daring is mistaken for will, but with time the will drops away and the automatic process takes its place, which again has to be broken or dropped and a new certitude established which has nothing to do with knowledge, skill, technique or faith. By daring one arrives at this mysterious X position of the artist, and it is this anchorage which no one can describe in words but yet subsists and exudes from every line that is written.

# THE WISDOM OF THE HEART

EVERY BOOK by an analyst gives us, in addition to the philosophy underlying his therapeutic, a glimpse into the nature of the analyst's own problem vis-à-vis life. The very fact of writing a book, indeed, is a recognition on the part of the analyst of the falsity of the patient-versus-analyst situation. In attempting, through the educative method, to enlarge his field of influence, the analyst is tacitly informing us of his desire to relinquish the unnecessary role of healer which has been thrust upon him. Though in fact he repeats every day to his patients the truth that they must heal themselves, actually what happens is that the list of patients grows with terrifying rapidity, so that sometimes the healer is obliged to seek another healer himself. Some analysts are just as pitiful and harassed specimens of humanity as the patients who come to them for relief. Many of them have confused the legitimate acceptance of a role with immolation, or vain sacrifice. Instead of exposing the secret of health and balance by example, they elect to adopt the lazier course, usually a disastrous one, of transmitting the secret to their patients. Instead of remaining human, they seek to cure and convert, to become life-giving saviors, only to find in the end that they have crucified themselves. If Christ died on the cross to inculcate the notion of sacrifice, it was to give significance to this inherent law of life, and not to have men follow his example. "Crucifixion is the law of life," says Howe, and it is true, but it must be understood symbolically, not literally.

Throughout his books* it is the indirect or Oriental way of life which he stresses, and this attitude, it may also be said, is that of art. The art of living is based on rhythm, on give and take, ebb and flow, light and dark, life and death. By acceptance of all the aspects of life, good and bad, right and wrong, yours and mine, the static, defensive life, which is what most people are cursed with, is converted into a dance, "the dance of life," as Havelock Ellis called it. The real function of the dance is—metamorphosis. One can dance to sorrow or to joy; one can even dance abstractly, as Helba Huara proved to the world. But the point is that, by the mere act of dancing, the elements which compose it are transformed; the dance is an end in itself, just like life. The acceptance of the situation, any situation, brings about a flow, a rhythmic impulse towards self-expression. To relax is, of course, the first thing a dancer has to learn. It is also the first thing

* *I and Me; Time and the Child; War Dance.* By E. Graham Howe.

a patient has to learn when he confronts the analyst. It is the first thing any one has to learn in order to live. It is extremely difficult, because it means surrender, full surrender. Howe's whole point of view is based on this simple, yet revolutionary idea of full and unequivocal surrender. It is the religious view of life: the *positive* acceptance of pain, suffering, defeat, misfortune, and so on. It is the long way round, which has always proved to be the shortest way after all. It means the assimilation of experience, fulfillment through obedience and discipline: the curved span of time through natural growth rather than the speedy, disastrous short-cut. This is the path of wisdom, and the one that must be taken eventually, because all the others only lead to it.

Few books dealing with wisdom—or shall I say, *the art of living?*—are so studded with profundities as these three books. The professional thinker is apt to look at them askance because of the utter simplicity of the author's statements. Unlike the analyst, the professional thinker seldom enjoys the opportunity of seeing his theories put to the test. With the analyst thinking is always vital, as well as an every-day affair. He is being put to the test every moment of his life. In the present case we are dealing with a man for whom writing is a stolen luxury, a fact which could be highly instructive to many writers who spend hours trying to squeeze out a thought.

Howe looks at the world as it is now, this moment. He sees it very much as he would a patient coming to him for treatment. "The truth is, we are sick," he says, and not only that, but— "we are sick of being sick." If there is something wrong, he infers, it is not a something which can be driven out with a stick, or a bayonet. The remedy is metaphysically achieved, not therapeutically: the cure does not lie in finding a cause and rooting it out. "It is as if we change the map of life itself by changing our attitude towards it," says Howe. This is an eternal sort of gymnastics, known to all wise men, which lies at the very root of metaphysics.

Life, as we all know, is conflict, and man, being part of life, is himself an expression of conflict. If he recognizes the fact and accepts it, he is apt, despite the conflict, to know peace and to enjoy it. But to arrive at this end, which is only a beginning (for we haven't begun to live yet!), man has got to learn the doctrine of acceptance, that is, of unconditional surrender, which is love. And here I must say that I think the author goes beyond any theory of life yet enunciated by the analysts; here he reveals himself as something more than a healer, reveals himself as an artist of life, a man capable of choosing the most perilous course in the certitude of faith. *Faith in life*, let me quickly add—a faith free and flexible, equal to any emergency and broad enough to include death, as well as other so-called evils. For in this broad and balanced view of life death appears neither as "the last enemy" nor the "end"; if the healer has a role, as he points out, it is "to play the part of gynaecologist to death." (For further delectation the reader might see the Tibetan *Book of the Dead*.)

The whole fourth-dimensional view of reality, which is Howe's metaphysic, hinges on this understanding of acceptance. The fourth element is Time, which is another way, as Goethe so well knew, of saying—*growth*. As a seed grows in the natural course of time, so the world grows, and so it dies, and so it is reborn again. This is the very antithesis of the current notion of "progress," in which are bound up the evil dragons of will, purpose, goal and struggle—or rather, they are not *bound* up, but unleashed. Progress, according to the Westerner, means a straight line through impenetrable barriers, creating difficulties and obstacles all along the line, and thus defeating itself. Howe's idea is the Oriental one, made familiar to us through the art of jujitsu, wherein the obstacle itself is made into an aid. The method is as applicable to what we call disease, or death or evil, as it is to a bullying adversary. The secret of it lies in the recognition that force can be directed as well as feared—more, that everything can be converted to good or evil, profit or loss, according to one's attitude. In his present fearsome state man seems to have but one attitude, escape, wherein he is fixed as in a nightmare. Not only does he refuse to accept his fears, but worse, *he fears his fears*. Everything seems infinitely worse than it is, says Howe, "just because we are trying to escape." This is the very Paradise of Neurosis, a glue of fear and anxiety, in which, unless we are willing to rescue ourselves, we may stick forever. To imagine that we are going to be saved by outside intervention, whether in the shape of an analyst, a dictator, a savior, or even God, is sheer folly. There are not enough lifeboats to go around, and anyway, as the author points out, what is needed more than lifeboats is lighthouses. A fuller, clearer vision—not more safety appliances!

Many influences, of astounding variety, have contributed to shape this philosophy of life which, unlike most philosophies, takes its stance in life, and not in a system of thought. His view embraces conflicting world-views; there is room in it to include all of Whitman, Emerson, Thoreau, as well as Taoism, Zen Buddhism, astrology, occultism, and so forth. It is a thoroughly religious view of life, in that it recognizes "the supremacy of the unseen." Emphasis is laid on the dark side of life, on all that which is considered negative, passive, evil, feminine, mysterious, unknowable. *War Dance* closes on this note—"there is nothing that it is not better to accept, even though it be the expression of our enemy's ill-will. There is no progress other than what is, if we could let it be. . . ." This idea of let be, of non-interference, of living now in the moment, fully, with complete faith in the processes of life, which must remain ever largely unknown to us, is the cardinal aspect of his philosophy. It means evolution versus revolution, and involution as well as evolution. It takes cognizance of insanity as well as sleep, dream and death. It does not seek to eliminate fear and anxiety, but to incorporate them in the whole plexus of man's emotional being. It does not offer a panacea for our ills, nor a paradise beyond: it recognizes that life's problems are fundamentally insoluble and accepts the fact graciously. It is in this full recognition and acceptance of conflict and paradox that Howe reconciles wisdom with common sense. At the heart of it is humor, gaiety, the sense of play—not morality, but reality. It is a lenitive, purgative, healing doctrine, based on the open palm rather than the closed fist; on surrender, sacrifice, renunciation, rather than struggle, conquest, idealism. It favors the slow, rhythmic movement of growth rather than the direct method which would attain an imaginary end through speed and force. (Is not the end always bound up with the means?) It seeks to eliminate the doctor as well as the patient, by accepting the disease itself rather than the medicine or the mediator; it puts the seed above the bomb, conversion before solution, and counsels uniqueness rather than normality.

It seems to be generally admitted by intelligent people, and even by the unintelligent, that we are passing through one of the darkest moments in history. (What is not so clearly recognized, however, is that man has passed through many such periods before, and survived!) There are those who content themselves with putting the blame for our condition on the "enemy," call it church, education, government, Fascism, Communism, poverty, circumstance, or what not. They waste their forces proving that they are "right" and the other fellow "wrong." For them society is largely composed of those who are against their ideas.

But society is composed of the insane and the criminals, as well as the righteous and the unrighteous. Society represents all of us, "what we are and how we feel about life," as Howe puts it. Society is sick, scarcely anybody will deny that, and in the midst of this sick world are the doctors who, "knowing little of the reason why they prescribe for us, have little faith in anything but heroic surgery and in the patient's quite unreasonable ability to recover." The medical men are not interested in health, but in combating sickness and disease. Like the other members of society, they function negatively. Similarly, no statesmen arise who appear capable of dealing with the blundering dictators, for the quite probable reason that they are themselves dictators at heart. . . . Here is the picture of our so-called "normal" world, obeying, as Howe calls it, the law of "infinite regress":

"Science carefully measures the seen, but it despises the unseen. Religion subdivides itself, protesting and nonconforming in one negative schism after another, pursuing the path of infinite regress while aggressively attaching itself to the altars of efficient organization. Art exploits a multiplication of accurate imitations; its greatest novelty is 'Surrealism,' which prides itself upon its ability to escape all the limitations imposed upon sanity by reality. Education is more or less free for all, but the originality of individualism suffers mechanization by mass-productive methods, and top marks are awarded for aggressive excellence. The limits of law aggressively insist that the aggressive should be aggressively eliminated, thus establishing the right by means of out-wronging the wrong-doer. Our amusements are catered for by mechanized methods, for we cannot amuse ourselves. Those who cannot play football themselves enthusiastically shout and boo the gallant but well-paid efforts of others in ardent partisanship. Those who can neither run nor take a risk, back horses. Those who cannot take the trouble to tolerate silence have sound brought to their ears without effort, or go to picture palaces to enjoy the vicarious advantages of a synthetic cinema version of the culture of our age. This system we call normality, and it is to live in this disordered world that we bring up our children so expensively. The system is threatened with disaster, but we have no thought but to hold it up, while we clamour for peace in which to enjoy it. Because we live in it, it seems to be as sacred as ourselves. This way of living as refugees from realism, this vaunted palace of progress and culture, it must never suffer change. It is normal to be so! Who said so? And what does this word normal mean?"

"Normality," says Howe, "is the paradise of escapeologists, for it is a fixation concept, pure and simple." "It is better, if we can," he asserts, "to stand alone and to feel quite normal about our abnormality, doing nothing whatever about it, except what needs to be done in order to be oneself."

It is just this ability to stand alone, and not feel guilty or harassed about it, of which the average person is incapable. The desire for a lasting external security is uppermost, revealing itself in the endless pursuit of health, happiness, possessions and so on, defense of what has been acquired being the obsessive idea, and yet no real defense being possible, because one cannot defend what is undefendable. All that can be defended are imaginary, illusory, protective devices. Who, for example, could feel sorry for St. Francis because he threw away his clothes and took the vow of poverty? He was the first man on record, I imagine, who asked for stones instead of bread. Living on the refuse which others threw away he acquired the strength to accomplish miracles, to inspire a joy such as few men have given the world, and, by no means the least of his powers, to write the most sublime and simple, the most eloquent hymn of thanksgiving that we have in all literature: *The Canticle to the Sun*. Let go and let be! Howe urges. Being is burning, in the truest sense, and if there is to be any peace it will come about through being, not having.

We are all familiar with the phrase—"life begins at forty." For the majority of men it is so, for it is only in middle age that the continuity of life, which death promises, begins to make itself felt and understood. The significance of renunciation, as the author explains it, lies in the fact that it is not a mere passive acquiescence, an ignominious surrender to the inevitable forces of death, but, on the contrary, a re-counting, a re-valuing. It is at this crucial point in the individual's life that the masculine element gives way to the feminine. This is the usual course, which Nature herself seems to take care of. For the awakened individual, however, life begins now, at any and every moment; it begins at the moment when he realizes that he is part of a great whole, and in the realization becomes himself whole. In the knowledge of limits and relationships he discovers the eternal self, thenceforth to move with obedience and discipline in full freedom. *Balance, discipline, illumination*—these are the key words in Howe's doctrine of wholeness, or holiness, for the words mean the same thing. It is not essentially new, but it needs to be rediscovered by each and every one individually. As I said before, one meets it in such poets and thinkers as Emerson, Thoreau, Whitman, to take a few recent examples. It is a philosophy of life which nourished the Chinese for thousands of years, a philosophy which, unfortunately, they have abandoned under Western influence.

That this ancient wisdom of life should be reaffirmed by a practicing analyst, by a "healer," seems to me altogether logical and just. What greater temptation is there for the healer than to play the role of God—and who knows better than he the nature and the wisdom of God? E. Graham Howe is a man in his prime, healthy, normal in the abnormal sense, successful, as the word goes, and desirous more than anything else of leading his own life. He knows that the healer is primarily an artist, and not a magician or a god. He seeks, by expressing his views publicly, to wean the public of a dependency which is itself an expression of disease. He is not interested in *healing*, but in *being*. He does not seek to cure, but to enjoy a life more abundant. He is not struggling to eliminate disease, but to accept it, and by devouring it, incorporate it in the body of light and health which is man's true heritage. He is not overburdened, because his philosophy of health would not permit him to assume tasks beyond his powers. He takes everything in his stride, with measure and balance, consuming only what he can digest and assimilate of experience. If he is a very capable analyst, as is generally admitted, even by his detractors, it is not because of what he *knows*, but because of what he *is*. He is constantly unloading himself of excess baggage, be it in the form of patients, friends, admirers or possessions. His mind is, as the Chinese well say, "alive-and-empty." He is anchored in the flux, neither drowned in it nor vainly trying to dam it. He is a very wise man who is at peace with himself and the world. One knows that instantly, merely by shaking hands with him.

"There is no need," he says, in concluding War Dance, "to be morbid about the difficulty in which we find ourselves, for there is no undue difficulty about it, if we will but realise that we bring the difficulty upon ourselves by trying to alter the inevitable. The Little Man is so afraid of being overwhelmed, but the Larger Man hopes for it; the Little Man refuses to swallow so much of his experience, regarding it as evil, but the Larger Man takes it as his everyday diet, keeping open pipe and open house for every enemy to pass through; the Little Man is terrified lest he should slip from light into darkness, from seen into unseen, but the Larger Man realises that it is but sleep or death and either is the very practice of his recreation; the Little Man depends upon 'goods' or golf for his well-being, seeking for doctors or other saviours, but the Larger Man knows by the deeper process of his inward conviction that truth is paradox and that he is safest when he is least defended. . . . The war of life is one thing; man's war is another, being war about war, war against war, in infinite regress of offensive and defensive argument."

It may seem, from the citations, that I favor War Dance above the other two books, but such is not the case. Perhaps because of the daily threat of war I was led instinctively to make reference to this book, which is really about Peace. The three books are equally valuable and represent different facets of this same homely philosophy, which is not, let me repeat, a system of thought expounded and defended in brilliant fashion, but a wisdom of life that increments life. It has no other purpose than to make life more life-like, strange as this may sound.

Whoever has dipped into the esoteric lore of the East must recognize that the attitude towards life set forth in these books is but a rediscovery of the Doctrine of the Heart. The element of Time, so fundamental in Howe's philosophy, is a restatement, in scientific language, of the esoteric view that one cannot travel on the Path before one has become that Path himself. Never, perhaps, in historic times, has man been further off the Path than at this moment. An age of darkness, it has been called—a transitional period, involving disaster and enlightenment. Howe is not alone in thus summarizing our epoch: it is the opinion of earnest men everywhere. It might be regarded as an equinoctial solstice of the soul, the furthest outward reach that can be made without complete disintegration. It is the moment when the earth, to use another analogy, before making the swing back, seems to stand stock still. There is an illusion of "end," a stasis seemingly like death. But it is only an illusion. Everything, at this crucial point, lies in the attitude which we assume towards the moment. If we accept it as a death we may be re-born and continue on our cyclical journey. If we regard it as an "end" we are doomed. It is no accident that the various death philosophies with which we are familiar should arise at this time. We are at the parting of the ways, able to look forwards and backwards with infinite hope or despair. Nor is it strange either that so many varied expressions of a fourth-dimensional view of life should now make their appearance. The negative view of life, which is really the death-like view of things, summed up by Howe in the phrase "infinite regress," is gradually giving way to a positive view, which is multi-dimensional. (Whenever the fourth-dimensional view is grasped multiple dimensions open up. The fourth is the symbolic dimension which opens the horizon in infinite "egress." With it time-space takes on a wholly new character: every aspect of life is henceforth transmuted.)

In dying the seed re-experiences the miracle of life, but in a fashion far beyond the comprehension of the individual organism. The terror of death is more than compensated for by the unknown joys of birth. It is precisely the difference, in my opinion, between the Eye and the Heart doctrines. For, as we all know, in expanding the field of knowledge we but increase the horizon of ignorance. "Life is not in the form, but in the flame," says Howe. For two thousand years, despite the real wisdom of Christ's teachings, we have been trying to live in the mold, trying to wrest wisdom from knowledge, instead of wooing it, trying to conquer over Nature instead of accepting and living by her laws. It is not at all strange, therefore, that the analyst, into whose hands the sick and weary are now giving themselves like sheep to the slaughter, finds it necessary to reinstate the metaphysical view of life. (Since Thomas Aquinas there has been no metaphysics.) The cure lies with the patient, not with the analyst. We are chained to one another by invisible links, and it is the weakest in whom our strength is revealed, or registered. "Poetry must be made by all," said Lautréamont, and so too must all real progress. We must grow wise together, else all is vain and illusory. If we are in a dilemma, it is better that we stand still and face the issue, rather than resort to hasty and heroic action. "To live in truth, which is suspense," says Howe, "is adventure, growth, uncertainty, risk and danger. Yet there is little opportunity in life today for experiencing that adventure, unless we go to war." Meaning thereby that by evading our real problems from day to day we have produced a schism, on the one side of which is the illusory life of comfortable security and painlessness, and on the other disease, catastrophe, war, and so forth. We are going through Hell now, but it would be excellent if it really were hell, and if we really go through with it. We cannot possibly hope, unless we are thoroughly neurotic, to escape the consequences of our foolish behavior in the past. Those who are trying to put the onus of responsibility for the dangers which threaten on the shoulders of the "dictators" might well examine their own hearts and see whether their allegiance is really "free" or a mere attachment to some other form of authority, possibly unrecognized. "Attachment to any system, whether psychological or otherwise," says Howe, "is suggestive of anxious escape from life." Those who are preaching revolution are also defenders of the *status quo—their status quo*. Any solution for the world's ills must embrace *all* mankind. We have got to relinquish our precious theories, our buttresses and supports, to say nothing of our defenses and possessions. We

**43**

have got to become more *inclusive*, not more exclusive. What is not acknowledged and assimilated through experience, piles up in the form of guilt and creates a real Hell, the literal meaning of which is—where the unburnt must be burnt! The doctrine of reincarnation includes this vital truth; we in the West scoff at the idea, but we are none the less victims of the law. Indeed, if one were to try to give a graphic description of this place-condition, what more accurate illustration could be summoned than the picture of the world we now "have on our hands"? The realism of the West, is it not negated by reality? The word has gone over into its opposite, which is the case with so many of our words. We are trying to live only in the light, with the result that we are enveloped in darkness. We are constantly fighting for the right and the good, but everywhere we see evil and injustice. As Howe rightly says, "if we must have our ideals achieved and gratified, they are not ideals at all, but phantasies." We need to open up, to relax, to give way, to obey the deeper laws of our being, in order to find a true discipline.

Discipline Howe defines as "the art of the acceptance of the negative." It is based on the recognition of the duality of life, of the relative rather than the absolute. Discipline permits a free flow of energy; it gives absolute freedom within relative limits. One develops *despite* circumstances, not because of them. This was a life wisdom known to Eastern peoples, handed down to us in many guises, not least of which is the significant study of symbols, known as astrology. Here time and growth are vital elements to the understanding of reality. Properly understood, there are no good or bad horoscopes, nor good or bad "aspects"; there is no moral or ethical examination of men or things, only a desire to get at the significance of the forces within and without, and their relationship. An attempt, in short, to arrive at a total grasp of the universe, and thus keep man anchored in the moving stream of life, which embraces known and unknown. Any and every moment, from this viewpoint, is therefore good or right, the best for whoever it be, for on how one orients himself to the moment depends the failure or fruitfulness of it. In a very real sense we can see today how man has really dislocated himself from the movement of life; he is somewhere on the periphery, whirling like a whirligig, going faster and faster and blinder and blinder. Unless he can make the gesture of surrender, unless he can let go the iron will which is merely an expression of his negation of life, he will never get back to the center and find his true being. It is not only the "dictators" who are possessed, but the whole world of men everywhere; we are in the grip of demonic forces created by our own fear and ignorance. We say No to everything, instinctively. Our very instincts are perverted, so that the word itself has come to lose all sense. The whole man acts not instinctively, but intuitively, because "his wishes are as much at one with the law as he is himself." But to act intuitively one must obey the deeper law of love, which is based on absolute tolerance, the law which suffers or permits things to be as they are. Real love is never perplexed, never qualifies, never rejects, never demands. It replenishes, by grace of restoring unlimited circulation. It burns, because it knows the true meaning of sacrifice. It is life illumined.

The idea of "unlimited circulation," not only of the necessities of life, but of everything, is, if there be such a thing, the magic behind Howe's philosophy. It is the most practical way of life, though seemingly impractical. Whether it be admitted or not, there are hierarchies of being, as well as of role. The highest types of men have always been those in favor of "unlimited circulation." They were comparatively fearless and sought neither riches nor security, except in themselves. By abandoning all that they most cherished they found the way to a larger life. Their example still inspires us, though we follow them more with the eye than with the heart, if we follow at all. They never attempted to lead, but only to guide. The real leader has no need to lead—he is content to point the way. Unless we become our own leaders, content to be what we are in process of becoming, we shall always be servitors and idolaters. We have only what we merit; we would have infinitely more if we wanted less. The whole secret of salvation hinges on the conversion of word to deed, with and through the whole being. It is this turning in wholeness and faith, *conversion*, in the spiritual sense, which is the mystical dynamic of the fourth-dimensional view. I used the word salvation a moment ago, but salvation, like fear or death, when it is accepted and experienced, is no longer "salvation." There is no salvation, really, only infinite realms of experience providing more and more tests, demanding more and more faith. Willy-nilly we are moving towards the Unknown, and the sooner and readier we give ourselves up to the experience, the better it will be for us. This very word which is so frequently on our lips today—*transition*—indicates increasing awareness, as well as apprehension. To become more aware is to sleep more soundly, to cease twitching and tossing. It is only when we get beyond phantasy, beyond wishing and dreaming, that the real conversion takes place and we awake re-born, the dream re-becomes reality. For reality is the goal, deny it how we will. And we can approach it only by an ever-expanding consciousness, by burning more and more brightly, until even memory itself vanishes.

# RAIMU

It is as an American living in France, who has seen practically all the important films produced by Russia, Germany, France and America, that I write this tribute to Raimu whom I consider the most human figure on the screen today. Though it seems that the French films have at last won the recognition which they deserve, in America, from the titles which I see discussed I realize that these films which my countrymen are beginning to appreciate, ten years too late, are by no means the best which the French have to offer. America is always twenty to fifty years behind time in accepting the true genius of Europe. Even today, for example, they are still discovering, through their avant-garde reviews, such writers as Jean Cocteau and Leon Paul Fargue. Recently an American who came to visit me had the naïveté to ask me if I did not consider the author of *Hommes de Bonne Volonté* the Dos Passos of Europe!

The fundamental difference between the French and American films, as everybody knows, lies in the understanding of what is human. A French film, when it is good, is unsurpassable, not only because it is more true to life but because this conception of life strikes a deeper note than anything conceived by Russians, Germans, or Americans. A fact often commented upon by foreigners is that French actors, male and female, are usually well advanced in years, usually quite unprepossessing, if not downright homely, and, when given the opportunity (which is not often enough), are capable of assuming the most diverse roles, including the comic as well as the tragic. In the American films, on the other hand, it is highly noticeable that there is not one great serious actor, unless it be the clown, Charlie Chaplin. (Men like Paul Muni and Edward Robinson, capable in their way, are always actors rather than men.) Anything verging on the tragic, in the American film, quickens into melodrama and sticky sentimentality. In the better French films (the poor ones are below every level!) there is always a sense of reality, of the tragicomedy of life. Where the French film fails is in the realm of imagination, of phantasy. It is the inherent weakness of the French character, the blind spot which accounts perhaps for the popularity of such a feeble masterpiece, in literature, as *Le Grand Meaulnes*. Among the French, one often hears it said that the American film, even if bad, is at any rate amusing. They are never thoroughly bored by a bad American film—so they say, at least. Myself, I am bored to tears often, even by the "great" American films. This attitude of the

French is explicable only because they do not expect too much of anything American. A man would be an imbecile, for example, to be disappointed in a work of Maurice Dekobra's. Somehow, much is expected of a good French film, even by the French.

In Raimu, whose rise I have watched now for several years, the French people, the soul quality, I might say, makes itself manifest. Raimu is the one truly human figure on the screen today, and whether he be considered a good actor or a bad one is relatively unimportant. He represents something which is vitally missing in the cinema, and he represents it forcefully. To appreciate his contribution one has only to take a sidelong glance at his American counterpart, Wallace Beery. The latter, together with Gary Cooper, represent the highest efforts of the American producers to give us a semblance of the human being and not the Hollywood figure in *papier-mâché*. But they are usually cast for adventure, for thrilling episodes, for *action*. Only once was Gary Cooper, for example, permitted to express anything like his real self—in *Mr. Deeds Goes to Town*. Wallace Beery has never been given a role which would permit him to reveal his full stature—nor has Barbara Stanwyck, except for one film, *Liliane*, which was banned in America. To understand this deliberate deterioration of character which Hollywood enforces one has only to reflect on what happens to the French actor whose services are impressed by Hollywood. Any ordinary French film starring Charles Boyer or Daniele Darrieux, for example, seems infinitely better than the sensational ones created for them in America. What is the constant plaint of the French artist after his arrival in Hollywood? "They want to make us over!" It is the American vice, the democratic disease which expresses its tyranny by reducing everything unique to the level of the herd. Think of "making

49

over" the heroine of *Mayerling!* Think of what it would mean to make over a Gabin or a Jouvet!

I do not mean to imply by the foregoing that the French producers are animated only by lofty artistic ideals. I think, taking them by and large, that they are as guilty as the American producers of complicity in foisting upon the public anything and everything which will bring quick returns. They are as bad as the French publishers who are deliberately, cold-bloodedly, ruining the taste for good literature by their shameless concentration on the till. They are as bad as the French politicians who, bar none, are the most corrupt in the world. But there is something in the French character which, despite the lowest intentions, prevents them from completely betraying their heritage. The Frenchman is first and foremost a *man*. He is likeable often just because of his weaknesses, which are always thoroughly human, even if despicable. As a rogue and a scoundrel he is more often than not misled by a perverted sense of reality which he calls realism. But even at his worst there always remains an area—of the soul, shall I say?—with which one can deal and hope for an ultimate understanding. It is difficult for a Frenchman to wholly defeat the human being in himself. Race, tradition, culture—these speak out even when the mind has been traduced. And so, even with the worst motives, it often happens that a mediocre French film offers something which the best films of other countries never take into account.

Study the faces of the American stars! Compare them with the French. At a glance one can spot the difference—the contrast between adolescence and maturity, between a fake idealism and a grim sense of reality, between puppets who will perform any insane stunt and individuals who cannot be trained to act like monkeys no matter what bait is held out to them. The American cannot help making an ass of himself, even when he is inspired; the Frenchman is always a human being, even when he caricatures himself. The American ideal is youth—handsome, empty youth. Russia too idolizes youth, but what a difference between the two conceptions of youth! Russia is young in spirit, because the spirit is still vital; in America youth means simply athleticism, disrespect, gangsterism, or sickly idealism expressing itself through thinly disguised and badly digested social science theories acted out by idiots who are desperadoes at heart. Think of the American idol, James Cagney; or of Robert Taylor, the matinee idol of the screen; or of Clark Gable, the symbol of American vigor and manliness! What do they bring to the screen besides good looks, a fast, pat lingo, the art of fisticuffs, or a suit of well-tailored clothes? Think of Victor MacLaglen, for whose work in *The Informer* I have the highest admiration. Think, however, what it is America truly admires in him! They have made him the symbol of their own brutish nature.

Let us get back to the human, to Raimu. . . . One of the things which impresses me most about Raimu is his habit of going about in shirt sleeves and suspenders, his struggles to lace his boots or to tie his cravat. He is always sweating (not perspiring!), always trying to unburden himself of his clothes, to give his body light and air. It is a quality which one almost never observes in an American actor. Raimu sweats, weeps, laughs, yells with pain. Raimu flies into a rage, an unholy rage, in which he is not ashamed to strike his wife or son, if deserving of his wrath. Wrath! Here again is something which is usually absent from the American's repertoire of emotions. The wrath of Raimu is magnificent; there is something Biblical, something godlike about it. It springs up from that sense of justice which is never entirely stifled in the French and which, when roused, permits them to accomplish

**51**

superhuman feats of strength and daring. When the American strikes it is really a reflex action. (The Englishman, be it noted, seldom resorts to violence; when he is sufficiently goaded he simply opens up, like the oyster, and devours his adversary. Yet the most sadistic picture I have ever seen, the only picture which I think should be banned, is the British production of *Broken Blossom*.) No, the American scarcely knows what anger is, nor joy, for that matter. He oscillates between cold-blooded murder, as depicted by the gangsters or those who are punishing them, and a bright, hard gaiety devoid of all sensitivity, all respect and consideration for the personality of the other. He is quick to kill or to laugh, but both his laughter and his murderousness are empty. The *"fraicheur"* which the French pretend to see in the impossible American farces is a hoax. The Americans are *not* young and fresh in spirit, but senile; their humor is hysterical, a reaction born of panic, of a refusal to look life in the face. The way they throw their bodies around, the way they pummel one another, the way they destroy themselves and the objects which they have created, what is it but a sort of ferocious nightmare activity? If this is "life," then life is absurd. If this is health and youthfulness, then give me old age and melancholy. The crimes they commit in their sleep outdo the atrocities perpetrated by the most tyrannical despots.

In Raimu I see the opposite of all this. In Raimu I see a heavy, sluggish figure, a man who is certainly not "refined," a man who is not a "heart-breaker," nor a "hero." Everything he says and does is human and understandable, even his crimes. He never tries to be more than he is, or other than he is; he is never ridiculous, even when he inspires laughter. He is *touching*, an old-fashioned word, but one that suits him well. It is not an actor one watches in his films, but a man living his life: he breathes, sleeps, snores, sweats, chews, spits, curses, and so on. He is unlovely to look at, and yet he is far from being ugly. He redeems the human figure by stripping it of its superfluities, its external paraphernalia. Think of his emotions and compare them with the frowsy bag of tricks employed by that broken-down hack, Lionel Barrymore, who is about the only old man America can rustle up to enact anything resembling tragedy. What a farce, the Barrymore tradition! For John, the great matinee idol of twenty-five years ago, is even worse than Lionel. What empty words and gestures! What drivel! Even an avowedly bad actor, such as Jules Berry, puts him to shame. Even Victor Francen, who is about as stagey and unreal as any French actor can hope to be, is infinitely superior to this antiquated tragedian.

It is when Raimu becomes violent that I like him best. His violence is slow in accumulating; it gathers like a storm-cloud and breaks with devastating fury, only to clear as quickly as it came. It is a purge, a creative purge, even to observe it as a spectator. This, I maintain, no American actor ever gives us. He can't, because his theory of dynamics is all wrong. Everything, including metabolism, is sacrificed to speed and effect. Everything moves like lightning—*but nothing ever happens*. There is no drama—there is only the heat of frenzy in a void of the mind. Raimu, on the other hand, when he saunters slowly down a street or through the corridor of a hotel, when he lowers himself into a seat or leans against a wall to tell a story, is like a refreshing bath. He allows time for what is human in the individual to gather and grow, to express itself finally, when the moment is ripe, by an appropriate gesture, by a gush of words or by an act of silence. He makes no attempt to conceal his tears—he weeps openly and unashamedly. When an American weeps—and usually no one but a silly young virgin or a stereotyped old mother ever weeps in the films!—no emotion whatever is aroused. They are all trained "tear-jerkers," to use an American expression. The tears do not well up from the feelings, but are pumped up by the will, or by the economic demands of the film director who values them at so much the ounce, like perfume. Why do the Americans envy and hate Garbo so? Because she is really a "tragic" figure, and because she has never concealed her scorn and contempt for their theories of art. To the American, Garbo, when she is not "grand" or "magnificent," is melodramatic—or else an anaemic, flat-footed, tired Swede. But they are proud to have given her to the world, and however much they ridicule and malign her, they want the credit for discovering her talent. As to learning anything from her, no, absolutely impossible. She represents another world, another mode of life, not only alien but hostile to theirs. They boast about absorbing the best from the world, but actually they take only what suits their own low level of life and then impose it on the world as their creation.

Only the other night I saw another Raimu film—*The Hero of the Marne*. Even without Raimu this picture would be the greatest of its genre ever produced. What a chasm between this quiet, moving spectacle and the false, trashy war films, such as those based on Remarque's books, for example, from America! Who can believe in these fabricated celluloid horrors of war? What silly, empty, hundred per cent American imbeciles they try to palm off as *Germans!* What a literary air of unreality about these films! In the *Hero of the Marne* the war is made out to be what every sensitive man knows it to be—a fateful horror, a butchery which nobody is responsible for, unless it be the statesmen and financiers. It is a mess in which both sides appear guilty and equally responsible, and for our colossal ignorance and sinfulness the innocent, as well as the guilty, are made to perish. What is heroic in man, as this film seems to indicate, is not born out of a sense of "righteousness" but of the power of endurance, of the courage which arises from accepting the worst in our nature. It is the common, undenominated man who, almost against his will, it would appear, rises to the heights of heroism. The deep resignation, the acceptance of that which is revolting and unbearable, is here revealed as of the very essence of heroism. In Raimu's portrayal of the dilemma one can see the spirit of the whole French people. He is a man of peace who is obliged to kill, and to offer his own flesh and blood to be killed too. He is not a patriot, but something far greater, far more inspiring: *he is a man*, and he acts like one. In his weakness he moves us even more than in his courageousness. He is what we all are, a mixture of good and bad, of wisdom and stupidity, of nobility and narrow-mindedness. He is not a paste-board figure pulled by the strings of an idealistic despot to prove the truth of an empty theory of life derived from a cheap *Saturday Evening Post* story which not even the editors themselves believe in.

In the French figures on the screen today, those who best know how to portray human emotions, there is that curious mixture, practically unheard of in the American, of tenderness and brutality combined. The American can give us one or the other, both in a more extreme degree, but never the two combined in the one personality. Wallace Beery and Victor MacLaglen come closest to it, perhaps, but they are rather crude specimens, *types* rather than human beings. In Emil Jannings we had the closest approximation to this great French quality, but marred by a hidebound German theatricality. Only once, to my recollection, was Jannings above criticism, and that was in an early silent film which was called in English *The Last Laugh*. Here he almost reached Dostoievskian proportions. But to achieve it he had to rely on burlesque, of which the French are altogether ignorant. As I say, this quality

55

of brutality and tenderness combined is the special characteristic of the French actor, and through it he reveals the meaning which the French give to the word "human." It is something passionate, and not the expression of a blind, senseless activity, of reflex muscular rage. It is something slumbering and capable of infinite mutations, destructive and creative, always dramatic because always expressive of the inherent antagonism in things. In a film such as *Geuele d'Amour* even the atmosphere reflects this quality. The street scene, in Orange I believe it was, when night is coming on and there is just the flapping of the awning in the breeze, so much is contained in this moment that it is like an act of poetry. In a trifling touch a whole world of feeling is conveyed. So it is too with Gabin's studied restraint, his abortive gestures, his muttering silences, his quick, dull look, which comes like a hammer-blow. Raimu and Jouvet also have this terrifying look at times; it is like a thick curtain of blood suddenly veiling the eye. They brood, they wait, they endure; but when they move, when they reach for their victim, it is like Fate itself striking, and nothing can hinder. In the American films murder is committed negligently, recklessly, unthinkingly: a button is touched and the sawed-off shot-guns squirt their fire. It matters little who gets in the way— women, children, priests, anybody who comes within range is mowed down. I remember the shock of a Parisian audience when in an American film a priest was shown as being struck down by a blow of the fist. But it might just as well have been a kick in the rear which he had received. Or he might have been boiled in oil. To the American, as their films well reveal, nothing is sacred, nothing taboo—except perhaps the act of going to bed with a woman. That is immoral, though it happens everywhere all the time, even in America. But it must never be openly shown—it must be imagined only. Thus, too, the dead are portrayed as drinking cocktails, something which is not altogether inconceivable, but which, if true, is only a minor virtue in the life of the dead.

But the real key to the American sense of grandeur lies in the glorification of catastrophes. Nature is the hero, not man! If it is not an earthquake it is a hurricane or a landslide or a flood, dramatic incidents which have their human counterpart in battle scenes, prison riots and so on. When it is really a grandiose theme, such as in *Lost Horizon*, for example, it is muffled with clowning and sensationalism. The Grand Lama spouts the Christian doctrine through the mouth of a Jewish actor. The French, who were as divided as the rest of the world about the merits of this film, reduced the theme to a comfortable bourgeois ideal with a little foreword containing some such clap-trap as this—"who has not dreamed of retiring some day to his little home in the country!" What rubbish! What a woeful depreciation of a grand theme! However . . . in the film based on that splendid human document, *The Good Earth*, the really important feature seems to have been the invasion of the locusts. In *San Francisco* it is the earthquake, an episode which requires about three minutes to render, and the rest of the film is sheer drivel, absolutely insupportable, especially Jeanette MacDonald. (The same is true for *The Charge of the Light Brigade* and *Gunga Din*; only the destructive scenes have value—the rest is hogwash.) Even when the film is a restoration film the street scenes are unconvincing. Whole corps of men and women are mobilized to study the history, costumes, architecture, furniture of a period—and yet the result is nil. The money spent on research, which is colossal, is sheer waste. The same for characters. In a Chinese film, when America of all countries is full of available types, Paul Muni, a Viennese Jew, is made a Chinese, and Luise Rainer, after her adorable portrayal of Anna Held in *The Great*

Ziegfeld, is converted into a Chinese peasant woman who speaks English with an Austrian accent. A Frenchman or a Hindu is always a caricature of the type. No country in the world has such a variety of racial types as America; no acting is required, because in the American film everybody is supposed "to be just himself." Yet in their frantic attempts at realism, at producing a semblance of something life-like, something authentic, they will choose, as if blindfolded, the very man or woman most unlike the one they are attempting to portray. When it comes to reciting the Gettysburg address an Englishman is chosen, because he is undoubtedly the most expert in the use of the English language. Charles Laughton's recital of the Gettysburg address was a memorable moment in the history of the cinema, but what a travesty of the homely diction Lincoln must have employed! When they admire good acting in a foreign film they choose an innocuous museum piece like *La Kermesse Héroique* or such a sham as *La Grande Illusion*, with that linguistic, physiognomic monstrosity, Eric von Stroheim, who is neither fish nor fowl. The French, in turn, are capable of applauding a fifth rate film such as *Back Street*, which was based upon the work of probably *the* worst writer in America, Fanny Hurst. They even fall so far, in their critical acumen, as to present it to the public through a little speech of pure asininity, by Henri Duvernois, one of their own bad writers. Of the two films which seem to be most frequently revived here—*Million Dollar Legs* and *The Whole Town's Talking*—the one is a burlesque-fantasy and the other a study of the "double." Robinson is a capable actor, in the old style, histrionic through and through. The film is excellent, and he is largely responsible for its excellence, but better films of this genre have been produced in Europe. As for *Million Dollar Legs*, with Jack Oakie, whom the French seem to adore, especially the intellectuals, it is hard to see what they so admire in this film which is put together in slapdash fashion and creaks with wheezy old gags that fill up the holes in a hollow scenario. The element of fantasy * in it perhaps appeals to the French, because they have none themselves, but the burlesque is shoddy and emasculated. What is called "burlesque" by French film fans is only the weak dregs, the coffee grounds, as it were, of a once strong brew. Real burlesque, as it was known in America before the Catholic Church intervened, would shock the French to death. The sexual element, which was its chief characteristic, has been eliminated; what remains is horse-play, wise-cracks, mountebank tricks of the carnival variety. This bastardized version of burlesque, which the American films now present, the French intelligentsia accept as a sort of American Surrealism, the spice of life in the great cultural desert. But they are mistaken. What is truly surrealistic the Americans understand nothing of, nor do the French themselves for that matter, excepting the pontificators and mystagogues.

What is truly American usually misses fire here, as I have noticed time and again. The really excellent things which America offers— in weak pills usually, I must confess—make no appeal to the French spirit. They fail to come within the scope of the Frenchman's understanding of reality. (What is truly Irish is similarly misunderstood or ignored, I notice, despite the Celtic bond. Poetry, when it is *lived*, is simply another form of insanity to the French.) The films I have in mind, when I speak of representative American themes, have to do with a "message." And this message has to do with the common man, with the great hope which Whitman gives sublime expression to throughout his works. This hope the Ameri-

* (P.S.) How explain the mysterious disappearance from the programs of the recent French attempt at fantasy—"*Monsieur Coccinelle*"? There is something *louche* about this!

can is blindly trying to give body to. It is something which the cultured European understands with his mind only; it never affects his behavior. But in America, despite the crass ignorance, despite the corruption in every walk of life, despite the seemingly permanent air of unreality in which everybody bathes, even when "up against it," as the saying goes, this message is nevertheless understood by the lowest man, is in his blood, so to speak. It marks the gulf between the New and the Old World, and all the blithe exchanges of fraternity and solidarity by the cunning politicians fail to hide it. The American *is* a different animal, and he is primarily a non-political, non-cultural animal. In his most Utopian dreams he is most truly himself. He is, despite all outward signs of practicality, a dreamer, one, unfortunately, who is capable of committing the most heinous crimes in his sleep.

In *Mr. Deeds Goes to Town* we have the American par excellence in the person of Gary Cooper who, interpreting in his own original way a thin story by a hack writer, permits the French to visualize the common man whose homely, shrewd common sense is very close to the wisdom of the cultured man. Between such a type as this and Raimu, who represents an ordinary man of the Midi, also a sound and solid type, though a "relapsed" one, there is a world of difference. Raimu symbolizes the tragedy of the common man of Europe who is forever being sacrificed to the political machinations of unscrupulous seekers after power. He is not a fool, but helpless, a pawn in a game which is beyond him. In Gary Cooper, as pure type of American, one feels that perhaps one day the common man will win out over the undeserving leaders, over the despots in every guise who lure him to death. Americans, though denying it in practice, have always clung to the belief in such a possibility. The European, on the other hand, does not believe, not deep down, even when he is a revolutionary. He is always thinking politically, strategically, ambitiously; he is animated more by envy and hatred than by any chimerical thought of real brotherhood. The peasant always wins out over the city man, and the peasant is at heart selfish and uninspired. The American is a born anarchist; he has no genuine concern with the ideals of the European. If, as an unwilling ally, he makes common cause with the European it is more out of a spirit of adventure, out of sheer love of fight, fight for its own sake. I speak of the man in the street, to be sure, and not those who "represent" America in official capacities by manipulating the passions of the mob.

When I see a character such as Raimu, I realize how solitary, how lonely, is the real man of Europe. In every gesture he makes Raimu enacts the tragedy of a life which has been imposed upon the common man of Europe and which, as an individual, he is powerless to alter because he cannot free himself from the mesh of national intrigues in which he is born and nurtured. But if this man has little or no hope, and it is that which I read in the faces of Europeans everywhere, he at least has grandeur and dignity, sometimes the noblesse which is born of sheer desperation. In all his roles, however, I have the feeling that it is not his own fight which I am witnessing; I feel that he has forfeited from birth the privilege of the pursuit of life and happiness which is theoretically, if not actually, supposed to be due every man. He lives on, as part of a group soul, a hero who is never recognized, except anonymously. The American, while moving with the herd, is instinctively a traitor—to group, country, race, tradition. He does not know clearly what he is striving for, but he does know that he wants a chance, and he means to grab that chance, when he can, even if it involves the destruction of the world. He is an unconscious Nihilist. Any real connection with the man of Europe is vague and tenuous, imagined rather than felt. He is far closer, in spirit, to the German and the Japanese than to the French. He is not democratic, not libertarian—he is a human bomb for the time being carefully wrapped like a mummy in swathes of idealistic bandages.

For me Raimu stands out as the symbol of the lone European who is doomed to disappear in the convulsions of internecine strife because he has never dared to believe in his destiny as an individual. He is the blood-brother whom the American left in the lurch in order to open up a New World.

# THE COSMOLOGICAL EYE

MY FRIEND Reichel is just a pretext to enable me to talk about the world, the world of art and the world of men, and the confusion and eternal misunderstanding between the two. When I talk about Reichel I mean any good artist who finds himself alone, ignored, unappreciated. The Reichels of this world are being killed off like flies. It will always be so; the penalty for being different, for being an artist, is a cruel one.

Nothing will change this state of affairs. If you read carefully the history of our great and glorious civilization, if you read the biographies of the great, you will see that it has always been so;

and if you read still more closely you will see that these exceptional men have themselves explained why it must be so, though often complaining bitterly of their lot.

Every artist is a human being as well as painter, writer or musician; and never more so than when he is trying to justify himself as artist. As a human being Reichel almost brings tears to my eyes. Not merely because he is unrecognized (while thousands of lesser men are wallowing in fame), but first of all because when you enter his room, which is in a cheap hotel where he does his work, the sanctity of the place breaks you down. It is not quite a hovel, his little den, but it is perilously close to being one. You cast your eye about the room and you see that the walls are covered with his paintings. The paintings themselves are holy. This is a man, you cannot help thinking, who has never done anything for gain. This man had to do these things or die. This is a man who is desperate, and at the same time full of love. He is trying desperately to embrace the world with this love which nobody appreciates. And, finding himself alone, always alone and unacknowledged, he is filled with a black sorrow.

He was trying to explain it to me the other day as we stood at a bar. It's true, he was a little under the weather and so it was even more difficult to explain than normally. He was trying to say that what he felt was worse than sorrow, a sort of sub-human black pain which was in the spinal column and not in the heart or brain. This gnawing black pain, though he didn't say so, I realized at once was the reverse of his great love: it was the black unending curtain against which his gleaming pictures stand out and glow with a holy phosphorescence. He says to me, standing in his little hotel room: "I want that the pictures should look back at me; if I look at them and they don't look at me too then they are no good." The remark came about because some one had observed that in all his pictures there was an eye, *the cosmological eye*, this person said. As I walked away from the hotel I was thinking that perhaps this ubiquitous eye was the vestigial organ of his love so deeply implanted into everything he looked at that it shone back at him out of the darkness of human insensitivity. More, that this eye had to be in everything he did or he would go mad. This eye had to be there in order to gnaw into men's vitals, to get hold of them like a crab, and make them realize that Hans Reichel exists.

This cosmological eye is sunk deep within his body. Everything he looks at and seizes must be brought below the threshold of consciousness, brought deep into the entrails where there reigns an absolute night and where also the tender little mouths with which he absorbs his vision eat away until only the quintessence remains. Here, in the warm bowels, the metamorphosis takes place. In the absolute night, in the black pain hidden away in the backbone, the substance of things is dissolved until only the essence shines forth. The objects of his love, as they swim up to the light to arrange themselves on his canvases, marry one another in strange mystic unions which are indissoluble. But the real ceremony goes on below, in the dark, according to the inscrutable atomic laws of wedlock. There are no witnesses, no solemn oaths. Phenomenon weds phenomenon in the way that atomic elements marry to make the miraculous substance of living matter. There are polygamous marriages and polyandrous marriages, but no morganatic marriages. There are monstrous unions too, just as in nature, and they are as inviolable, as indissoluble as the others. Caprice rules, but it is the stern caprice of nature, and so divine.

There is a picture which he calls "The Stillborn Twins." It is an ensemble of miniature panels in which there is not only the embryonic flavor but the hieroglyphic as well. If he likes you, Reichel will show you in one of the panels the little shirt which the mother of the stillborn twins was probably thinking of in her agony. He says it so simply and honestly that you feel like weeping. The little shirt embedded in a cold pre-natal green is indeed the sort of shirt which only a woman in travail could summon up. You feel that with the freezing torture of birth, at the moment when the mind seems ready to snap, the mother's eye inwardly turning gropes frantically towards some tender, known object which will attach her, if only for a moment, to the world of human entities. In this quick, agonized clutch the mother sinks back, through worlds unknown to man, to planets long since disappeared, where perhaps there were no baby's shirts but where there was the warmth, the tenderness, the mossy envelope of a love beyond love, of a love for the disparate elements which metamorphose through the mother, through her pain, through her death, so that life may go on. Each panel, if you read it with the cosmological eye, is a throw-back to an undecipherable script of life. The whole cosmos is moving back and forth through the sluice of time and the stillborn twins are embedded there in the cold pre-natal green with the shirt that was never worn.

When I see him sitting in the armchair in a garden without bounds I see him dreaming backward with the stillborn twins. I see him as he looks to himself when there is no mirror anywhere in the world: when he is caught in a stone trance and has to *imagine* the mirror which is not there. The little white bird in the corner near his feet is talking to him, but he is deaf and the voice of the bird is inside him and he does not know whether he is talking to himself or whether he has become the little white bird itself. Caught like that, in the stony trance, the bird is plucked to the quick. It is as though the idea, *bird*, was suddenly arrested in the act of passing through the brain. The bird and the trance and the bird *in* the trance are transfixed. It shows in the expression on his face. The face is Reichel's, but it is a Reichel that has passed into a cataleptic state. A fleeting wonder hovers over the stone mask. Neither fear nor terror is registered in his expression—only an inexpressible wonder, as though he were the last witness of a world sliding down into darkness. And in this last minute vision the little white bird comes to speak to him—but he is already deaf. The most miraculous words are being uttered inside him, this bird language which no one has ever understood; he has it now, deep inside him. But it is at this moment when everything is clear that he sees with stony vision the world slipping away into the black pit of nothingness.

There is another self-portrait—a bust which is smothered in a mass of green foliage. It's extraordinary how he bobs up out of the still ferns, with a more human look now, but still drunk with wonder, still amazed, bedazzled and overwhelmed by the feast of the eye. He seems to be floating up from the paleozoic ooze and, as if he had caught the distant roar of the Flood, there is in his face the premonition of impending catastrophe. He seems to be anticipating the destruction of the great forests, the annihilation of countless living trees and the lush green foliage of a spring which will never happen again. Every variety of leaf, every shade of green seems to be packed into this small canvas. It is a sort of bath in the vernal equinox, and man is happily absent from his preoccupations. Only Reichel is there, with his big round eyes, and the wonder is on him and this great indwelling wonder saturates the impending doom and casts a searchlight into the unknown.

In every cataclysm Reichel is present. Sometimes he is a fish hanging in the sky beneath a triple-ringed sun. He hangs there like a God of Vengeance raining down his maledictions upon man. He is the God who destroys the fishermen's nets, the God who brings down thunder and lightning so that the fishermen may be drowned. Sometimes he appears incarnated as a snail, and you may see him at work building his own monument. Sometimes he is a gay and happy snail crawling about on the sands of Spain. Sometimes he is only the dream of a snail, and then his world already phantasmagorical becomes musical and diaphanous. You are there in his dream at the precise moment when everything is melting, when only the barest suggestion of form remains to give a last fleeting clue to the appearance of things. Swift as flame, elusive, perpetually on the wing, nevertheless there is always in his pictures the iron claw which grasps the unseizable and imprisons it without hurt or damage. It is the dexterity of the master, the visionary clutch which holds firm and secure its prey without ruffling a feather.

There are moments when he gives you the impression of being seated on another planet making his inventory of the world. Conjunctions are recorded such as no astronomer has noted. I am thinking now of a picture which he calls "Almost Full Moon." The *almost* is characteristic of Reichel. This *almost* full is not the almost full with which we are familiar. It is the almost-full-moon which a man would see from Mars, let us say. For when it will be full, this moon, it will throw a green, spectral light reflected from a planet just bursting into life. This is a moon which has somehow strayed from its orbit. It belongs to a night studded with strange configurations and it hangs there taut as an anchor in an ocean of pitchblende. So finely balanced is it in this unfamiliar sky that the addition of a thread would destroy its equilibrium. This is one of the moons which the poets are constantly charting and concerning which, fortunately, there is no scientific knowledge. Under these new moons the destiny of the race will one day be determined. They are the anarchic moons which swim in the latent protoplasm of the race, which bring about baffling disturbances, angoisse, hallucinations. Everything that happens now and has been happening for the last twenty thousand years or so is put in the balance against this weird, prophetic cusp of a moon which is traveling towards its optimum.

The moon and the sea! What cold, clean attractions obsess him! That warm, cosy fire out of which men build their petty emotions seems almost unknown to Reichel. He inhabits the depths, of ocean and of sky. Only in the depths is he content and in his element. Once he described to me a Medusa he had seen in the waters of Spain. It came swimming towards him like a sea-organ playing a mysterious oceanic music. I thought, as he was describing the Medusa, of another painting for which he could not find words. I saw him make the motion with his arms, that helpless, fluttering stammer of the man who has not yet named everything. He was *almost* on the point of describing it when suddenly he stopped, as if paralyzed by the dread of naming it. But while he was stuttering and stammering I heard the music playing; I knew that the old woman with the white hair was only another creature from the depths, a Medusa in female guise who was playing for him the music of eternal sorrow. I knew that she was the woman who inhabited "The Haunted House" where in hot somber tones the little white bird is perched, warbling the pre-ideological language unknown to man. I knew that she was there in the "Remembrance of a Stained Glass Window," the being which inhabits the window, revealing herself in silence only to those who have opened their hearts. I knew that she was in the wall on which he had painted a verse of Rilke's, this gloomy, desolate wall over which a smothered sun casts a wan ray of light. I knew that what he could not name was in everything, like his black sorrow, and that he had chosen a language as fluid as music in order not to be broken on the sharp spokes of the intellect.

In everything he does color is the predominant note. By the choice and blend of his tones you know that he is a musician, that he is preoccupied with what is unseizable and untranslatable. His colors are like the dark melodies of César Franck. They are all weighted with black, a live black, like the heart of chaos itself. This black might also be said to correspond to a kind of beneficent ignorance which permits him to resuscitate the powers of magic. Everything he portrays has a symbolic and contagious quality: the subject is but the means for conveying a significance which is deeper than form or language. When I think, for example, of the picture which he calls "The Holy Place," one of his strikingly unobtrusive subjects, I have to fall back on the word enigmatic. There is nothing in this work which bears resemblance to other holy places that we know of. It is made up of entirely new elements which through form and color suggest all that is called up by the title. And yet, by some strange alchemy, this little canvas, which might also have been called "Urim and Thummim," revives the memory of that which was lost to the Jews upon the destruction of the Holy Temple. It suggests the fact that in the consciousness of the race nothing which is sacred has been lost, that on the contrary it is we who are lost and vainly seeking, and that we shall go on vainly seeking until we learn to see with other eyes.

In this black out of which his rich colors are born there is not only the transcendental but the despotic. His black is not oppressive, but profound, producing a *fruitful* disquietude. It gives one to believe that there is no rock bottom any more than there is eternal truth. Nor even God, in the sense of the Absolute, for to create God one would first have to describe a circle. No, there is no God in these paintings, unless it be Reichel himself. There is no need for a God because it is all one creative substance born out of darkness and relapsing into darkness again.

70

# THE PHILOSOPHER WHO
# PHILOSOPHIZES

As A species the philosophers have always bored me to death. The profession has always seemed to me to be an unnatural one, an activity removed from life. (This is a criticism which does not come to my head, for example, when thinking of a Hindu or a Tibetan sage.) At the same time philosophy itself excites me, much as good wine does: I accept it not only as a legitimate part of life but as a *sine qua non*, a without which no life. Nothing, however, is sadder, more dismal, dingy, mingy, picayune than the lives of certain philosophers. It is as if they had become, or rebecome, queasy, quaky, archaic little men whose whole lives are mortgaged by the obsession for constructing miniature soul-houses to be occupied only after death. The man can be one thing, a tiny louse, let us say, and the philosophy another, perhaps a crushing, devastating world conception which nobody can swallow, not even the philosopher himself. The process of refining and segregating Idea, of making it "pure," so to speak, inevitably brings about a muddiness which is fortunately lacking in the original chaos. I have a mental image of the philosophic systems of the world lying like a net above the surface of human activity; from his remote and lofty perch the philosopher looks down through the curd-like net and discovers in the affairs of men nothing but dreck.

All this is not by way of saying that Keyserling is the first philosopher whom I can stomach. No, there are times when Keyserling too bores me to death. But with Keyserling there comes a new element, an heroic and adulterative one which, like the discovery of the microbe world in the human organism, stimulates and complicates the problem of health and clarity. Keyserling is the first philosopher to use a sky-light—or a periscope. He may plunge as deep as the whale but he never forgets the sky above, nor the fact that it is the sky towards which men are turning instinctively for relief and assuagement. Keyserling comes at a time when both sea and sky are being heavily explored. He is the new type of spiritual adventurer, the Plutonic heralder who faces both ways, who is at home above and below, who reconciles East and West and yet never loses hold of the tiller. Built like a Viking, with an unquenchable fire in his guts and a pantheon for a brain, he has dedicated his life to quest and conquest. For me he represents the genuine metamorphic thinker, one capable of navigating in any medium. He is endowed with an indestructible skeletal structure and a crystalline transparency usually observable only in lower forms of life.

I first came upon Keyserling's vast symphonic musings at a fortuitous moment in my life. For forty years I had been sound asleep and thrashing about with furious activity. Life had become nothing but this noisy breathing which signifies nothing. Through a *rencontre* with an extraordinary person I suddenly awoke, looked about, and saw what I had never seen before—*the cosmos*. And then, right to hand, was one of Keyserling's books—*Creative Understanding*—which I devoured ravenously. It was like the first mouthful of bread after a long fast; even the hard, tough crust tasted good. I allowed this food to roll about in my guts a long while before venturing to taste another morsel. The next time I picked up Keyserling, I remember, was during a sea voyage. This time it was *The Travel Diary*. I did not begin at the beginning, but glanced here and there at the chapters dealing with those countries which most interest me—China and India. I saw the philosopher in his undershirt, a frail weather-beaten man, puzzled, ravished, perplexed, roving amidst a fauna and flora which were constantly changing and shifting; I saw that he was most extraordinarily fallible, permeable, malleable. I rejoiced for him, and even enjoyed his occasional discomfiture.

Another time, in bed, I began the great South American saga of the soul. I was privileged to experience that indescribable pleasure of being electrified in the midst of a heavy torpor. The whole cosmos suddenly began to wheel before me. I felt the blood which the earth has given to man restored to earth to run in tumultuous subterranean rivers, to flow sluggishly among the constellations, to burst the trunks of fat tropical trees, to dry and bake in the peaked Andes, to slumber in the land-and-water beasts, the shell-backed monsters, the hypnotic and fatalistic ophidians: I saw a man take

**73**

a continent by the scalp and wash it in the sea, shaking loose its hair-like dreams and silences, laying its blood out in thick slabs and dissecting it, selecting with a most dexterous digital manipulation its fragile, doomed inhabitants one by one, group by group, race by race, generation by generation, the whole multimillenary ancestral horde living and dead, ghastly and ghostly, full-blown, fly-blown, scoriated, striated, truncated, pulped, battered, a rich plasma of dead and living, of souls, ghosts, mummies, spirits, noumena, phenomena, succubi, incubi, and plough them through with the iron harrow of thought's brutal logic; then taking gold and dross together, with the goldsmith's finest balance, weigh, assay, test and attest, in order, like a dreaming Titan, to set moving in the sleep of thought a timeward litter of words which would arrange itself in the form of a significant whole. This I glimpsed whilst falling asleep one night, and it was a special dress rehearsal put on for me by the same gaunt Viking in swallow-tail coat who prefers champagne with his evening meal, who gesticulates like a god of thunder, who strokes his beard meditatively and sits alone sometimes, ofttimes, to reflect, meditate and pray, or to gather back into him the vast sperm and spew which he is capable of ejecting on the slightest provocation.

Such an experience is definitely not in the philosophic scheme of things. I had to recast my notion of "philosopher." I had to take the situation philosophically. I had to admit, above all, that for the first time in my life I was witnessing a philosopher lose himself in the world—not only lose himself, but drown himself, and not only drown, but immolate himself: had to confess that more miraculous still was the sight of him rising from the grave with the stake through his body, the sight of him defiantly flinging it off—stake, world, water, waves, heavy ether, soporific excrescences, end dreams, blood vistas, horoscopic hallucinations, dead thought clinkers, social pus habits, all, all, the while making an airy music above in the pink clouds drenching the mountain top. Nor was I any longer surprised when I heard him blow the conch and roll the kettle drum, nor when whooping it up along the Appalachian spine he suddenly burst into the Rig-Veda.

This is what I call philosophizing. It is something other than making philosophy—*something plus.* Here the creative becomes the thing-in-itself, and not vice versa: the exercise of a faculty and not the product of the exercise. Living the every-day life whilst spinning the most tenuous tough web. Not the soul-house of incarceration but the light-meshed web of the divine diaphane. In this transparent garb studded with dead flies, dead thought matter, dead meteoric systems, dead mouse-traps, dead pass-keys, we advance page after page, foot by foot, millimeter by millimeter, through the Keyserling underworld sea. At times we are lifted clean out of the waters and rushed aloft like a screaming condor. The world systems pass in review, those already formulated and those not yet formulated. With myriad-minded mythological eye we pierce the stale imperfections that cement life to life and death to death. We become habituated to all climates, all conditions of weather, all forms of blight, pestilence, sorrow and suffering; we peregrinate in non-peripatetic style, eschewing the perimeter, the axes, the hypotenuse, avoiding angles, squares, triangles: instead we adopt the lymphatic slide, follow the interstitial, interstellar parabolas. In the deep-holed world conceptions scattered between star births and star deaths we shimmer with spangled webs, radiant, dewy, misty, effulgent with philosophic dust. Where now the god who was nailed to the cross? Where the man with the lantern? Where the ferryman, the fire-eater, the logos dealer, the lotus healer, the Gorgon, the flat-footed Moloch? What has become of man, mollusc of molluscs?

Keyserling's style . . . there is something prehistoric about it. Of a morning he awakes in a volcanic mood, and he erupts. What is terrifying and unbearable, in his style, is not the heavy Baltic or Pomeranian redundancy, but the inundating effect. We are enlightened, blessed, baptized and drowned. There is every variety of inundation—by air, fire, earth and water, by lava, slag, cinders, by relics, monuments, symbols, signs and portents. The very secrets of the earth are belched forth and with them the scintillating prediluvial records of man. Throughout the convulsive record there are pages of oceanic calm in which one can hear the breathing of whales and other leviathans of the deep; there are celestial sunrises too, as on the morning of creation when even the fledgling lark can be heard caroling in the blue. And there are great frozen tracts in which the air itself turns blue as a knuckle and the marrow of wisdom is held in icy suspense.

Keyserling is a sort of red-feathered giant from the tundras, a megalithic Mameluke of the Lemurian Age who has created his own polyphonetic, polyphylacteric alphabet. His language is something forged by hand out of meteoric rock; there is no sensuality, no humor in it. It contains the seeds of all that was dreamed of by man in the cataclysmic beginnings of the world: it is not a blood language but a schist-cyst-and-quartz medium. And yet, like all those of royal strain, he is capable of showing tenderness, humility, true humility. He will take the pains, in a letter, to answer a microscopic point, if the point is worth answering. He will begin on a post-card and end by presenting you with an album. With the superabundant energy of a colossus he will uncover a ton of debris in order to bring to light an infinitesimal speck of radium with which to illumine the question. He does not impose his verdict; he turns his searchlight on the problem. He is a visionary of heavy substance, a seer who looks into the bowels of the earth as well as into the blue. He is equipped with the most sensitive antennae and the boring tusk of a rhinoceros to boot.

The ordinary reader is killed off—not by the back-breaking *longueurs* à la Proust or Henry James, nor by the learned abracadabra of a Joyce, but by the unaccustomed variety of media through which the muscular flow of thought cleaves and surges. People have accused him of being derivative, assimilative, synthetic. The truth is that he is analgesic and amalgamatic. As the thought flows it congeals, imprisoning in the most marvelous veined clots the hemorrhages produced by the terrifying lesions which his impetuous ardor opens up. He is a thinker who attacks with the whole body, who emerges at the end of a book bleeding from every pore. With Keyserling the spirit goes berserker. It is the rage of the giants who, weary of earthly conquests, flung themselves at the heavens. He makes a blood marriage with the spirit: Apis the Bull goring the Holy Ghost in ecstasy. Sometimes it seems more like God lying down on the operating table with his adopted son Hermann and exchanging vital fluids: a last minute operation in preparation for the final ordeal, the quest and conquest of death.*

* Written in Corfu as a tribute to Keyserling on the occasion of his 60th birthday this July 1940.

# THE ABSOLUTE COLLECTIVE*

"WE CAN no longer live to live, but to create the new. That is the hymn of modernity; that is the new need. But how came the new need? It came because star and fire, rose and tiger died within us . . . Should our time grasp this, it would be a spiritual revolution which would lead right into the midst of the new time."

This, from an essay called "World Conquest" which appeared in *Purpose* back in 1932, is reminiscent of D. H. Lawrence. Like Lawrence, Gutkind is of the line of Akhenaton, Hermes Trismegis-

* The Absolute Collective: A Philosophical Attempt to overcome our broken state. By Erich Gutkind. Translated by Marjorie Gabain.

tus, Plotinus, Paracelsus, Blake, Nietzsche: he is a visionary, a prophet, a man ahead of his time. And yet, like all these figures, a man supremely of his time too. No man is born out of time! But the men who are most representative of their time, those who situate themselves in the creative flux, are always and inevitably rejected, if not crucified. For such men are of sidereal time, which is the poet's chronology and not the astronomer's. The visionary *predicts* the stars and the planets which will be discovered, for he is of the stars as well as of the earth.

Gutkind is obsessed, in a superbly healthy way, by the new world which is in the making. He is obsessed too by the possibility of the miraculous which the birth of a new world-condition always engenders. The miracle this time, in Gutkind's opinion, is *the birth of man*. As a philosopher and diagnostician he has strong affinities with Nietzsche, Spengler and Lawrence: he too has had his vision of the end. But he has also a clear vision of the future, an absolute faith in the new world-condition, which is not to be merely a new cultural cycle but a complete new integration marked by a polarity which will establish the *vertical* axis of man. Man will come into his own by establishing a *cosmic* relationship with the universe, that is Gutkind's idea. It is a very old and tenacious idea, this, one which has been given us repeatedly from the most varied sources. It comes now with new force because even the dullest professor, even the philosopher, is aware that the dissolution of our world is certain. In the grip of a paralysis such as the world has never known before, filled with a premonitory dread such as perhaps only the Atlanteans experienced, we live from day to day, from hour to hour, awaiting the debacle. In our very midst a great people is preparing the execution of the most revolting part of this program of annihilation. The world watches indignantly and fascinatedly, too bewildered perhaps or too deeply aware of the significance of this activity to do anything to counteract it. Before our very eyes the Germans are creating the bomb which will destroy what is called our "civilization." With it they will destroy themselves, that is certain. Even the Germans are aware of that, hence their fervor and exaltation, their arrogance and reck-lessness. In another part of the world the Japanese are educating the Chinese in our footsteps, paving the way to make their enemy the masters of the Oriental world and in turn to destroy it. These are patent facts which only the stern misguided "realists" refuse to see.

Gutkind, who is a German Jew (now in exile), because perhaps of the situation in which he was placed, is able to "violently de-mand that we may bodily experience the abysses instead of only philosophizing thereon." It is a refreshing antidote to the apostasy of Freud, who tried to erect a metaphysics on the recognition of fear, creating a gray realism of scientific hue instead of a Dantesque reality of black and white. Gutkind, living in the midst of the Teutonic world of technic, becomes an out-and-out Jew, a Jew of the Essenes stamp such as Christ was, a realist of the first water, as was Christ again, able to recognize the world for what it is and to embrace it for what it is in process of becoming. In the midst of the non-human world he proclaims the human world, proclaims the transcendent in man which will not only free him from murder and death but enable him to live completely in the present. For the world of man, he says, is *the world that is com-pletely alive!* In such a world there is no place for murder, nor can there be a human world until murder is eliminated from man's consciousness. How is such a world possible? The question cannot be settled forthwith, he answers. "We are only beginning to open the world, for we have never yet lived in an unbroken state . . .

The opener of man is Reality . . . Everything can be both itself and a means to something else."

The world we are now living in is what Gutkind calls the Mamser world of confusion, idols, ghosts, the world of things, oriented towards death, a world in which man is nothing but an object waiting for redemption. It is a world in which there is nothing but a dreary sequence of predictable events. God becomes an empty concept, man an isolated individual, the world a collection of things. It is the very picture of evil, with the most hideous of all punishments as penalty: death in life. Against this false worldliness, in which all nations of the earth alike are guilty of living, Gutkind opposes a real "worldliness." Man's roots do not lie in consciousness, he asserts, but in reality. He goes on again to speak of death, stating that death is not an essential part of man, that he can separate himself from it as from an accident. "In the midst of life," he writes, "we are filled with death, and to die will bring us no release . . . Immortality does not yet exist. Immortality follows from the complete aliveness of man when, purged of Tuma, the original corruption, he has been changed from a being locked up in himself to one that is opened and can speak . . . The isolated individual cannot, by dying, work himself free of the world of death. We are all inextricably bound together. So long as one still belongs to death all will belong." And then he speaks of the Hebrew meaning of the word "eternity," which is that of victory rather than duration. "To die means to be cut off, it does not mean to cease. One who is bound to others is free from the fear of death, for fear has its roots in separation. Where there is fear it is quickly followed by the flight to possessions. Far deadlier than any bodily decay," he concludes, "is the insidious principle of death within our souls."

It is impossible to overstress the importance of this theme.

Death is the paramount obsession of our time, and it is the knowledge of death which is destroying us. The great exponents of reality today—of a false worldliness, that is—are all advocates of murder. Even the pacifists are murderers at heart. The world is divided into idealistic camps, and not one ideal is proclaimed but means death to the other, death to all concerned. Men are fanatically ready, it would seem, to kill and to be killed. Never was a whole world so devoted to the cause of death and destruction. Nowhere in the whole world is there a people exempt from reproach. Even the neutral countries, through their heartless profiteering, through their supine indifference, contribute to the death racket. This is the supreme reality of our death-like world, and this is a horror which must be faced by every individual, and not by legislatures and governments alone. But where are the individuals? Who is an individual? Who has the courage to say No at the crucial moment—or even to meet the challenge in advance with a No! It is not to the men of this order and generation, I feel, that Gutkind's book is addressed. Gutkind, like Lawrence, is a man of the transition stage, the double-faced "hero-metaphysician" who looks backward with deep understanding and forward with exultation. He is the Pluto-Janus type of which the German astrologers have been talking ever since the discovery of that new planet. Only, whereas the German people have identified themselves with the hero-death impulse, Gutkind identifies himself with the daring metaphysician, the man of the future whose face is set towards the established kingdom of man. The keynote of this coming type of man is totality, integration, oneness. The man of today, the man of the transition period, split and straddled as he is between two worlds, pregnant with the germ of the future, is veritably crucified by his duality.

The great exploration of the Unconscious which was begun by

Dostoievski, and subsequently pursued systematically by Freud and his disciples, bears a curious resemblance to the exploration and development of the New World in the time of the Renaissance. The expansion of the known universe always entails a split in the consciousness. We know how the Renaissance faded out—in an orgy of megalomania. The "modern" nations today—Japan, Germany, America—are going mad in a similar way. No more wonderful examples of schizophrenia are to be found than in these "progressive" countries. The fury and enormity of their activity is the symbol of their impotence, their inability to bridge the split. This stupendous activity, disguised as progress and enlightenment, is only a means of spreading the death which they carry within them. It is the function of such peoples to make the egg rotten through and through, to sever the bondage of the womb in order that the real human being may emerge. Themselves doomed, they act as carriers of the deadly germ which will sweep the ground clear for a new way of life. As Gutkind says: "Only the dead things in the world exercise power and restraint. The fully opened world that has been cleansed of idols is a deathless world."

It is indeed difficult for me to look at this book impartially, or criticize it objectively. It is the sort of book which I write every day of my life in my off moments. Only about a hundred pages long, its language is at once true, precise, necessitous. It carries far beyond its scope and intention, as every vital book should. In my mind it situates itself exactly at that angle of time and space which is most portentous. More than any book I have ever read this one is born at precisely the right time. Turning its pages is like turning the pages of life itself, the life which we all know and deny, the life which has never been realized. The prophetic is not set forth in the usual prophetic manner; on the contrary, the deep certitude which inspired the work creates a sort of axiomatic ecstasy, a residue of truth which is implicit and unshakeable. The book is true in the highest sense, because based on acceptance, which is to say that it is entirely on the side of life. This acceptance of life is again merely to say recognition of the cosmic principle. The climate of this opus is a sort of spiritual equinox in which life and death are seen to be at balance. Is it necessary to add that it is precisely at such moments that the miraculous nature of life reveals itself, at just such moments that the whole order of life can be reversed, or transcended? The men who exerted the greatest influence over the world were those who stood at just such junctures and revealed the truths which were vouchsafed them. In their wake they brought about devastating changes; they altered the face of the world—and more than the face of the world, the heart of the world! In each case the miracle almost happened; yet somehow something always intervened, the message was aborted, the vision lost. This has happened so repeatedly as to create in the majority of men an ingrained pessimism as to the destiny of the race. The world is perpetually divided on the question of truth versus illusion. The two co-exist in man, creating a perpetual duality, a seemingly unhealable schism. More tragic still is that the example which the lives of these great pioneers of the human spirit have given us sputters out in empty symbol and servile fetishism. The tremendous impulse which these great spirits unleashed stiffens into hobbling fetters and manacles imposed by stupid cult and religion. Every inspired man has been at some time aware of the real significance of these great figures, but the inspiration passes off, unfortunately, into religiousness or into art. Art has been just as crippling as religion, because like religion it has always represented the triumph of man over an imaginary world. The man of action, it is true, places himself in a real world, but his world is a diminished one and becomes finally even more illusory than the imagined world of the artist or the religious-minded individual. "We have not yet dared to face the world as we should!" writes Gutkind, and that is so. The history of cultural man is one long tale of evasion, of trial by error, of repetition, of cul-de-sac. Here and there the isolated man of genius has had a vision of the way, but no one man can lead the way! Sacrifice, if it has any meaning, reveals to us that true progress can only be made by all simultaneously.

Today, from the most irreconcilable quarters, there is coagulating the conviction that this futile repetition which has marked the era of "civilization" is destined to cease. We stand at the threshold of a new way of life, one in which MAN is about to be realized. The disturbances which characterize this age of transition indicate clearly the beginnings of a new climate, a spiritual climate in which the body will no longer be denied, in which, on the contrary, the body of man will find its proper place in the body of the world. Man's domination over nature is only now beginning to be understood as something more than a mere technical triumph: behind the brutal assertion of power and will there lies a smoldering sense of the awesomeness, the majesty, the grandeur of his responsibility. Is he perhaps just faintly beginning to realize that "all the ways of the earth lead to heaven?"

Thus, the complete destruction of our cultural world, which seems more than ever assured now by the impending smashup, is really a blessing in disguise. The old grooves of race, religion and nationality are destined to go, and in their place we shall see, for the first time in the history of man, a community of interest based not on the animal in him but on the human being which he has so long denied. The fight is between the death instinct and the life instinct. It has nothing to do with culture, or bread, or ideology, or peace or security. The schism has grown so wide that it is either self-destruction or a totality never before imagined. With each new conflict one is made increasingly aware of the real battle, which is inner, and which is nothing but a warfare between the real and the ideal man. The ideal man must perish, and the ideal man will certainly perish, for the last props are now giving way. Man must open up, prepared to live the life of the world in all its worldliness, if he is to survive. For, as Gutkind cogently points out, even worse than the wholesale slaughter in which we indulge is what he calls "sublimated murder," or the refusal to overflow. I stress this aspect of the book particularly, because it has always seemed to me incontrovertible that war is just and necessary, so long as men insist on repressing their murderous instincts. War is not an economic affair, nor a curse of the gods, nor an inevitability: it is the reflection of an inner split, the projection of our continuous repressed lusts and hatreds.

That man has always lived in what Gutkind calls "a broken state" seems only too evident. Moreover, man has always known that this condition was evil and unnecessary. The sense of guilt which has accumulated throughout centuries of struggle towards enlightenment and liberation has at last become overwhelming. It is absurd and wrong to wish to remove this sense of guilt. The sense of guilt is the spiritual barometer which we carry in our blood. It is not only useless to deny sin, it is impossible. Man has been throttling and strangling himself ever since the dawn of history. He has been fear-stricken—more daring in his panic sometimes than God Almighty, and again more cowardly than the worm. He has never understood what the conflict was about precisely. He has never wanted to accept his real nature, his responsibility, which is creation, and which must begin with himself. All the forces of coercion are maintained on the false theory of protection—protection against the wicked, or the insane, or the greedy. But the

truly insane, the truly wicked, the truly greedy ones are we ourselves, we who try to bolster up the crumbling edifice with external
remedies, with prisons, asylums and instruments of war. Whom
are we trying to protect? And against what? The real ghost is
fear—we are confronted with it at every step. The whole movement of the social order is a retrograde movement, a retreat, a
panic in the face of reality. The man who decides to live his own
life is without fear; he lives positively, not negatively. That is why
men like Hitler and Mussolini, who are one with their destiny,
move with lightning-like rapidity and assurance. What is there to
hinder them? There is no resistance—there is only on the part of
their opponents fear, which expresses itself in terms of "peace and
security." The moment one is on the side of life "peace and security" drop out of consciousness. The only peace, the only security, is in fulfillment. On the other hand, whatever needs to be
maintained through force is doomed. There can be no real life until
murder ceases, that is incontestable. "The highest activity," says
Gutkind, "is an effect rather than an act." In the highest type of
activity there is a radiation of energy, as from the sun itself, he
adds. *From a center that is at rest.* To overcome the world is to
make it transparent, I believe he says, which is a remarkable statement and of a simplicity which is profound. It is precisely here that
one detects the abysmal gulf which separates a Christ or a Buddha,
let us say, from a Hitler or a Mussolini. With the latter it is sheer
Will which manifests itself, and which in the end destroys itself.
In the case of the former it is a vital emanation from a being at
peace with himself and the world, and consequently irresistible.
The use of the will is the sign of death; it is only as a half-being
that the man of will triumphs. What lives on, when he has worked
his will, is the death which was in him. It is this exaltation of the
will, the mark of the divided self, which emasculates the world of

87

men and women. Thus, whereas the strong leader may or may not have been "wicked," his followers certainly are never wicked, but simply weak. The instinctive nature of man gets used up: he tends to function more and more as a machine, a robot. The proletarian, for example—is he not the last cog in the human equation, the lowest symbol of man that ever was? Who can deny that he is infinitely less than the most primitive man? And in what sense is he less? Because he has not enough food, clothing, shelter, security, leisure, learning? Some would like to have us believe that such is the case. To me it seems that the real diminution of his power and substance has come about through his dividedness. He is without passion and without hope, a pawn in a game whose rules he knows nothing of. "A de-humanized commodity," Gutkind calls him. "An object waiting for redemption." No, there are no individuals any longer. There are monstrous tyrants—and the mob, the "masses."

The progress of humanity is so infinitesimally slow that it almost seems like no progress at all. But there is that which is called "conscience," which is not an empty concept but a very real factor in the human make-up, and this conscience does indicate the existence of another and a higher urge. In its negative aspect it makes itself known through fatality, punishment, etc., but in its positive aspect it reveals the existence of an Absolute, of law. It indicates the hidden axis of our vertical life without which the "dreary round of predictable events" would make the world appear like a rat-trap. As Gutkind rightly says, we have never dared to face the world as we should—or one might say with equal truth that we have never dared to face the world-as-it-is. Why does the word "reality" always have such a sinister, gray, fatalistic ring? It is the realists—that is to say, the death-eaters—who are responsible for the pall which has come over the word. But the men who are thoroughly wide-awake and completely alive are in reality, and for these reality has always been close to ecstasy, partaking of a life of fulfillment which knows no bounds. Of them only may it be said that they live in the present. Through them is it permitted us to grasp the meaning of timelessness, of eternity which is victory. It is they who are truly of this world. Their victory is one which each man must win for himself: it is a private and at the same time a universal affair. Nothing which is of value can be handed down, bequeathed, preserved—as with our lamentable treasures of art. What happens must be realized anew by each man. The history of religions emphasizes the stupendous difficulty which man has in realizing this truth. Truth crystallizes quickly into idolatry, servility, surrender. Everywhere we see life being lived vicariously. And yet life everywhere and at all times for any and everybody is simple, startlingly simple. We live on the edge of the miraculous every minute of our lives. The miracle is in us, and it blossoms forth the moment we lay ourselves open to it. The miracle of miracles is the stubbornness with which men refuse to open themselves up. Our whole life seems to be nothing but a frantic effort to evade that which is constantly within our grasp. This which is the very reverse of the miraculous is nothing else but FEAR. Man has no other real enemy than this which he carries within him. Somewhere a French poet has written: "No daring is fatal." *Provided*, he should have added, that one is unified. Divided, everything is fatal and leads to catastrophe. This has been the history of mankind, yet no man of vision and integrity has ever accepted it as ordained and ineluctable. Man has the power to renounce and to accept; he can refuse to be a pawn and he can make of himself a god. He holds his fate in his own hands—and not only his own fate, but the fate of the world. There is a justice which, fortunately, surpasses the comprehension of most men, else the world would go mad immediately. It is at the edge of madness that we attain to a glimpse of the overwhelming truth and simplicity of life. What confounds the mob, when confronted with a great figure, is the simplicity of the man's behavior. I repeat, it is the utter simplicity of life which defeats man. He has turned the earth inside out in a frantic effort to attain security, to arrive at wisdom. But he has never really attached himself to the earth, never sufficiently venerated it. He has tried to subjugate when he has had only to observe and enjoy. Suffering is not the only way to victory—it is a way. And knowledge is the poorest way of all, for it means that only a part of man's being is struggling forward. The whole man must be there, ready at all times to act (or not to act), to move with the certitude of a sleepwalker, to dare anything because he is convinced that life is now, this very moment, and that it is inexhaustible and unknowable.

Up to the present man has been an embryo, a unique one nevertheless, in that he possesses the power at any moment to leap forth into full being. At one jump he can leap clear of the clockwork, to borrow a phrase of Gutkind's. I believe it absolutely. I know it to be so from my own experience. All growth is a leap in the dark, a spontaneous, unpremeditated act without benefit of experience. Every sign of growth is a revolt against death. Even death itself, finally, is regarded as the means to another kind of growth. In one form or another man has always regarded death as a portal opening the way to a new and greater life. Man has postponed his real life here on earth for a life to come. Once he begins to realize that death is present here and now, in each and all of us, and that it is only necessary to open the door to have life immediately and in unqualified abundance and magnificence, what could possess him to withhold, to remain closed, to fear, to kill, to cling to his miserable possessions? Compared with the splendor and magnificence of that life which we are constantly denying this life which we now lead is a nightmare. Perhaps this alone explains why it is easier to enlist men in the cause of death, why they prefer to be dead heroes, dead saints, dead martyrs in every sense of the word. Life itself has lost its value, its attraction. In a real sense, life is something which has not yet begun. Men are seeking life thirstily, but their eyes are in the back of their heads. Life can only be seized by the whole organism, as something felt, something which demands neither proof nor justification. Nobody can point the way. *Life is*, and in this sense a man is or he is not. Life is not an "it" to be grasped by the mind. "Whoever has not been fully alive in this life," says Gutkind, "will not become so through death." Or, as Jacob Boehme put it: "Who dies not before he dies is ruined when he dies." It is the same thing.

This is the Apocalyptic Era when all things will be made manifest unto us. I am not dippy. I have not become what is erroneously called "religious." I am against all the religions of the world as I am against all the nations of the world and all the teachings of the world. I speak illogically, intuitively, and with absolute certitude. Nothing will prevent the world from realizing its worst fears—nothing but the elimination of fear itself. The destruction of the world we have foolishly tried to preserve is at hand. The death which had been rotting away in us secretly and disgracefully must be made manifest, and to a degree never before heard of. As Father Perrault said to "Glory" Conway—"It will be such a storm, my son, as the world has not seen before. There will be no safety by arms, no help from authority, no answer in science. It will rage till every flower of culture is trampled, and all human things are levelled in a vast chaos . . . The Dark Ages to come will cover the whole world in a single pall; there will be neither escape nor sanctuary, save such as are too secret to be found or too humble to be noticed." This is the dread prospect which faces us and which is our hope at the same time. The wheel turns slowly, but it turns and turns, and not even death can arrest it. For death is a part of the endless process. For the time being there is no ceiling; if we are to make a real ascent we must break through the "metaphysical zenith." We have remained too long at the level of culture subject to the law of evaporation by which everything freezes into the stagnant flux of civilization. "Our action," says Gutkind, "must have its root in the mysterious center of our dumb, unconscious being . . . Our ascent must take its start in the depths of the body."

All about us we see a world in revolt; but revolt is negative, a mere finishing-off process. In the midst of destruction we carry with us also our creation, our hopes, our strength, our urge to be fulfilled. The climate changes as the wheel turns, and what is true for the sidereal world is true for man. The last two thousand years have brought about a duality in man such as he never experienced before, and yet the man who dominates this whole period was one who stood for wholeness, one who proclaimed the Holy Ghost. No life in the whole history of man has been so misinterpreted, so woefully misunderstood as Christ's. If not a single man has shown himself capable of following the example of Christ, and doubtless none ever will for we shall no longer have need of Christs, nevertheless this one profound example has altered our climate. Unconsciously we are moving into a new realm of being; what we have brought to perfection, in our zeal to escape the true reality, is a complete arsenal of destruction; when we have rid ourselves of the suicidal mania for a beyond we shall begin the life of here and now which is reality and which is sufficient unto itself. We shall have no need for art or religion because we shall be in ourselves a work of art. This is how I interpret realistically what Gutkind has set forth philosophically: this is the way in which man will overcome his broken state. If my statements are not precisely in accord with the text of Gutkind's thesis, I nevertheless am thoroughly in accord with Gutkind and his view of things. I have felt it my duty not only to set forth his doctrine, but to launch it, and in launching it to augment it, activate it. Any genuine philosophy leads to action and from action back again to wonder, to the enduring fact of mystery. I am one man who can truly say that he has understood and acted upon this profound thought of Gutkind's—"the stupendous fact that we stand in the midst of reality will always be something far more wonderful than anything we do."

# THE ENORMOUS WOMB

As THE dictionary says, the womb is the place where anything is engendered or brought to life. As far as I can make out, there is never anything but womb. First and last there is the womb of Nature; then there is the mother's womb; and finally there is the womb in which we have our life and being and which we call the world. It is the failure to recognize the world as womb which is the cause of our misery, in large part. We think of the child unborn as living in a state of bliss; we think of death as an escape from life's ills; but life itself we still refuse to regard as bliss and security. And yet, in this world about is not everything being engendered and brought to life? Perhaps it is only another of our illusions that the grave be regarded as a refuge and the nine months preceding birth as bliss. Who knows anything about the uterine life or the life hereafter? Yet somehow the idea has caught hold, and probably it will never perish, that these two states of unconsciousness mean freedom from pain and struggle, and hence bliss. On the other hand we know from experience that there are people alive and moving about who live in what is called a state of bliss. Are they more unconscious than the rest, or less so? I think most of us would agree that they are less unconscious. Wherein are their lives different then from that of the ordinary run of mankind? To my way of thinking the difference lies in their attitude towards the world, lies in the supreme fact that they have accepted the world as a womb, and not a tomb. For they seem neither to regret what has passed nor to fear what is to come. They live in an intense state of awareness and yet are apparently without fear.

It has been said that fear, which plays such a dominant role in our lives, was once a vague, nameless thing, an echo, one might almost say, of the life instinct. It has been said that with the development of civilization this nameless fear gradually crystallized into a fear of death. And that in the highest reaches of civilization this fear of death becomes a fear of life, as exemplified by the behavior of the neurotic. Now there is nothing strange about fear: no matter in what guise it presents itself it is something with which we are all so familiar that when a man appears who is without it we are at once enslaved by him. There have been less than a handful of such men in the history of man. Whether they were forces for good or evil matters little: the fear which they awaken is the fear of the monster. In truth they were all monsters, whether they be called Tamerlane, Buddha, Christ or Napoleon. They were heroic figures, and the hero, according to myths, was always born supernaturally. The hero, in short, is one who was spared the shock of birth.

The hero then is a sort of monster who is immune to pain and suffering: he is on the side of life. The world is for him a place where things are engendered, brought to life. Life reveals itself to him as art, and not as an ordeal. He enjoys life by rearranging it according to his own needs. He may say that he is doing it for others, for humanity, but we know that he is also a liar. The hero is a man who says to himself—*this* is where things happen, not somewhere else. He acts as if he were at home in the world. Such behavior, of course, brings about a terrific confusion, for as you may have noticed, people are seldom at home, always somewhere else, always "absent." Life, as it is called, is for most of us one long postponement. And the simple reason for it is: FEAR.

As we see whenever a war breaks out, the fear of war is overcome the moment one is really in it. If war were really as terrible as people imagine it to be it would have been wiped out long ago. To make war is as natural for human beings as to make love. Love can make cowards of men just as much as the fear of war. But once desperately in love a man will commit any crime and not only feel justified, but feel good about it. It is in the order of things.

The wisest men are those who speak of illusion: MAYA. Illusion is the antidote to fear. In harness they render life absurdly illogical. But it is just this antinomian quality of life which keeps us going, which sends us shuttling back and forth from one womb to another. The world, which is not just the *human* world, is the womb of all, of birth and of life and of death.

It is this third and all-inclusive womb, THE WORLD, which man is perpetually striving to make himself a part of. It is the original chaos, the seat of creation itself. No man ever fully attains it. It is a condition of IS known neither to the foetus nor to the corpse. But it is known to the soul, and if it be unrealizable it is none the less true.

Curiously enough the verb which expresses being is in our language an intransitive verb. Most people think it quite natural that the verb *to be* should be an intransitive one. And yet there are languages, as we know, which make no distinction between transitive and intransitive. The spirit of these languages is more deeply rooted in symbol. Since it is only through symbolism that we apprehend anything profoundly, the more precise and conceptual a language becomes the more sterile does it become. The modern tongues, all of them, reflect more and more the death in us. They reflect only too clearly the fact that we regard life itself as a vestibule, whether to heaven or to hell makes little difference. It was against this stagnant automatism which Lawrence fought all his life; it is this surrender to the death instincts which enrages a man like Céline.

Real death is not a source of terror for the ordinary, intelligent, sensitive being. It is living death which is the great nightmare. Living death means the interruption of the current of life, the forestalling of a natural death process. It is a negative way of recognizing that the world is really nothing but a great womb, the place where everything is brought to life.

Everything that lives has will, that is, creativeness. Will is in the verb, which is the most important adjunct of our speech: a verb is *ipso facto* transitive. A verb, however, can be made intransitive, as the will can be rendered powerless, by the mind. But by its nature a verb is the symbol of action, regardless of whether the action be doing, having, breathing, or being.

Actually there is nothing but a steady stream of activity, a movement towards or away from life. This activity continues even in death, therein proving often to be the most fructifying of all activity. We have no real language for death, since we know nothing of it, have never experienced it; we have only thought concepts, counter-symbols which are expressive of life in a negative fashion. All that we really know is becoming, the endless change and transformation. Things are constantly being recreated. The real fear, the real terror, lies in the idea of arrest. It is a living idea of death.

Some people are born dead. Some people impress us as only half-alive. Others again seem radiant with energy. Whether one is on the side of life or on the side of death makes no difference. Life is just as wonderful on the minus side as on the plus side. The real miracle is to stand still. That would mean becoming God, or dead-alive. That is the only possible escape from the womb, and that of course is why the notion of God is so ingrained in the human consciousness. God is summation, which is the same as saying cessation. God does not represent life, but fulfillment, which is the only legitimate form of death.

In this legitimate form of death, which I say lies behind the notion of fulfillment, there is the completest subservience to the life instinct. This is the idea which has obsessed all the religious maniacs, the very sensible one that only in living a thing out to the full can there be an end. It is a wholly unmoral idea, a thoroughly artistic one. The greatest artists have been the immoralists, that is, the ones who have been in favor of living it out. Of course they were immediately misunderstood by their disciples, by those who go about preaching in their name, disseminating the gospel of this or that. The idea with which these great religious figures were imbued is that of bringing things to an end. They were all ridden with an obsession about suffering.

The idea that the womb might be a place of torture or punishment is a fairly recent one. I mean by that only a few thousand years old. It goes hand in hand with the loss of innocence. All ideas of Paradise involve the conquest of fear. Paradise is always a condition that is earned or won through struggle. The elimination of struggle is the greatest struggle of all—the struggle not to struggle. For struggle, whether erroneously or not, has to do with birth. But there was a time when birth was easy. That time is now as much as then.

To get beyond pain and suffering, beyond struggle, one must learn the equilibrist's art. ("God does not want men to overtax themselves," said Nijinsky. "He wants men to be happy.") In walking the slack wire above the opposites one becomes thoroughly and keenly aware—perilously aware. The consciousness expands to embrace the apparently conflicting opposites. To be supremely aware, which means accepting life for what it is, eliminates the terrors of life and kills false hopes. I should say rather, kills hope, for seen from a beyond hope appears as an evil rather than a good.

I say nothing about being happy. When one really understands what happiness is one goes out like a light. (Vide Kirillov!) All arrangements for a better life here on earth mean increased suffering and misery. Everything that is being planned for tomorrow means the destruction of that which now exists. *The best world is that which is now this very moment.* It is the best because it is absolutely just—which does not mean that it has anything to do with *justice.* If we wish something better or worse we have only to want it and we shall damned well have it. The world is a dream which is being realized from moment to moment, only man is sound asleep in the midst of his creation. Birth and rebirth, and the monsters as much a part of the process as the angels. The world becomes interesting and livable only when we accept it in toto with eyes wide open, only when we live it out as the foetus lives out its uterine life. Apropos, has any one ever heard of an "immoral" foetus? Or a "cowardly" corpse? Can any one say whether the Bushmen in Australia are leading the right life, the good life? And the flowers, do they make for progress and invention? These are little questions which often disturb the philosophers. Intellectual sabotage. But it is good to ask unanswerable questions now and then—it makes life more livable.

I remember a phrase which haunted me when I was younger: "man on his way to ordination." I didn't know what it meant precisely, but it fascinated me. I believed. Today, though I am frank to say I don't know what such a phrase means, I believe more than ever. I believe everything, good and bad. I believe more and less than what is true. I believe beyond the whole corpus of man's thinking. *I believe everything.* I believe in a collective life and in the individual life also. I believe in the life of the world, the uterus which it is. I believe in the contradictions of the uterine life of this world. I believe in having money and in not having money too. And whether I believe or don't believe I always act. I act first and inquire afterwards. For nothing seems more certain to me than that everything which exists, exists by fiat. If the world is anything it is an act. Thinking too is an act. The world is not a thought, but it may well be an act of thought. Those who act create reactions, as we say. In the throes of giving birth the mother is only reacting: it is the foetus which acts. And whether the mother lives or dies is one and the same to the foetus. For a foetus the important thing is birth.

Similarly for man, the important thing is to get born, born into the world-as-is, not some imaginary, wished for world, not some better, brighter world, but this, the only world, the world of NOW. There are many people today who imagine that the way to do this is to pay another man to permit them to lie down on a couch and have him listen to their tale of woe. Others again think that the midwives who perform this task ought themselves pay to be born again.

There are always Saviours and somehow the Saviours always get it in the neck. Nobody has yet found out how to save those who refuse to save themselves. And then again—a little uterine question —do we really want to be saved? And if so, for what, why, what is there to save?

We see how the banks spend the money which we save for them; we see how governments spend the taxes which they compel us to pay, in order, as they say, to "protect" us. We see how the philosophers dispense of their wisdom, and how prodigal the artist is of his strength. And do we not know that God is constantly giving us of his boundless love? In the highest places there is giving and spending galore. Why then do we not give ourselves—recklessly, abundantly, completely? If we realized that we were part of an endless process, that we had neither to lose nor to gain, but only to live it out, would we behave as we do? I can imagine the man of the year 5,000 A. D. opening the door of his home and stepping out into a world infinitely better than this; I can also imagine him stepping out into a world infinitely worse than ours. But for him, Mr. John Doe personally, I believe in the bottom of my heart that it will be exactly the same world as this which we now inhabit. The fauna and flora may be different, the climate may be different, the ideologies may be different, God may be different, everything may be different—but John Doe will himself be different and so it will be the same. I feel as close to John Doe of the year 5,000 A. D. as I do to John Doe of the year 5,000 B. C. I would be incapable of choosing between them. Each has his own world to which he belongs. Whoever does not realize what a wonderful world it is, *tant pis* for him. The world is the world, and the world is more interested in its own birth and death than in the opinion which Mr. John Doe may have about it.

Most of the active workers of the world today look upon our life on earth as a Purgatory or a Hell. They are sweating and struggling to make it a Heaven for the man to come. Or if they refuse to put it quite that way to themselves, then they say that it is to make a Heaven for themselves—a little later. Time passes. Five Year Plans. Ten Year Plans. (Dinosaurs, dynasties, dynamos.) Meanwhile the teeth decay, rheumatism comes, then death. (Death never fails.) But it's never Heaven. Somehow Heaven is always in the offing, always just around the corner. Tomorrow, tomorrow, tomorrow. . . .

IT'S BEEN GOING ON THAT WAY FOR A MILLION YEARS OR SO. In the midst of this crazy treadmill I refuse to budge an inch. I stand still. Stock still. Now or never! I say. *Peace brothers, it's wonderful!* Meanwhile the big guns are booming, in Abyssinia, in China, in Spain, and besides the usual routine slaughter of harmless animals, birds, fish, insects, snails, oysters et cetera, man is slaughtering man to pave the way for the millennium. Tomorrow the guns may be roaring here in Paris, or in New York, or in Timbuctoo. They may even roar in Scandinavia, in Holland, in Switzerland, where all is sleep and contentment whilst the cows silently chew the cud. But they will soon roar and belch their fire, that is sure. Still I will not budge. I will stand stock still and shout: *Peace! It's wonderful!* I have nothing to lose, nothing to gain. Even though I did not make the cannon with my own hands, nevertheless I assisted at their birth. The cannons belong, like everything else. Everything belongs. It's the world, comrades—the world of birth and rebirth, and long may it wave!

# THE ALCOHOLIC VETERAN
# WITH THE WASHBOARD CRANIUM

In Tulsa not long ago I saw a shorty short movie called "The Happiest Man on Earth." It was in the O. Henry style but the implications were devastating. How a picture like that could be shown in the heart of the oil fields is beyond my comprehension. At any rate it reminded me of an actual human figure whom I encountered some weeks previously in New Orleans. He too was trying to pretend that he was the happiest mortal alive.

It was about midnight and my friend Rattner and I were returning to our hotel after a jaunt through the French Quarter. As we were passing the St. Charles Hotel a man without a hat or overcoat fell into step with us and began talking about the eyeglasses he had just lost at the bar.

"It's hell to be without your glasses," he said, "especially when you're just getting over a jag. I envy you fellows. Some fool drunk in there just knocked mine off and stepped on them. Just sent a telegram to my oculist in Denver—suppose I'll have to wait a few days before they arrive. I'm just getting over one hell of a binge: it must have lasted a week or more, I don't know what day it is or what's happened in the world since I fell off the wagon. I just stepped out to get a breath of air—and some food. I never eat when I'm on a bat—the alcohol keeps me going. There's nothing to do about it, of course; I'm a confirmed alcoholic. Incurable. I know all about the subject—studied medicine before I took up law. I've tried all the cures, read all the theories. . . . Why look here—" and he reached into his breast pocket and extricated a mass of papers along with a thick wallet which fell to the ground—"look at this, here's an article on the subject I wrote myself. Funny, what? It was just published recently in. . ." (he mentioned a well-known publication with a huge circulation).

I stooped down to pick up the wallet and the calling cards which had fluttered out and fallen into the gutter. He was holding the loose bundle of letters and documents in one hand and gesticulating eloquently with the other. He seemed to be utterly unconcerned about losing any of his papers or even about the contents of the wallet. He was raving about the ignorance and stupidity of the medical profession. They were a bunch of quacks; they were hijackers; they were criminal-minded. And so on.

It was cold and rainy and we, who were bundled up in overcoats, were urging him to get moving.

"Oh, don't worry about that," he said, with a good-natured grin, "I never catch cold. I must have left my hat and coat in the bar.

The air feels good," and he threw his coat open wide as if to let the mean, penetrating night wind percolate through the thin covering in which he was wrapped. He ran his fingers through his shock of curly blond hair and wiped the corners of his mouth with a soiled handkerchief. He was a man of good stature with a rather weather-beaten face, a man who evidently lived an outdoor life. The most distinctive thing about him was his smile—the warmest, frankest, most ingratiating smile I've ever seen on a man's face. His gestures were jerky and trembly, which was only natural considering the state of his nerves. He was all fire and energy, like a man who has just had a shot in the arm. He talked well, too, exceedingly well, as though he might have been a journalist as well as doctor and lawyer. And he was very obviously not trying to make a touch.

When we had walked a block or so he stopped in front of a cheap eating house and invited us to step in with him and have something to eat or drink. We told him we were on our way home, that we were tired and eager to get to bed.

"But only for a few minutes," he said. "I'm just going to have a quick bite."

Again we tried to beg off. But he persisted, taking us by the arm and leading us to the door of the café. I repeated that I was going home but suggested to Rattner that he might stay if he liked. I started to disengage myself from his grasp.

"Look," he said, suddenly putting on a grave air, "you've got to do me this little favor. I've got to talk to you people. I might do something desperate if you don't. I'm asking you as a human kindness—you wouldn't refuse to give a man a little time, would you, when you knew that it meant so much to him?"

With that of course we surrendered without a word. "We're in for it now," I thought to myself, feeling a little disgusted with myself for letting myself be tricked by a sentimental drunkard.

"What are you going to have?" he said, ordering himself a plate of ham and beans which, before he had even brought it to the table, he sprinkled liberally with ketchup and chili sauce. As he was about to remove it from the counter he turned to the server and ordered him to get another plate of ham and beans ready. "I can eat three or four of these in a row," he explained, "when I begin to sober up." We had ordered coffee for ourselves. Rattner was about to take the checks when our friend reached for them and stuck them in his pocket. "This is on me," he said, "I invited you in here."

We tried to protest but he silenced us by saying, between huge gulps which he washed down with black coffee, that money was one of the things that never bothered him.

"I don't know how much I've got on me now," he continued. "Enough for this anyway. I gave my car to a dealer yesterday to sell for me. I drove down here from Idaho with some old cronies from the bench—they were on a jamboree. I used to be in the legislature once," and he mentioned some Western State where he had served. "I can ride back free on the railroad," he added. "I have a pass. I used to be somebody once upon a time. . . ." He interrupted himself to go to the counter and get another helping.

As he sat down again, while dousing the beans with ketchup and chili sauce, he reached with his left hand into his breast pocket and dumped the whole contents of his pocket on the table. "You're an artist, aren't you?" he said to Rattner. "And you're a writer, I can tell that," he said, looking at me. "You don't have to tell me, I sized you both up immediately." He was pushing the papers about as he spoke, still energetically shoveling down his food, and apparently poking about for some articles which he had written and which he wanted to show us. "I write a bit myself," he said, "whenever I need a little extra change. You see, as soon as I get my allowance I go on a bat. Well, when I come out of it I sit down and write some crap for"—and here he mentioned some of the leading magazines, those with the big circulation. "I can always make a few hundred dollars that way, if I want to. There's nothing to it. I don't say it's literature, of course. But who wants literature? Now where in the hell is that story I wrote about a psychopathic case . . . I just wanted to show you that I know what I'm talking about. You see. . . ." He broke off suddenly and gave us a rather wry, twisted smile, as though it were hopeless to try to put it all in words. He had a forkful of beans which he was about to shovel down. He dropped the fork, like an automaton, the beans spilling all over his soiled letters and documents, and leaning over the table he startled me by seizing my arm and placing my hand on his skull, rubbing it roughly back and forth. "Feel that?" he said, with a queer gleam in his eye. "Just like a washboard, eh?" I pulled my hand away as quickly as I could. The feel of that corrugated brainpan gave me the creeps. "That's just one item," he said. And with that he rolled up his sleeve and showed us a jagged wound that ran from the wrist to the elbow. Then he pulled up the leg of his trousers. More horrible wounds. As if that were not enough he stood up quickly, pulled off his coat and, quite as if there were no one but just us three in the place, he opened his shirt and displayed even uglier scars. As he was putting on his coat he looked boldly around and in clear, ringing tones he sang with terrible bitter mockery "America, I love you!" Just the opening phrase. Then he sat down as abruptly as he had gotten up and quietly proceeded to finish the ham and beans. I thought there would be a commotion but no, people continued eating and talking just as before, only now we had become the center of attention. The man at the cash register seemed rather nervous and thoroughly undecided as to what to do. I wondered what next.

I half expected our friend to raise his voice and begin a melo-dramatic scene. Except however for the fact that he had grown a little more high-strung and more voluble his behavior was not markedly different from before. But his tone had altered. He spoke now in jerky phrases punctuated with the most blasphemous oaths and accompanied by grimaces which were frightening to behold. The demon in him seemed to be coming out. Or rather, the mutilated being who had been wounded and humiliated beyond all human endurance.

"*Mister* Roosevelt!" he said, his voice full of scorn and contempt. "I was just listening to him over the radio. Getting us in shape to fight England's battles again, what? Conscription. *Not this bird!*" and he jerked his thumb backwards viciously. "Decorated three times on the field of battle. The Argonne . . . Chateau Thierry . . . the Somme . . . concussion of the brain . . . fourteen months in the hospital outside Paris . . . ten months on this side of the water. Making murderers of us and then begging us to settle down quietly and go to work again. . . . Wait a minute, I want to read you a poem I wrote about our Fuehrer the other night." He fished among the papers lying about on the table. He got up to get him-self another cup of coffee and as he stood with cup in hand, sip-ping it, he began to read aloud this vituperative, scabrous poem about the President. Surely now, I thought, somebody will take umbrage and start a fight. I looked at Rattner who believes in Roosevelt, who had traveled 1200 miles to vote for him at the last election. Rattner was silent. He probably thought it useless to remonstrate with a man who had obviously been shell shocked. Still, I couldn't help thinking, the situation was a little unusual, to say the least. A phrase I had heard in Georgia came back to my head. It was from the lips of a woman who had just been to see "Lincoln in Illinois." "What are they trying to do—make a he-ro of that man Lincoln?" Yes, something distinctly pre-Civil War about the atmosphere. A president re-elected to office by a great popular vote and yet his name was anathema to millions. Another Woodrow Wilson perchance? Our friend wouldn't even accord him that ranking. He had sat down again and in a fairly moderate tone of voice he began making sport of the politicians, the members of the judiciary, the generals and admirals, the quartermaster generals, the Red Cross, the Salvation Army, the Y. M. C. A. A withering play of mockery and cynicism, larded with personal experiences, grotesque encounters, buffoonish pranks which only a battle-scarred veteran would have the audacity to relate.

"And so," he exploded, "they wanted to parade me like a monkey, with my uniform and medals. They had the brass band out and the mayor all set to give us a glorious welcome. The town is yours, boys, and all that hokum. Our heroes! God, it makes me vomit to think of it. I ripped the medals off my uniform and threw them away. I burned the damned uniform in the fireplace. Then I got myself a quart of rye and I locked myself in my room. I drank and wept, all by myself. Outside the band was playing and people cheering hysterically. I was all black inside. Everything I had believed in was gone. All my illusions were shattered. They broke my heart, that's what they did. They didn't leave me a goddamned crumb of solace. Except the booze, of course. Sure, they tried to take that away from me too, at first. They tried to shame me into giving it up. Shame me, huh! Me who had killed hundreds of men with the bayonet, who lived like an animal and lost all sense of human decency. They can't do anything to shame me, or frighten me, or fool me, or bribe me, or trick me. I know them inside out, the dirty bastards. They've starved me and beaten me

109

and put me behind the bars. That stuff doesn't frighten me. I can put up with hunger, cold, thirst, lice, vermin, disease, blows, insults, degradation, fraud, theft, libel, slander, betrayal . . . I've been through the whole works . . . they've tried everything on me . . . and still they can't crush me, can't stop my mouth, can't make me say it's right. I don't want anything to do with these honest, God-fearing people. They sicken me. I'd rather live with animals—or cannibals." He found a piece of sheet music among his papers and documents. "There's a song I wrote three years ago. It's sentimental but it won't do anyone any harm. I can only write music when I'm drunk. The alcohol blots out the pain. I've still got a heart, a big one, too. My world is a world of memories. Do you remember this one?" He began to hum a familiar melody. "You wrote that?" I said, taken by surprise. "Yes, I wrote that—and I wrote others too"—and he began to reel off the titles of his songs.

I was just beginning to wonder about the truth of all these statements—lawyer, doctor, legislator, scrivener, song writer—when he began to talk about his inventions. He had made three fortunes, it seems, before he fell into complete disgrace. It was getting pretty thick even for me, and I'm a credulous individual, when presently a chance remark he made about a friend of his, a famous architect in the Middle West, drew a surprising response from Rattner. "He was my buddy in the army," said Rattner quietly. "Well," said our friend, "he married my sister." With this there began a lively exchange of reminiscences between the two of them, leaving not the slightest doubt in my mind that our friend was telling the truth, at least so far as the architect was concerned.

From the architect to the construction of a great house in the center of Texas somewhere was but a step. With the last fortune he made he had bought himself a ranch, married and built himself a fantastic chateau in the middle of nowhere. The drinking was gradually tailing off. He was deeply in love with his wife and looking forward to raising a family. Well, to make a long story short, a friend of his persuaded him to go to Alaska with him on a mining speculation. He left his wife behind because he feared the climate would be too rigorous for her. He was away about a year. When he returned—he had come back without warning, thinking to surprise her—he found her in bed with his best friend. With a whip he drove the two of them out of the house in the dead of night, in a blinding snowstorm, not even giving them a chance to put their clothes on. Then he got the bottle out, of course, and after he had had a few shots he began to smash things up. But the house was so damned big that he soon grew tired of that sport. There was only one way to make a good job of it and that was to put a match to the works, which he did. Then he got in his car and drove off, not bothering to even pack a valise. A few days later, in a distant State, he picked up the newspaper and learned that his friend had been found dead of exposure. Nothing was said about the wife. In fact, he never learned what happened to her from that day since. Shortly after this incident he got in a brawl with a man at a bar and cracked his skull open with a broken bottle. That meant a stretch at hard labor for eighteen months, during which time he made a study of prison conditions and proposed certain reforms to the Governor of the State which were accepted and put into practice.

"I was very popular," he said. "I have a good voice and I can entertain a bit. I kept them in good spirits while I was there. Later I did another stretch. It doesn't bother me at all. I can adjust myself to most any conditions. Usually there's a piano and a billiard table and books—and if you can't get anything to drink you can always get yourself a little dope. I switch back and forth. What's the difference? All a man wants is to forget the present. . . ."

"Yes, but can you ever really forget?" Rattner interjected.

"I can! You just give me a piano, a quart of rye and a sociable little joint and I can be just as happy as a man wants to be. You see, I don't need all the paraphernalia you fellows require. All I carry with me is a toothbrush. If I want a shave I buy one; if I want to change my linen I get new linen; when I'm hungry I eat; when I'm tired I sleep. It doesn't make much difference to me whether I sleep in a bed or on the ground. If I want to write a story I go to a newspaper office and borrow a machine. If I want to go to Boston all I have to do is show my pass. Any place is home sweet home so long as I can find a place to drink and meet a friendly fellow like myself. I don't pay taxes and I don't pay rent. I have no boss, no responsibilities. I don't vote and I don't care who's President or Vice-President. I don't want to make money and I don't look for fame or success. What can you offer me that I haven't got, eh? I'm a free man—are you? And happy. I'm happy because I don't care what happens. All I want is my quart of whiskey every day—a bottle of forgetfulness, that's all. My health? I never worry about it. I'm just as strong and healthy as the next man. If there's anything wrong with me I don't know it. I might live to be a hundred whereas you guys are probably worrying whether you'll live to be sixty. There's only one day—today. If I feel good I write a poem and throw it away the next day. I'm not trying to win any literary prizes—I'm just expressing myself in my own cantankerous way. . . ."

At this point he began to go off the track about his literary ability. His vanity was getting the best of him. When it got to the point where he insisted that I glance at a story he had written for some popular magazine I thought it best to pull him up short. I much preferred to hear about the desperado and the drunkard than the man of letters.

"Look here," I said, not mincing my words, "you admit that this is all crap, don't you? Well, I never read crap. What's the use of showing me that stuff—I don't doubt that you can write as badly as the next fellow—it doesn't take genius to do that. What I'm interested in is good writing: I admire genius not success. Now if you have anything that you're proud of that's another thing. I'd be glad to read something that you yourself thought well of."

He gave me a long, down-slanting look. For a few long moments he looked at me that way, silently, scrutinizingly. "I'll tell you," he said finally, "there's just one thing I've ever written which I think good—and I've never put it down on paper. But I've got it up here," and he tapped his forehead with his forefinger. "If you'd like to hear it I'll recite it for you. It's a long poem I wrote one time when I was in Manila. You've heard of Morro Castle, haven't you? All right, it was just outside the walls of Morro Castle that I got the inspiration. I think it's a great poem. I know it is! I wouldn't want to see it printed. I wouldn't want to take money for it. Here it is. . . ."

Without pausing to clear his throat or take a drink he launched into this poem about the sun going down in Manila. He recited it at a rapid pace in a clear musical voice. It was like shooting down the rapids in a light canoe. All around us the conversation had died down; some stood up and moved in close the better to hear him. It seemed to have neither beginning nor end. As I say, it had started off at the velocity of a flood, and it went on and on, image upon image, crescendo upon crescendo, rising and falling in musical cadences. I don't remember a single line of it, more's the pity. All I remember is the sensation I had of being borne along on the swollen bosom of a great river through the heart of a tropical zone in which there was a constant fluttering of dazzling plumage, the sheen of wet green leaves, the bending and swaying of lakes of grass,

113

the throbbing midnight blue of sky, the gleam of stars like coruscating jewels, the song of birds intoxicated by God knows what. There was a fever running through the lines, the fever not of a sick man but of an exalted, frenzied creature who had suddenly found his true voice and was trying it out in the dark. It was a voice which issued straight from the heart, a taut, vibrant column of blood which fell upon the ear in rhapsodic, thunderous waves. The end was an abatement rather than a cessation, a diminuendo which brought the pounding rhythm to a whisper that prolonged itself far beyond the actual silence in which it finally merged. The voice had ceased to register, but the poem continued to pulsate in the echoing cells of the brain.

He broke the silence which ensued by alluding modestly to his unusual facility for memorizing whatever caught his eye. "I remember everything I read in school," he said, "from Longfellow and Wordsworth to Ronsard and François Villon. Villon, there's a fellow after my own heart," and he launched into a familiar verse in an accent that betrayed he had more than a textbook knowledge of French. "The greatest poets were the Chinese," he said. "They made the little things reveal the greatness of the universe. They were philosophers first and then poets. They lived their poetry. We have nothing to make poetry about, except death and desolation. You can't make a poem about an automobile or a telephone booth. To begin with, the heart has to be intact. One must be able to believe in something. The values we were taught to respect when we were children are all smashed. We're not men any more—we're automatons. We don't even get any satisfaction in killing. The last war killed off our impulses. We don't respond; we react. We're the lost legion of the defeated archangels. We're dangling in chaos and our leaders, blinder than bats, bray like jackasses. You wouldn't call Mister Roosevelt a great leader, would you? Not if you know your history. A leader has to be inspired by a great vision; he has to lift his people out of the mire with mighty pinions; he has to rouse them from the stupor in which they vegetate like stoats and slugs. You don't advance the cause of freedom and humanity by leading poor, feeble dreamers to the slaughterhouse. What's he belly-aching about anyway? Did the Creator appoint him the Saviour of Civilization? When I went over there to fight for Democracy I was just a kid. I didn't have any great ambitions, neither did I have any desire to kill anybody. I was brought up to believe that the shedding of blood was a crime against God and man. Well, I did what they asked me to, like a good soldier. I murdered every son of a bitch that was trying to murder me. What else could I do? It wasn't all murder, of course. I had some good times now and then—a different sort of pleasure than I ever figured I would like. In fact, nothing was like what I thought it would be before I went over. You know what those bastards make you into. Why, your own mother wouldn't recognize you if she saw you taking your pleasure—or crawling in the mud and sticking a bayonet in a man who never did you any harm. I'm telling you, it got so filthy and poisonous I didn't know who I was any more. I was just a number that lit up like a switchboard when the order came to do this, do that, do the other thing. You couldn't call me a man—I didn't have a god-damned bit of feeling left. And I wasn't an animal because if I had been an animal I'd have had better sense than to get myself into such a mess. Animals kill one another only when they're hungry. We kill because we're afraid of our own shadow, afraid that if we used a little common sense we'd have to admit that our glorious principles were wrong. Today I haven't got any principles—I'm an outlaw. I have only one ambition left—to get enough booze under my belt every day so as to forget what the world looks like. I never sanctioned this setup. You can't convince

115

me that I murdered all those Germans in order to bring this unholy mess about. No sir, I refuse to take any part in it. I wash my hands of it. I walk out on it. Now if that makes me a bad citizen why then I'm a bad citizen. So what? Do you suppose if I ran around like a mad dog, begging for a club and a rifle to start murdering all over again, do you suppose that would make me into a good citizen, good enough, what I mean, to vote the straight Democratic ticket? I suppose if I did that I could eat right out of their hand, what? Well, I don't want to eat out of anybody's hand. I want to be left alone; I want to dream my dreams, to believe as I once believed, that life is good and beautiful and that men can live with one another in peace and plenty. No son of a bitch on earth can tell me that to make life better you have to first kill a million or ten million men in cold blood. No sir, those bastards haven't got any heart. I know the Germans are no worse than we are, and by Christ, I know from experience that some of them at least are a damned sight better than the French or the English.

"That schoolteacher we made a President of, he thought he had everything fixed just right, didn't he? Can you picture him crawling around on the floor at Versailles like an old billygoat, putting up imaginary fences with a blue pencil? What's the sense of making new boundaries, will you tell me? Why tariffs and taxes and sentry boxes and pillboxes anyway? Why doesn't England part with some of her unlawful possessions? If the poor people in England can't make a living when the government possesses the biggest empire that ever was how are they going to make a living when the empire falls to pieces? Why don't they emigrate to Canada or Africa or Australia?

"There's another thing I don't understand. We always assume that we're in the right, that we have the best government under the sun. How do we know—have we tried the others out? Is everything running so beautifully here that we couldn't bear the thought of a change? Supposing I honestly believed in Fascism or Communism or polygamy or Mohammedanism or pacifism or any of the things that are now tabu in this country? What would happen to me if I started to open my trap, eh? Why you don't even dare to protest against being vaccinated, though there's plenty of evidence to prove that vaccination does more harm than good. Where is this liberty and freedom we boast about? You're only free if you're in good odor with your neighbors, and even then it's not a hell of a lot of rope they give you. If you happen to be broke and out of a job your freedom isn't worth a button. And if you're old besides then it's just plain misery. They're much kinder to animals and flowers and crazy people. Civilization is a blessing to the unfit and the degenerate— the others it breaks or demoralizes. As far as the comforts of life go I'm better off when I'm in jail than when I'm out. In the one case they take your freedom away and in the other they take your manhood. If you play the game you can have automobiles and town houses and mistresses and pâté de foie gras and all the folde-rol that goes with it. But who wants to play the game? Is it worth it? Did you ever see a millionaire who was happy or who had any self-respect? Did you ever go to Washington and see our law-breakers—excuse me, I mean lawmakers—in session? There's a sight for you! If you dressed them in striped dungarees and put them behind the bars with pick and shovel nobody on earth could tell but what they belonged there. Or take that rogues' gallery of Vice-Presidents. I was standing in front of a drug store not so long ago studying their physiognomies. There never was a meaner, craftier, uglier, more fanatical bunch of human faces ever assembled in one group. And that's the stuff they make presidents of whenever there's an assassination. Yes, assassinations. I was sitting in a restaurant the day after the election—up in Maine it was—and the fellow next to me

117

was trying to lay a bet with another guy that Roosevelt wouldn't last the term out. He was laying five to one—but nobody would take him up. The thing that struck me was that the waitress, whom nobody had paid any attention to, suddenly remarked in a quiet tone that 'we were about due for another assassination.' Assassinations seem ugly when it's the President of the United States but there's plenty of assassinating going on all the time and nobody seems to get very riled up about it. Where I was raised we used to flog a nigger to death just to show a visitor how it's done. It's still being done, but not so publicly, I suppose. We improve things by covering them up.

"You take the food they hand us. . . . Of course I haven't got any taste left, from all the booze I pour down my system. But a man who has any taste buds left must be in a hell of a way eating the slop they hand you in public places. Now they're discovering that the vitamins are missing. So what do they do? Do they change the diet, change the chef? No, they give you the same rotten slop only they add the necessary vitamins. That's civilization—always doing things assways. Well, I'll tell you, I'm so god-damned civilized now that I prefer to take my poison straight. If I had lived what they call a 'normal' life I'd be on the dump heap by fifty anyway. I'm forty-eight now and sound as a whistle, always doing just the opposite of what they recommend. If you were to live the way I do for two weeks you'd be in the hospital. So what does it add up to, will you tell me? If I didn't drink I'd have some other vice—a baby-snatcher, maybe, or a refined Jack-the-Ripper, who knows? And if I didn't have any vices I'd be just a poor sap, a sucker like millions of others, and where would that get me? Do you think I'd get any satisfaction out of dying in harness, as they say? Not me! I'd rather die in the alcoholic ward among the has-beens and no-goods. At least, if it happens that way, I'll have the satisfaction of saying that I had only one master—John Barleycorn.

118

You have a thousand masters, perfidious, insidious ones who torment you even in your sleep. I've only got one, and to tell the truth he's more like a friend than a taskmaster. He gets me into some nasty messes, but he never lies to me. He never says 'freedom, liberty, equality' or any of that rot. He just says, 'I will make you so stinking drunk that you won't know who you are,' and that's all I crave. Now if Mister Roosevelt or any other politician could make me a promise and keep it I'd have a little respect for him. But who ever heard of a diplomat or a politician keeping his word? It's like expecting a millionaire to give his fortune away to the men and women he robbed it from. It just ain't done."

He went on at this rate without a letup—long monologues about the perfidy, the cruelty and the injustice of man towards man. Really a grand fellow at heart, with good instincts and all the attributes of a citizen of the world, except for the fact that somewhere along the line he had been flung out of the societal orbit and could never get back into it again. I saw from the queries which Rattner interjected now and then that he had hopes for the man. At two in the morning he was optimistic enough to believe that with a little perseverance there might be sown in this rugged heart the seed of hope. To me, much as I liked the fellow, it seemed just as futile as to attempt to reclaim the bad lands of Arizona or Dakota. The only thing society can do with such people, and it never does, is to be kind and indulgent to them. Just as the earth itself, in its endless experiments, comes to a dead end in certain regions, gives up, as it were, so with individuals. The desire to kill the soul, for that's what it amounts to, is a phenomenon which has an extraordinary fascination for me. Sometimes it lends a grandeur to an individual which seems to rival the sublime struggles of those men whom we consider superior types. Because the gesture of negation, when pure and uncompromising, has also in it the qualities of the

119

heroic. Weaklings are incapable of flinging themselves away in this manner. The weakling merely succumbs while the other, more single-minded character works hand and glove with Fate, egging it on, as it were, and mocking it at the same time. To invoke Fate is to expose oneself to the chaos which the blind forces of the universe are ever ready to set in motion once the will of man is broken. The man of destiny is the extreme opposite: in him we have an example of the miraculous nature of man, in that those same blind forces appear to be harnessed and controlled, directed towards the fulfillment of man's own microscopic purpose. But to act either way one has to lift himself completely out of the set, reactionary pattern of the ordinary individual. Even to vote for self-destruction demands something of a cosmic approach. A man has to have some definite view of the nature of the world in order to reject it. It is far easier to commit suicide than to kill the soul. There remains the doubt, which not even the most determined destroyer can annihilate, that the task is impossible. If it could be accomplished by an act of will then there would be no need to summon Fate. But it is precisely because the will no longer functions that the hopeless individual surrenders to the powers that be. In short he is obliged to renounce the one act which would deliver him of his torment. Our friend had delivered himself up to John Barleycorn. But beyond a certain point John Barleycorn is powerless to operate. Could one succeed in summoning all the paralyzing and inhibiting forces of the universe there would still remain a frontier, a barrier which nothing but man himself can surmount and invade. The body can be killed, but the soul is imperishable. A man like our friend could have killed himself a thousand times had he the least hope of solving his problem thereby. But he had chosen to relapse, to lie cold and inert like the moon, to crush every fructifying impulse and, by imitating death, finally achieve it in the very heart of his being.

120

When he spoke it was the heart which cried out. They had broken his heart, he said, but it was not true. The heart cannot be broken. The heart can be wounded and cause the whole universe to appear as one vast writhing place of anguish. But the heart knows no limits in its ability to endure suffering and torment. Were it otherwise the race would have perished long ago. As long as the heart pumps blood it pumps life. And life can be lived at levels so utterly disparate one from another that in some cases it would appear to be almost extinct. There are just as violent contrasts in the way life is lived by human beings as there are startling contrasts in the fish, the mineral or the vegetable worlds. When we use the term human society we speak of something which defies definition. No one can encompass the thought and behavior of man with a word or phrase. Human beings move in constellations which, unlike the stars, are anything but fixed. A story, such as I am relating, can be of interest or significance to certain clusters of men and totally devoid of any charm or value to others. What would Shakespeare mean to a Patagonian, assuming he could be taught to read the words? What can "The Varieties of Religious Experience" mean to a Hopi Indian? A man goes along thinking the world to be thus and so, simply because he has never been jolted out of the rut in which he crawls like a worm. For the civilized man war is not always the greatest jolt to his smug every day pattern. Some men, and their number is greater I fear than most of us would like to believe, find war an exciting if not altogether agreeable interruption to the toil and drudgery of common life. The presence of death adds spice, quickens their usually torpid brain cells. But there are others, like our friend who, in their revolt against wanton killing, in the bitter realization that no power of theirs will ever put an end to it, elect to withdraw from society and if possible destroy even the chance of returning to earth again

121

at some distant and more propitious moment in human history. They want nothing more to do with man; they want to nip the experiment in the bud. And of course they are just as powerless here as in their efforts to eliminate war. But they are a fascinating species of man and ultimately of value to the race, if for no other reason than that they act as semaphores in those periods of darkness when we seem to be rushing headlong to destruction. The one who operates the switchboard remains invisible and it is in him we put our trust, but as long as we hug the rails the flashing semaphores offer a fleeting consolation. We hope that the engineer will bring us safely to our destination. We sit with arms folded and surrender our safekeeping to other hands. But even the best engineer can only take us over a charted course. Our adventure is in uncharted realms, with courage, intelligence and faith as our only guides. If we have a duty it is to put our trust in our own powers. No man is great enough or wise enough for any of us to surrender our destiny to. The only way in which any one can lead us is to restore to us the belief in our own guidance. The greatest men have always reaffirmed this thought. But the men who dazzle us and lead us astray are the men who promise us those things which no man can honestly promise another—namely safety, security, peace, etc. And the most deceptive of all such promisers are those who bid us kill one another in order to attain the fictive goal.

Like our friend, thousands, perhaps millions of men, awaken to the realization of their error on the battlefield. When it is too late. When the men whom they no longer have a desire to kill are already upon them, ready to cut their throats. Then it is kill or be killed and whether one kills in the knowledge of the truth or without that knowledge makes little difference The murdering goes on —until the day the sirens scream their announcement of a truce. When peace comes it descends upon a world too exhausted to show any reaction except a dumb feeling of relief. The men at the helm, who were spared the horrors of combat, now play their ignominious role in which greed and hatred rival one another for mastery. The men who bore the brunt of the struggle are too sickened and disgusted to show any desire to participate in the rearrangement of the world. All they ask is to be left alone to enjoy the luxury of the petty, workaday rhythm which once seemed so dull and barren. How different the new order would be if we could consult the veteran instead of the politician! But logic has it that we ordain innocent millions to slaughter one another, and when the sacrifice is completed, we authorize a handful of bigoted, ambitious men who have never known what it is to suffer to rearrange our lives. What chance has a lone individual to dissent when he has nothing to sanction his protest except his wounds? Who cares about wounds when the war is over? Get them out of sight, all these wounded and maimed and mutilated! Resume work! Take up life where you left off, those of you who are still strong and able! The dead will be given monuments; the mutilated will be pensioned off. Let's get on—business as usual and no feeble sentimentality about the horrors of war. When the next war comes we'll be ready for them! *Und so weiter.* . . .

I was reflecting thus while he and Rattner were exchanging anecdotes about their experiences in France. I was dying to get to bed. Our friend, on the other hand, was obviously becoming more awake; I knew that with the least encouragement he would regale us till dawn with his stories. The more he talked about his misfortunes, oddly enough, the more cheerful he seemed to grow. By the time we managed to persuade him to leave the place he was positively radiant. Out in the street he began bragging again about his wonderful condition—liver, kidneys, bowels, lungs all perfect, eyes super-normal. He had forgotten evidently about his broken glasses, or perhaps that was just an invention by way of breaking the ice.

We had a few blocks to walk before reaching our hotel. He said he would accompany us because he was going to turn in soon himself. There were some thirty-five cent lodging houses in the vicinity, he thought, where he'd get a few hours sleep. Every few steps, it seemed, he stopped dead and planted himself in front of us to expatiate on some incident which he evidently thought it important for us to hear. Or was it an unconscious desire to delay us in nestling down to our warm cozy beds? More than once, when we finally neared the hotel, we held out our hands to say good night, only to drop them again and stand patiently with one foot in the gutter and one on the curb hearing him out to the end.

At last I began to wonder if he had the necessary pence to get himself a flop. Just as I was about to inquire Rattner, whose thoughts were evidently running in the same direction, anticipated me. Had he the money for a room? Why, he was pretty certain he did; he had counted his change at the restaurant. Yes, he was quite sure he had enough—and if he hadn't he would ask us to make it up. Anyhow, that wasn't important. What was he saying? Oh yes, about Nevada . . . about the crazy ghost towns he had lived in . . . the saloon made of beer bottles and the mechanical piano from the Klondike which he rolled out to the desert one night just to hear how it would sound in that great empty space. Yes, the only people worth talking to were the bar flies. They were all living in the past, like himself. Some day he'd write the whole thing out. "Why bother to do that?" I interposed. "Maybe you're right," he said, running his tobacco-stained fingers through his thick curly hair. "I'm going to ask you for a cigarette now," he said. "I'm all out of mine." As we lit the cigarette for him he launched into another tale. "Listen," I said, "make it short, will you, I'm dead tired." We moved at a snail-like pace across the street to the door of the hotel.

As he was winding up his story I put my hand on the handle of the door in readiness to make a break. We started to shake hands again when suddenly he took it into his head to count his change. "I guess I'll have to borrow three cents from you," he said. "You can have a couple of bucks if you like," we both started to say simultaneously. No, he didn't want that—that might start him drinking all over again. He didn't want to begin that now—he wanted a little rest first.

There was nothing to do but give him the three cents and what cigarettes we had left. It hurt Rattner to hand him three pennies. "Why don't you take a half dollar at least?" he said. "You might use it for breakfast tomorrow."

"If you give me a half dollar," he said, "I'll probably buy some candles and put them at Robert E. Lee's monument up the street. It was his birthday today, you know. People have forgotten about him already. Everybody's snoring now. I sort of like Lee; I revere his memory. He was more than a great general—he was a man of great delicacy and understanding. As a matter of fact, I think I'll wander up there anyway before turning in. It's just the sort of fool thing a fellow like me would do. Sleep isn't so important. I'll go up there to the monument and talk to him a little while. Let the world sleep! You see, I'm free to do as I please. I'm really better off than a millionaire. . . ."

"Then there's nothing more we can do for you?" I said, cutting him short. "You've got everything you need, you've got your health, you're happy. . . ."

I had no more than uttered the word happy when his face suddenly changed and, grasping me by both arms with a steely grip, he wheeled me around and gazing into my eyes with a look I shall never forget, he broke forth: "Happy? Listen, you're a writer—you should know better than that. You know I'm lying like hell.

125

Happy? Why, brother, you're looking at the most miserable man on earth." He paused a moment to brush away a tear. He was still holding me firmly with both hands, determined apparently that I should hear him out. "I didn't bump into you accidentally to-night," he continued. "I saw you coming along and I sized you both up. I knew you were artists and that's why I collared you. I always pick the people I want to talk to. I didn't lose any glasses at the bar, nor did I give my car to a dealer to sell for me. But everything else I told you is true. I'm just hoofing it from place to place. I've only been out of the pen a few weeks. They've got their eye on me still—somebody's been trailing me around town, I know it. One false move and they'll clap me back in again. I'm giving them the runaround. If I should go up to the circle now and acci-dentally fall asleep on a bench they'd have the goods on me. But I'm too wary for that. I'll just amble about leisurely and when I'm good and ready I'll turn in. The bartender'll fix me up in the morning. . . . Look, I don't know what kind of stuff you write, but if you'll take a tip from me the thing to do is to learn what it is to suffer. No writer is any good unless he's suffered. . . ."

At this point Rattner was about to say something in my behalf, but I motioned to him to be silent. It was a strange thing for me to be listening to a man urging me to suffer. I had always been of the opinion that I had had more than my share of suffering. Evi-dently it didn't show on my face. Or else the fellow was so en-grossed with his own misfortunes that he was unable or unwilling to recognize the marks in another. So I let him ramble on. I lis-tened to the last drop without once seeking to interrupt him. When he had finished I held out my hand for the last time to say good-bye. He took my hand in both of his and clasped it warmly. "I've talked your head off, haven't I?" he said, that strange ecstatic smile lighting up his face. "Look, my name is So-and-So." It

126

sounded like Allison or Albertson. He began digging for his wallet. "I'd like to give you an address," he said, "where you could drop me a line." He was searching for something to write on, but couldn't seem to find a card or blank piece of paper among the litter of documents he carried in that thick wallet. "Well, you give me yours," he said. "That will do. I'll write you some time."

Rattner was writing out his name and address for the fellow. He took the card and put it carefully in his wallet. He waited for me to write mine.

"I have no address," I said. "Besides, we've got nothing more to say to each other. I don't think we'll ever meet again. You're bent on destroying yourself, and I can't stop you, nor can anybody else. What's the good of pretending that we'll write one another? Tomorrow I'll be somewhere else and so will you. All I can say is I wish you luck." With that I pulled the door open and walked into the lobby of the hotel. Rattner was still saying good-bye to him.

As I stood there waiting for the elevator boy he waved his hand cheerily. I waved back. Then he stood a moment, swaying on his heels and apparently undecided whether to go towards the monument or turn round and look for a flop. Just as the elevator boy started the lift going he signalled for us to wait. I signalled back that it was too late. "Go on up," I said to the boy. As we rose up out of sight our friend stood there in front of the hotel door peering up at us with a blank expression. I didn't feel that it was a lousy thing to do, leave him standing there like that. I looked at Rattner to see how he felt about it. He sort of shrugged his shoulders. "What can you do with a guy like that?" he said, "he won't let you help him." As we entered the room and turned on the lights, he added: "You surely did give him a jolt when you told him he was happy. Do you know what I thought he was going to do? I thought he was going to crack you. Did you notice the look

127

that came over him? And when you refused to give him your name and address, well that just about finished him. I couldn't do that. I'm not reproaching you—I just wonder why you acted that way. You could just as well have let him down easy, couldn't you?"

I was about to smile, but so many thoughts entered my head at once that I forgot and instead I frowned.

"Don't get me wrong," said Rattner, misinterpreting my expression. "I think you were damned patient with him. You hardly said a word all evening. . . ."

"No, it's not that," I said. "I'm not thinking of myself. I'm thinking of all the fellows like him I've met in one short lifetime. Listen, did I ever tell you about my experience with the telegraph company? Hell, it's late and I know you're fagged out. So am I. But I just want to tell you one or two things. I'm not trying to defend myself, mind you. I'm guilty, if you like. Maybe I could have done something, said something—I don't know what or how. Sure, I did let him down. And what's more I probably hurt him deeply. But I figured it would do him good, if you can believe that. I never crossed him once, did I, or criticized him, or urged him to change his ways? No, I never do that. If a man is determined to go to the dogs I help him—I give him a little push if needs be. If he wants to get on his feet I help him to do that. Whatever he asks for. I believe in letting a man do as he pleases, for good or bad, because eventually we'll all wind up in the same place. But what I was starting to tell you is this—I've heard so many terrible tales, met so many guys like this Allison or Albertson, that I've hardly got an ounce of sympathy left in me. That's a horrible thing to say, but it's true. Get this—in one day, sometimes, I've had as many as a half-dozen men break down and weep before me, beg me to do something for them, or if not for them, for their wives and children. In four years I hardly ever had more than four or five hours'

128

sleep a night, largely because I was trying to help people who were helpless to help themselves. What money I earned I gave away; when I couldn't give a man a job myself I went to my friends and begged them to give a man the work he needed. I brought them home and fed them; I fixed them up on the floor when the beds were full. I got hell all around for doing too much and neglecting my own wife and child. My boss looked upon me as a fool, and instead of praising me for my efforts bawled hell out of me continually. I was always between two fires, from above and from below. I saw finally that no matter how much I did it was just a drop in the bucket. I'm not saying that I grew indifferent or hardened. No, but I realized that it would take a revolution to make any appreciable change in conditions. And when I say a revolution I mean a real revolution, something far more radical and sweeping than the Russian revolution, for instance. I still think that, but I don't think it can be done politically or economically. Governments can't bring it about. Only individuals, each one working in his own quiet way. It must be a revolution of the heart. Our attitude towards life has to be fundamentally altered. We've got to advance to another level, a level from which we can take in the whole earth with one glance. We have to have a vision of the globe, including all the people who inhabit it—down to the lowest and the most primitive man.

"To come back to our friend. . . . I wasn't too unkind to him, was I? You know damned well I've never refused a man help when he asked for it. But he didn't want help. He wanted sympathy. He wanted us to try to dissuade him from accomplishing his own destruction. And when he had melted us with his heartbreaking stories he wanted to have the pleasure of saying no and leaving us high and dry. He gets a kick out of that. A quiet sort of revenge, as it were, for his inability to cure himself of his sorrows. I figure it doesn't help a man any to encourage him in that direction. If a woman gets hysterical you know that the best thing to do is to slap her face good and hard. The same with these poor devils: they've got to be made to understand that they are not the only ones in the world who are suffering. They make a vice of their suffering. An analyst might cure him—and again he might not. And in any case, how would you get him to the analyst? You don't suppose he'd listen to a suggestion of that sort, do you? If I hadn't been so tired, and if I had had more money, I'd have tried another line with him. I'd have bought him some booze—not just a bottle, but a case of whiskey, two cases or three, if I were able to afford it. I tried that once on a friend of mine—another confirmed drunkard. Do you know, he was so damned furious when he saw all that liquor that he never opened a single bottle. He was insulted, so he pretended. It didn't faze me in the least. I had gotten rather fed up with his antics. When he was sober he was a prince, but when he got drunk he was just impossible. Well, thereafter, every time he came to see me, as soon as he suggested a little drink, I poured out a half dozen glasses at once for him. While he was debating whether to touch it or not I would excuse myself and run out to buy more. It worked—in his case, at least. It cost me his friendship, to be sure, but it stopped him from playing the drunkard with me. They've tried similar things in certain prisons I know of. They don't force a man to work, if he doesn't want to. On the contrary, they give him a comfortable cell, plenty to eat, cigars, cigarettes, wine or beer, according to his taste, a servant to wait on him, anything he wants save his freedom. After a few days of it the fellow usually begs to be permitted to work. A man just can't stand having too much of a good thing. Give a man all he wants and more and you'll cure him of his appetites in nine cases out of ten. It's so damned simple—it's strange we don't take advantage of such ideas."

130

When I had crawled into bed and turned out the light I found that I was wide awake. Often, when I've listened to a man for a whole evening, turning myself into a receiving station, I lie awake and rehearse the man's story from beginning to end. I like to see how accurately I can retrace the innumerable incidents which a man can relate in the course of several hours, especially if he is given free rein. I almost always think of such talks as a big tree with limbs and branches and leaves and buds. Roots, too, which have their grip in the common soil of human experience and which make any story, no matter how fantastic or incredible, quite plausible, provided you give the man the time and attention he demands. The most wonderful thing, to carry the image further, is the buds: these are the little incidents which like seeds a man will often plant in your mind to blossom later when the memory of him is almost lost. Some men are particularly skillful in handling these buds; they actually seem to possess the power to graft them on to your own story-telling tree so that when they blossom forth you imagine that they were your own, though you never cease marveling that your own little brain could have produced such astonishing fruit.

As I say, I was turning it all over in my mind and chuckling to myself to think how clever I was to have detected certain definite falsifications, certain distortions and omissions which, when one is listening intently, one seldom catches. Presently I recalled how he had admitted some slight fabrications only to emphasize that the rest of his yarn was pure wool. At this point I chuckled aloud. Rattner was tossing about, evidently no more able than I to close his eyes.

"Are you still awake?" I asked quietly.

He gave a grunt.

"Listen," I said, "there's one thing I want to ask you—do you believe he was telling the truth about himself?"

Rattner, too tired I suppose to go into any subtleties of analysis, began to hem and haw. In the main he thought the fellow had been telling us the truth. "Why, didn't you believe him?" he asked.

"You remember," I said, "when I touched him to the quick . . . you remember how sincerely he spoke? Well, it was at that moment that I doubted him. At that moment he told us the biggest lie of all—when he said that the rest was all true. I don't believe that any of it was true, not even the story about knowing your friend. You remember how quickly he married him off to his sister? That was sheer spontaneous invention. I was tracing it all back just now. And I remembered very distinctly how, when you were discussing your friend the architect, he always told his part after you had made a few remarks. He was getting his clue from you all the time. He's very agile and he's certainly fertile, I'll say that for him, but I don't believe a damned thing he told us, except perhaps that he was in the army and got badly bunged up. Even that, of course, could have been trumped up. Did you ever feel a head that was trepanned? That seems like solid fact, of course, and yet somehow, I don't know just why, I could doubt even what my fingers told me. When a man has an inventive brain like his he could tell you anything and make it sound convincing. Mind you, it doesn't make his story any less real, as far as I'm concerned. Whether all those things happened or not, they're true just the same. A minute ago, when I was mulling it over to myself, I caught myself deforming certain incidents, certain remarks he made, in order to make the story a better story. Not to make it more truthful, but more true, if you see the difference. I had it all figured out, how I would tell it myself, if I ever got down to it. . . ."

Rattner began to protest that I was too sweeping in my judgment, which only served to remind me of the marvelous poem he had recited for us.

"I say," I began again, "what would you think if I told you that the poem which he got off with such gusto was somebody else's? Would that shock you?"

"You mean you recognized it—you had heard it before?"

"No, I don't mean to say that, but I'm damned sure he was not the author of it. Why did he talk about his unusual memory immediately afterwards—didn't that strike you as rather strange? He could have spoken about a thousand things, but no, he had to speak of that. Besides, he recited it too well. Poets aren't usually so good at reciting their own things. Very few poets remember their verses, particularly if they're long ones such as his was. To recite a poem with such feeling a man has to admire it greatly and a poet, once he's written a poem out, forgets it. In any case, he wouldn't be going around spouting it aloud to every Tom, Dick and Harry he meets. A bad poet might, but then that poem wasn't written by a bad poet. And furthermore, a poem like that couldn't have been written by a man like our friend who boasted so glibly about turning out crap for the magazines whenever he needed to earn an honest or a dishonest penny. No, he memorized that poem because it was just the sort of thing he would like to have written himself and couldn't. I'm sure of it."

"There's something to what you say there," said Rattner sleepily. He sighed and turned over, his face towards the wall. In a jiffy he had turned round again and was sitting bolt upright.

"What's the matter," I asked, "what hit you?"

"Why my friend what's his name . . . you know, the architect who was my buddy. Who mentioned his name first—he did, didn't he? Well, how could he be lying then?"

"That's easy," I said. "Your friend's name is known to millions of people. He selected it just because it was a well-known name; he thought it would add tone to his story. That was when he was talking about his inventions, you remember? He just made a stab in the dark—and happened to strike your friend."

"He seemed to know a hell of a lot about him," said Rattner, still unconvinced.

"Well, don't you know lots of things about people whom you've never met? Why, if a man is any kind of celebrity we often know more about him than he does himself. Besides, this bird may have run into him at a bar some time or other. What sounded fishy to me was marrying him off to his sister right away."

"Yep, he was taking a big chance there," said Rattner, "knowing that I had been such an intimate friend."

"But you had already told him you hadn't seen each other since you were buddies together, don't forget that. Why he could have given him not only a wife but a half dozen children besides—you wouldn't be able to disprove it. Anyway, that's one thing we can check up on. I do wish you'd write to your friend and see if he knows this guy or not."

"You bet I will," said Rattner, getting out of bed at once and looking for his notebook. "You've got me all worked up about it now. Jesus, what licks me is that you could have entertained such suspicions and listened to him the way you did. You looked at him as though he were handing you the Gospel. I didn't know you were such an actor."

"I'm not," I hastened to put in. "At the time I really believed every word he was telling us. Or, to be more exact, I never stopped to think whether what he was saying was so or not so. When a story is good I listen, and if it develops afterwards that it was a lie why so much the better—I like a good lie just as much as the truth. A story is a story, whether it's based on fact or fancy."

134

"Now I'd like to ask you a question," Rattner put in. "Why do you suppose he was so sore at Roosevelt?"

"I don't think he was half so sore as he pretended to be," I answered promptly. "I think his sole motive for introducing Roosevelt's name was to get us to listen to that scurrilous poem he had cooked up. You noticed, I hope, that there was no comparison between the two poems. He wrote the one on Roosevelt, that I'm positive of. Only a bar-fly could cook up such ingenious nonsense. He probably hasn't anything against Roosevelt. He wanted us to admire the poem and then, failing to get a reaction from us, he got his wires crossed and connected Roosevelt with Woodrow Wilson, the demon who sent him to hell."

"He certainly had a vicious look when he was talking about the war," said Rattner. "I don't doubt him for a minute when he said he had murdered plenty of men. I wouldn't want to run across him in the dark when he was in a bad mood."

"Yes, there I agree with you," I said. "I think the reason he was so bitter about killing was that he was a killer himself . . . I was almost going to say a killer by nature, but I take that back. What I do think, though, is that the experience in the trenches often brings out the killer in a man. We're all killers, only most of us never get a chance to cultivate the germ. The worst killers, of course, are the ones who stay at home. They can't help it, either. The soldier gets a chance to vent his feelings, but the man who stays at home has no outlet for his passions. They ought to kill off the newspaper men right at the start, that's my idea. Those are the men who inspire the killing. Hitler is a pure, clean-hearted idealist compared to those birds. I don't mean the correspondents. I mean the editors and the stuffed shirts who order the editors to write the poison that they hand out."

"You know," said Rattner, in a soft, reflective voice, "there was only one man I felt like killing when I was in the service—and that was the lieutenant, the second-lieutenant, of our company."

"Don't tell me," I said. "I've heard that same story a thousand times. And it's always a lieutenant. Nobody with any self-respect wants to be a lieutenant. They all have inferiority complexes. Many of them get shot in the back, I'm told."

"Worse than that sometimes," said Rattner. "This chap I'm telling you about, why I can't imagine anyone being hated more than he was—not only by us but by his superiors. The officers loathed him. Anyway, let me finish telling you about him. . . . You see, when we were finally demobilized everybody was gunning for him. I knew some fellows who came all the way to New York from Texas and California to look him up and take a poke at him. And when I say a poke I don't mean just a poke—I mean to beat the piss out of him. I don't know whether it's true or not, but the story I heard later on was this, that he was beaten up so often and so badly that finally he changed his name and moved to another state. You can imagine what what's his name would have done to a guy like that, can't you? I don't think he's have bothered to soil his hands. I think he'd have plugged him or else cracked him over the head with a bottle. And if he'd have had to swing for it I don't think he would have batted an eyelash. Did you notice how smoothly he passed over that story about cracking a friend with a broken bottle? He told it as though it were incidental to something else—it rang true to me. If it had been a lie he would have made more of it. But he told it as though he were neither ashamed nor proud of doing what he did. He was just giving us the facts, that's all."

I lay on my back, when we had ceased talking, with eyes wide open, staring at the ceiling. Certain phrases which our friend had dropped returned obsessively to plague me. The collection of vice-presidents of the United States, which he had so accurately described, was a most persistent image. I was trying my damnedest to recall in what town I too had seen this collection in a drugstore window. Chattanooga, most likely. And yet it couldn't have been Chattanooga either, because in the same window there was a large photograph of Lincoln. I remembered how my eye had flitted back and forth from the rogues' gallery of vice-presidents to the portrait of Lincoln's wife. I had felt terribly sorry for Lincoln at that moment, not because he had been assassinated but because he had been saddled with that crazy bitch of a wife who almost drove him insane. Yes, as the woman from Georgia had said, we were trying to make a he-ro of him. And yet for all the good he had tried to do he had caused a lot of harm. He almost wrecked the country. As for Lee, on the other hand, there was no division of opinion throughout the country as to the greatness of his soul. As time goes on the North becomes more enamored of him. . . . *The killing*—that's what I couldn't fathom. What had it accomplished? I wondered if our friend had really gone up to the circle and held communion with the spirit of the man he revered. And then what? Then he had gone to a cheap lodging house and fought with the bed bugs until dawn, was that it? And the next day and the day after? Legions of them floating around. And me priding myself on my detective ability, getting all worked up because I uncovered a few flaws in his story. A revolution of the heart! Fine phrase, that, but meanwhile I'm lying comfortably between clean warm sheets. I'm lying here making emendations in his story so that when I come to put it down on paper it will sound more authentic than the authentic one. Trying to kid myself that if I tell the story real well perhaps it will make people more kindly and tolerant towards such poor devils. Rot! All rot! There are the people who give and forgive without stint, without question, and there are the other

137

kind who always know how to muster a thousand reasons for withholding their aid. The latter never graduate into the former class. Never. The gulf between them is as wide as hell. One is born kind, indulgent, forgiving, tolerant, merciful. One isn't made that way through religion or education. Carry it out to the year 56,927 A.D. and still there will be the two classes of men. And between the two there will always be a shadow world, the world of ghostly creatures who toss about in vain, walking the streets in torment while the world sleeps. . . .

It wasn't so long ago that I was walking in that same shadow world myself. I used to walk around in the dead of night begging for coppers so that I could fill my empty belly. And one night in the rain, walking with head down and full of nothing but misery, I run plump into a man with a cape and an opera hat and in a faint, cheerless voice I beg in my customary way for a few pence. And without stopping, without even looking at me, the man from the opera digs in his vest pocket, pulls out a handful of change and flings it at me. The money rolls all over the sidewalk and into the gutter. Suddenly I straightened up, stiff and taut with anger. Suddenly I was completely out of the coma, snorting like a bull and ready to charge. I waved my fist and shouted in the direction the man had taken, but there was no sight or sound of him. He had vanished as mysteriously as he had appeared. I stood there a moment or so undecided what to do, whether to run after him and vent my spleen or quietly set about searching for the shower of coins he had flung at me. Presently I was laughing hysterically. Run after him, bawl him out, challenge him to a duel? Why, he wouldn't even recognize me! I was a nonentity to him, just a voice in the dark asking for alms. I drew myself up still more erect and took a deep breath. I looked around calmly and deliberately. The street was empty, not even a cab rolling along. I felt strong and chastened, as if I had just taken a whipping I deserved. "You bastard," I said aloud, looking in the direction of my invisible benefactor, "I'm going to thank you for this! You don't know what you've done for me. Yes sir, I want to thank you from the bottom of my heart. I'm cured." And laughing quietly, trembling with thanksgiving, I got down on my hands and knees in the rain and began raking in the wet coins. Those which had rolled into the gutter were covered with mud. I washed them carefully in a little pool of rain water near a post of the elevated line. Then I counted them slowly and deliciously. Thirty-six cents altogether. A tidy sum. The cellar where we lived was near by. I brought the bright clean coins home to my wife and showed them to her triumphantly. She looked at me as if I had gone out of my head.

"Why did you wash them?" she said nervously.

"Because they had fallen in the gutter," I answered. "An angel with an opera hat left them there for me. He was in too much of a hurry to pick them up for me. . . ."

"Are you sure you're all right?" said my wife, eyeing me anxiously.

"I never felt better in my life," I said. "I've just been humiliated, beaten, dragged in the mud and washed in the blood of the Lamb. I'm hungry, are you? Let's eat."

And so at 3:10 of an Easter morning we sallied forth from the dungeon arm in arm and ordered two hamburgers and coffee at the greasy spoon cafeteria on Myrtle Avenue corner of Fulton Street. I was never so wide awake in my life, and after I had offered up a short prayer to St. Anthony I made a vow to remain wide awake and if possible to wake up the whole world, saying in conclusion Amen! and wiping my mouth with a paper napkin.

139

# MADEMOISELLE CLAUDE

Previously, when I began to write this tale, I set out by saying that Mlle. Claude was a whore. She is a whore, of course, and I'm not trying to deny it, but what I say now is—if Mlle. Claude is a whore then what name shall I find for the other women I know? Somehow the word whore isn't big enough. Mlle. Claude is more than a whore. I don't know what to call her. Maybe just Mlle. Claude. *Soit.*

There was the aunt who waited up for her every night. Frankly, I couldn't swallow that story. Aunt hell! More likely it was her *maquereau.* But then that was nobody's business but her own. . . .

Nevertheless, it used to gall me—that pimp waiting up for her, getting ready perhaps to clout her if she didn't come across. And no matter how loving she was (I mean that Claude really knew how to love) there was always in the back of my head the image of that blood-sucking, low-browed bastard who was getting all the gravy. No use kidding yourself about a whore—even when they're most generous and yielding, even if you've slipped them a thousand francs (who would, of course?)—there's always a guy waiting somewhere and what you've had is only a taste. He gets the gravy, be sure of that!

But then, all this, as I afterwards discovered, was just so much wasted emotion. There was no *maquereau*—not in Claude's case. I'm the first *maquereau* Claude has ever had. And I don't call myself a *maquereau* either. Pimp's the word. I'm her pimp now. O. K.

I remember distinctly the first time I brought her to my room, —what an ass I made of myself. Where women are concerned I always make an ass of myself. The trouble is I worship them and women don't want to be worshiped. They want . . . well, anyway, about that first night, believe it or not, I behaved just as if I had never slept with a woman before. I don't understand to this day why it should have been so. But that's how it was.

Before she even attempted to remove her things, I remember, she stood beside the bed looking up at me, waiting for me to do something, I suppose. I was trembling. I had been trembling ever since we left the café. I gave her a peck—on the lips, I think. I don't know—maybe I kissed her brow—I'm just the guy to do that sort of thing . . . with a woman I don't know. Somehow I had the feeling that she was doing me a tremendous favor. Even a whore can make a guy feel that way sometimes. But then, Claude isn't just a whore, as I said.

Before she had even removed her hat she went to the window, closed it, and drew the curtains to. Then she gave me a sort of sidelong look, smiled, and murmured something about getting undressed. While she fooled around with the bidet I went through the business of stripping down. As a matter of fact, I was nervous. I thought perhaps she'd be embarrassed if I watched her, so I fiddled around with the papers on my table, made a few meaningless notes, and threw the cover over the typewriter. When I turned she was standing in her chemise, near the sink, wiping her legs.

"Hurry! Get in bed!" she said. "Warm it up!" And with this she gave herself a few extra dabs.

Everything was so damned natural that I began to lose my uneasiness, my nervousness. I saw that her stockings were rolled down carefully, and from her waist there dangled some sort of harness which she flung presently over the back of the chair.

The room was chilly all right. We snuggled up and lay silently for a while, a long while, warming each other. I had one arm around her neck and with the other I held her close. She kept staring into my eyes with that same expectant look that I had observed when we first entered the room. I began to tremble again. My French was fading away.

I don't remember now whether I told her then and there that I loved her. Probably I did. Anyway, if I did, she probably forgot it immediately. As she was leaving I handed her a copy of *Aphrodite*, which she said she'd never read, and a pair of silk stockings that I had bought for some one else. I could see she liked the stockings.

When I saw her again I had changed my hotel. She looked about in her quick, eager way and saw at a glance that things weren't going so well. She asked very naïvely if I was getting enough to eat.

"You mustn't remain here long," she said. "It's very sad here." Maybe she didn't say *sad*, but that's what she meant, I'm sure.

142

It was sad all right. The furniture was falling apart, the window-panes were broken, the carpet was torn and dirty, and there was no running water. The light too was dim, a dim, yellow light that gave the bedspread a gray, mildewed look.

That night, for some reason or other, she pretended to be jealous. "There is somebody else whom you love," she said.

"No, there's nobody else," I answered.

"Kiss me, then," she said, and she clung to me affectionately, her body warm and tingling. I seemed to be swimming in the warmth of her flesh . . . not swimming either, but drowning, drowning in bliss.

Afterwards we talked about Pierre Loti, and about Stamboul. She said she'd like to go to Stamboul some day. I said I'd like to go too. And then suddenly she said—I think this was it—"you're a man with a soul." I didn't try to deny it—I was too happy, I guess. When a whore tells you you've got a soul it means more somehow. Whores don't usually talk about souls.

Then another strange thing happened. She refused to take any money.

"You mustn't think about money," she said. "We are comrades now. And you are very poor. . . ."

She wouldn't let me get out of bed to see her to the landing. She spilled a few cigarettes out of her bag and laid them on the table beside the bed; she put one in my mouth and lit it for me with the little bronze lighter that some one had given her as a gift. She leaned over to kiss me good-night.

I held her arm. "Claude," I said, "*vous êtes presque un ange.*"

"*Ah non!*" she replied, quickly, and there was almost a look of pain in her eyes, or terror.

That "presque" was really the undoing of Claude, I do believe. I sensed it almost immediately. And then the letter which I handed her soon after—the best letter I ever wrote in my life, though the French was execrable. We read it together, in the café where we usually met. As I say, the French was atrocious, except for a paragraph or two which I lifted from Paul Valéry. She paused a moment or two when she came to these passages. "Very well expressed!" she exclaimed. "Very well, indeed!" And then she looked at me rather quizzically and passed on. Oh, it wasn't Valéry that got her. Not at all. I could have done without him. No, it was the angel stuff that got her. I had pulled it again—and this time I embroidered it, as subtly and suasively as I knew how. By the time we had reached the end, though, I was feeling pretty uncomfortable. It was pretty cheap, taking advantage of her like that. I don't mean to say that it wasn't sincere, what I wrote, but after that first spontaneous gesture—I don't know, it was just literature. And then, too, it seemed shabbier than ever when, a little later, sitting on the bed together, she insisted on reading it over again, this time calling my attention to the grammatical errors. I became a little impatient with her and she was offended. But she was very happy just the same. She said she'd always keep the letter.

About dawn she slipped out. The aunt again. I was getting reconciled to the aunt business. Besides, if it wasn't an aunt I'd soon know now. Claude wasn't very good at dissembling—and then that angel stuff . . . that sank in deep.

I lay awake thinking about her. She certainly had been swell to me. The maquereau! I thought about him, too, but not for long, I wasn't worrying about him any more. Claude—I thought only about her and how I could make her happy. Spain . . . Capri . . . Stamboul. . . . I could see her moving languidly in the sunshine, throwing crumbs to the pigeons or watching them bathe, or else lying back in a hammock with a book in her hands, a book that I would recommend to her. Poor kid, she probably had never been further than Versailles in her life. I could see the expression on her face as we boarded the train, and later, standing beside a fountain somewhere. . . . Madrid or Seville. I could feel her marching beside me, close, always close, because she wouldn't know what to do with herself alone and even if it was dumb I liked the idea. Better a damned sight than having some god-damned flapper with you, some lightheaded little bastard who's always figuring out a way of ditching you even when she's lying with you. No, I could feel sure of Claude. Later it might get tiresome—later . . . later. I was glad I had picked a whore. *A faithful whore!* Jesus, I know people who'd laugh like hell if I ever said that.

I was planning it all out in detail: the places we'd stop at, the clothes she'd wear, what we'd talk about . . . everything . . . everything. She was Catholic, I supposed, but that didn't matter a damn to me. In fact, I rather liked it. It was lots better going to church to hear mass than to study architecture and all that crap. If she wanted, I'd become a Catholic too . . . what the hell! I'd do anything she asked me to—if it gave her a kick. I began to wonder if she had a kid somewhere, as most of them have. Imagine, Claude's kid! Why I'd love that kid more than if it were my own. Yes, she must have a kid, Claude—I'm going to see about it. There'd be times, I knew, when we'd have a big room with a balcony, a room looking out on a river, and flowers on the windowsill and birds singing. (I could see myself coming back with a birdcage on my arm. O. K. So long as it made her happy!) But the river—there must be rivers once in a while. I'm nuts about rivers. Once, in Rotterdam, I remember — — —. The idea, though, of waking up in the morning, the sun streaming in the windows and a good, faithful whore beside you who loves you, who loves the guts out of you, the birds singing and the table all spread, and while she's washing up and combing her hair all the men she's been

145

with and now you, just you, and barges going by, masts and hulls, the whole damned current of life flowing through you, through her, through all the guys before you and maybe after, the flowers and the birds and the sun streaming in and the fragrance of it choking you, annihilating you. O Christ! Give me a whore always, all the time!

I've asked Claude to live with me and she's refused. This is a blow. I know it's not because I'm poor—Claude knows all about my finances, about the book I'm writing, etc. No, there must be some other, deeper reason. But she won't come out with it.

And then there's another thing—I've begun to act like a saint. I take long walks alone, and what I'm writing now has nothing to do with my book. It seems as if I were alone in the universe, that my life is complete and separate, like a statue's. I have even forgotten the name of my creator. And I feel as if all my actions are inspired, as if I were meant to do nothing but good in this world. I ask for nobody's approval.

I refuse to take any charity from Claude any more. I keep track of everything I owe her. She looks sad these days, Claude. Sometimes, when I pass her on the *terrasse*, I could swear that there are tears in her eyes. She's in love with me now, I know it. She loves me desperately. For hours and hours she sits there on the *terrasse*. I go with her sometimes because I can't bear to see her miserable, to see her waiting, waiting, waiting. . . . I have even spoken to some of my friends about her, tipped them off, as it were. Yes, anything is better than to see Claude sitting there waiting, waiting. What does she think about when she sits there all by herself?

I wonder what she would say if I walked up to her one day and slipped her a thousand franc note. Just walk up to her, when she's got that melancholy look in her eyes, and say: "*Voici quelque*

chose que *j'ai oublié l'autre jour.*" Sometimes, when we lie together and there come those long brimming silences, she says to
me: "*Que pensez-vous maintenant?*" And I always answer "*Rien!*"
But what I'm really thinking to myself is—"*Voici quelque chose
que....*" This is the beautiful part of *l'amour à credit.*

When she takes leave of me the bells ring out wildly. She makes
everything so right inside me. I lie back on the pillow and luxu-
riously enjoy the weak cigarette which she has left me. I don't
have to stir for a thing. If I had a plate in my mouth I'm sure
she wouldn't forget to put it in the tumbler on the table beside
my bed, together with the matches and the alarm clock and all
the other junk. My trousers are carefully folded and my hat and
coat are hanging on a peg near the door. Everything in its place.
Marvelous! When you get a whore you get a jewel....

And the best of it is, the fine feeling endures. A mystic feeling
it is, and to become mystic is to feel the unity of life. I don't
care particularly any more whether I am a saint or not. A saint
struggles too much. There is no struggle in me any longer. I have
become a mystic. I impart good, peace, serenity. I am getting
more and more customers for Claude and she no longer has that
sad look in her eyes when I pass her. We eat together most every
day. She insists on taking me to expensive places, and I no longer
demur. I enjoy every phase of life—the expensive places as well as
the inexpensive places. If it makes Claude happy — — —.

*Pourtant je pense à quelque chose.* A little thing, to be sure,
but lately it has grown more and more important in my mind.
The first time I said nothing about it. An unwonted touch of
delicacy, I thought to myself. Charming, in fact. The second time
—was it delicacy, or just carelessness? However, *rien à dire.* Between the second and third times I was unfaithful, so to speak.
Yes, I was up on the *Grands Boulevards* one night, a little tight.

147

After running the gauntlet all the way from the Place de la République to *Le Matin*, a big, scabby buzzard whom I ordinarily wouldn't have pissed on grabbed me off. A droll affair. Visitors knocking at our door every few minutes. Poor little ex-Folies girls who begged the kind monsieur to give them a little tip—thirty francs or so. For what, pray? *Pour rien . . . . pour le plaisir.* A very strange, and very funny night. A day or so later irritation. Worries. Hurried trip to the American Hospital. Visions of Ehrlich and his black cigars. Nothing wrong, however. Just worry.

When I broach the subject to Claude she looks at me in astonishment. "I know you have every confidence in me, Claude, but. . . ." Claude refuses to waste any time on such a subject. A man who would consciously, deliberately give a woman a disease is a criminal. That's how Claude looks upon it. "*C'est vrai, n'est-ce pas?*" she asks. It's *vrai* all right. However. . . . But the subject is closed. Any man who would do that is a criminal.

Every morning now, when I take my paraffin oil—I always take it with an orange—I get to thinking about these criminals who give women diseases. The paraffin oil makes the spoon very sticky. It is necessary to wash it well. I wash the knife and the spoon very carefully. I do everything carefully—it is my nature. After I have washed my face I look at the towel. The patron never gives out more than three towels a week; by Tuesday they are all soiled. I dry the knife and the spoon with a towel; for my face I use the bedspread. I don't rub my face—I pat it gently with the edge of the bedspread, near the feet.

The Rue Hippolyte Mandron looks vile to me. I detest all the dirty, narrow, crooked streets with romantic names hereabouts. Paris looks to me like a big, ugly chancre. The streets are gangrened. Everybody has it—if it isn't clap it's syphilis. All Europe is diseased, and it's France who's made it diseased. This is what comes of admiring Voltaire and Rabelais! I should have gone to Moscow, as I intended. Even if there are no Sundays in Russia, what difference does it make? Sunday is like any other day now, only the streets are more crowded, more victims walking about contaminating one another.

Mind you, it's not Claude I'm raving against. Claude is a jewel, un ange, and no presque about it. There's the bird-cage hanging outside the window, and flowers too—though it ain't Madrid or Seville, no fountains, no pigeons. No, it's the clinic every day. She goes in one door and I in the other. No more expensive restaurants. Go to the movies every night and try to stop squirming. Can't bear the sight of the Dôme or the Coupole any more. These bastards sitting around on the terrasse, looking so clean and healthy with their coats of tan, their starched shirts and their eau-de-cologne. It wasn't entirely Claude's fault. I tried to warn her about these suave looking bastards. She was so damned confident of herself—the injections and all that business. And then, any man who would. . . . Well, that's just how it happened. Living with a whore—even the best whore in the world—isn't a bed of roses. It isn't the numbers of men, though that too gets under your skin sometimes, it's the everlasting sanitation, the precautions, the irrigations, the examinations, the worry, the dread. And then, in spite of it all — — —. I told Claude . . . . I told her repeatedly—"watch out for the swell guys!"

No, I blame myself for everything that's happened. Not content with being a saint I had to prove that I was a saint. Once a man realizes that he's a saint he should stop there. Trying to pull the saint on a little whore is like climbing into heaven by the back stairs. When she cuddles up to me—she loves me now more than ever—it seems to me that I'm just some damned microbe that's wormed its way into her soul. I feel that even if I am living with an angel I ought to try to make a man of myself. We ought to get out of this filthy hole and live somewhere in the sunshine, a room with a balcony overlooking a river, birds, flowers, life streaming by, just she and me and nothing else.

# TRIBUTE TO BLAISE CENDRARS

*Je suis un homme inquiet, dur vis à vis de soi-même, comme tous les solitaires.* From *Une Nuit dans la Forêt*.

THE REASON I always think of Cendrars with affection and admiration is that he resembles so closely that Chinese rock-bottom man of my imagination whom I have probably invented because of my hatred and contempt for the men I see about me in the world today. Cendrars himself gives the clue to his enigmatic character in an autobiographical fragment, a little book called *Une Nuit dans la Forêt*. *"De plus en plus, je me rends compte que j'ai toujours pratiqué la vie contemplative."*

Turbulent and chaotic though his writing seems, the meaning nevertheless is always crystal clear. Cendrars anchors himself in the

151

very heart of things. He is the most active of men and yet serene as a lama. To bemoan the contradictoriness of his nature is to misjudge him. The man is all of a piece, one inexhaustible creative substance which enjoys a continuous fulfillment through giving. Many people would say that he is generous to a fault. I would not use the word generous in connection with Cendrars. He is beyond that. He is a vital force, a blind and pitiless urge, closer to nature than to man. He is tender and ruthless at the same time. He is antinomian. And always uniquely himself, always uniquely Blaise Cendrars.

If you will look at a list of his works you will see that more than half of them are exhausted. And if you study the titles of his works you will see that the man himself is inexhaustible. He is the most contemporary of contemporaries, dated and undated at the same time. He is so well informed that he is absolutely oblivious of what is going on. Cendrars is the crude ore of which the finest metals are made. He can tell the most monstrous lies and remain absolutely truthful. In every yarn he spins there is more of vital substance and genuine fact than you can find in the whole panorama, for example, of Jules Romains' magnum opus. In every book he gives us Cendrars seems to be making the gesture of bending down and picking up a handful of earth with his good left hand. In every book he seems to be embracing us with that mutilated arm through which the blood still courses warm and red. Cendrars knows only the reality and honesty of the heart. His gestures, often rough and awkward, are nevertheless manly gestures. He never tries to please or to conciliate. He is the worst diplomat in the world, and consequently the best. He is not a realist, but real. In his peculiar inhuman way he does only what is human, responds only to what is human. If sometimes he seems like a charge of dynamite it is because his sincerity, his integrity, is incorruptible.

Cendrars is a voyager. There is hardly a corner of the globe whereon he has not set foot. He has not only voyaged about the world, but beyond the world. He has been to the moon, to Mars, to Neptune, Vega, Saturn, Pluto, Uranus. He is a visionary who does not spurn the ordinary means of travel, of locomotion. Usually he travels incognito, adopting the manners and the speech of the people he is visiting. He carries no passport and no letters of credit, neither letters of introduction, to be sure. He knows that wherever he lands it is the same rigmarole. It is not a question of confidence in himself, nor even of faith in his lucky star—it is a question of accuracy. When he describes his celestial voyages he proceeds simply and honestly, as if he were describing a trip to Formosa or Patagonia. The world is one, the same in dream as in waking life. One plasma and one magma. Frontiers exist only for the timid ones, for the poor and mean at heart. Cendrars never uses the word "frontier": he speaks of latitude and longitude. He inquires about the climate, or the nature of the soil, what do you use for food, and so on. He is almost frighteningly natural, almost inhumanly human. "*L'action seule libère. Elle dénoue tout.*"

He has friends everywhere, even among the Hottentots. And yet he is the most solitary of men. Of all the men I have ever met he is the most liberated—yet thoroughly earthbound. To use the word "cosmic" with reference to him would be to insult him; it would imply that he accepted life. Cendrars does not accept. He accepts nothing. He says neither "Yes" nor "No." He walks over such questions rough-shod. He becomes terrifyingly silent. And that is why perhaps he is the most marvellous talker I have ever listened to. His talk is not of loneliness, as with most men—it is of the absolute moment, of nothingness, of evanescence and metamorphosis. And so it is fecund, magical, toxic. His talk is pure destruction to everything that is not of the moment; it is a mirage

153

born of the peculiar spiritual atmosphere which he has created about him and in which he lives. He follows it thirstily, like the wanderer in the desert. But he is never lost, nor is he ever deceived. Nor does he ever leave his body, as do those strange seekers of wisdom in Tibet. Wherever Cendrars goes his body accompanies him—and his hunger and his thirst. If it has been a tight squeeze he returns looking emaciated; if it was plain sailing he comes back with ruddy face and that sort of starry gleam in his eyes which is unforgettable. One is tempted to say of him that he is hallucinating. Cendrars not only creates longing, he answers it too. His talk is that of a man ceaselessly emptying his pockets. He does not talk words; he talks things, facts, deeds, experiences. He needs no adjectives, just verbs and nouns—and conjunctions and conjunctions and conjunctions.

His nationality is obscure. He is a melting-pot of all races, all peoples. Once I was going to dedicate a book to him—"*To Blaise Cendrars, the first Frenchman to make me a royal gesture!*"—but I realized as I wrote the phrase that it would be an injustice to Cendrars to call him a Frenchman. No, he is, as I said before, the Chinese rock-bottom man of my imagination, the man that D. H. Lawrence would like to have been, the man of the cosmos who remains forever unidentified, the man who renews the race by putting humanity back into the crucible. "*Je méprise tout ce qui est. J'agis. Je revolutionne,*" says Cendrars.

I remember reading *Moravagine*, one of my very first attempts to read French. It was like reading a phosphorescent text through smoked glasses. I had to divine what he was saying, Cendrars, but I got it. If he had written it in Tegalic I would have gotten it. Even in such a work as *L'Eubage* one gets it, gets it quick in the guts—or never. Everything is written in blood, but a blood that is saturated with starlight. Cendrars is like a transparent fish swimming in a planetary sperm; you can see his backbone, his lungs, his heart, his kidneys, his intestines; you can see the red corpuscles moving in the blood-stream. You can look clean through him and see the planets wheeling. The silence he creates is deafening. It takes you back to the beginning of the world, to that hush which is engraved on the face of mystery.

I always see him there in the hub of the universe, slowly revolving with the vortex. I see his slouch hat and battered mug beneath it. I see him "revolutionizing," because there is no help for it, because there is nothing else to do. Yes he is a sort of Brahman à rebours, as he says of himself, a Brahman who is the envoy plenipotentiary of the active principle itself. He is the man of the dream which he is dreaming, and he will be that until the dream ends. There is no subject and object. *There is.* A transitive mode which is expressed by the intransitive; action which is the negation of activity. Cendrars is the eye of the navel, the face in the mirror which remains after you have turned your back on it.

Another interesting thing about him—he does as little as possible. It is not that he is lazy—far from it!—nor that he is gripped by the futility of things. It is rather because he is a piece of human radium buried in the maggot pile of humanity. At the very bottom of the pile he can still assert his full strength. He does not need to get up and walk or shout; he has only to be, only to radiate his inexhaustible vitality. He is the incarnation of the very opposite principle which governs the world, like the lie which reveals the truth. He is all those things which we know only by contrast, and so he has not even to move his little finger. The slightest *voluntary* movement and he would be done for, he would explode. And Cendrars knows it. He has an almost geologic wisdom, which is why he is never logical, never truthful, never serious, never hopeful, never confident, never trustful, never anything. He is never, never, never *He is*. You reach to him by leaning backward, by receding, by putting minus in front of you. You can never meet him face to face, never seize him by putting your arms out. You must relinquish, sink back, close your eyes. He is at the beginning of the road, not at the end. Meet me yesterday, he says, or the day before yesterday. It is no use setting the alarm—you will never get up early enough to meet him.

If he had wanted to be anything he could have been it most successfully. He does not want. He is like the sage in the Chinese story who, when asked why he never performed the miracles attributed to his disciple, replied: "The Master is able to do these things, but he is also able to refrain from doing them." His disinterestedness is always a positive, active quality. He is not inactive —*he refuses, he rejects.*

It is this instinctive, ordained defiance in Cendrars which makes the word "rebel" sound ridiculous when applied to him. He is not a rebel, he is an absolute traitor to the race, and as such I salute him. The salute is wasted, of course, because Cendrars doesn't give a damn whether you salute him or not. Would you salute a tree for spreading its foliage? Whether you are at the bottom or the top is all the same to Cendrars. He doesn't care to know what you are trying to do; he is only interested in what you are. He looks you through and through, pitilessly. If you are meat for the gristle, fine! he devours you. If you are just suet, then down the sewer you go—unless that day he happens to be in need of a little fat. He is the epitome of injustice, which is why he appears so magnanimous. He does not forgive, or pardon, or condemn, or condone. He puts you in the scales and weighs you. He says nothing. He lets you do the talking. With himself he is equally rigorous. "*Moi, l'homme le plus libre du monde, je reconnais que l'on est toujours lié par quelque chose, et que la liberté, l'indépen-*

*dance n'existe pas, et je me méprise autant que je peux, tout en rejouissant de mon impuissance."*

He has been accused of writing trash. It is true that he does not always write on the same level—but Cendrars never writes trash. He is incapable of writing trash. His problem is not whether to write well or badly, but whether to write or not write. Writing is almost a violation of his way of living. He writes against the grain, more and more so as the years go on. If, on the impulse of the moment, or through dire necessity, he takes the notion to do a piece of reportage, he goes through with it with good grace. He goes about even the most trivial task with pains, because fundamentally he does not recognize that one thing is trivial and another important. If it is not anti-human, his attitude, it is certainly anti-moral. He is as much ashamed of being disgusted or revolted as of being exalted or inspired. He has known what it is to struggle, but he despises struggle too.

His writing, like his life, is on different levels. It changes color, substance, tempo, just as his life changes rhythm and equilibrium. He goes through metamorphoses, without however surrendering his identity. His behavior seems to be governed not merely by internal changes—psychic, chemical, physiologic—but by external ones also, chiefly by interstellar configurations. He is tremendously susceptible to changes of weather—the spiritual weather. He experiences in his soul genuine eclipses; he knows what it means to fly off at a tangent, or to sweep across the sky like a flaming comet. He has been put on the rack, drawn and quartered; he has pursued his own shadow, tasted madness. It seems to me that his greatest tribulation has been to accept the quality of the grandiose which is written in his destiny. His struggle has been with his own fate, with the grandeur which for some reason he has never wholly accepted. Out of desperation and humility he has created for himself the more human role of the antagonist. But his destiny was laid down in royal colors. He does not fit in anywhere because his whole life has been lived in defiance of the pattern which was ordained. And desperate and tragic, even foolish as such a course may seem, it is the very inmost virtue of Cendrars, the link which binds him to the human family, which makes him the wonderful copain he is, the marvellous man among men whom even the unseeing recognize immediately. It is this challenge which he carries around in him, which he hurls now and then in his mad, drunken moments; it is this which really sustains those about him, those who have had even the least contact with him. It is not the blustering, heroic attitude, but the blind, tragic defiance of the Greeks. It is the resistance to fate which is always aroused by a super-endowment of strength, by a super-wisdom. It is the Dionysian element which is created at the moment of greatest lucidity: the frail, human voice denying the god-impulse because to accept it would mean the death of all that is creative, all that is truly human. It is on this wheel of creation and destruction that Cendrars turns, as the globe itself turns. It is this which isolates him, makes him a solitary. He refuses to spread himself thin over an illusory pattern of grandeur; he muscles deeper and deeper into the hub, into the everlasting no-principle of the universe.

# INTO THE FUTURE

To APPROACH the world of Lawrence two things must be steadily borne in mind: first, the nature of his individual temperament, and second, the relation between such a temperament and the times. For Lawrence was both distinctively unique and at the same time a figure representative of our time. He stands out among the constellations as a tiny, blazing star; he glows more brilliantly in the measure that we understand our age. Had he not reflected his epoch so thoroughly he would have already been forgotten. As it is, his importance increases with time. It is not that he grows bigger, or that he moves nearer the earth. No, he remains where he was at the beginning: he remains just a tiny bit above the horizon, like an evening star, but as night comes on, and it is the night which is coming on stronger and stronger, he waxes more brilliant. We understand him better as we go down into the night.

Before me lie the notes from which this book on Lawrence will emerge. They make a huge, baffling pile. Some of them I don't understand myself any more. Some of them I see already in a new light. The notes are full of contradictions. Lawrence was full of contradictions. Life itself is full of contradictions. I want to impose no higher order upon the man, his works, his thought, than life imposes. I do not want to stand outside life, judging it, but in it, submitting to it, reverencing it.

I speak of contradictions. And immediately I feel impelled to contradict this. For example, I wish to make it clear at the outset that a man like Lawrence was right, right in everything he said, in everything he did, even when what he said or did was obviously wrong, obviously stupid, obviously prejudiced or unjust. (He is at his very best, to illustrate what I mean, in such writing as the studies on Poe and on Melville.) Lawrence was opposed to the world as is. The world is wrong, always was wrong, always will be wrong. In this sense Lawrence was right, is still right, and always will be right. Every sensitive being aware of his own power, his own right, senses this opposition. The world however is there and will not be denied. The world says NO. The world is eternally wagging its head NO.

The most important figure for the entire Western world has been for two thousand years the man who was the quintessence of contradictoriness: Christ. He was a contradiction to himself and to the world. And yet those who were opposed to him, or to the world, or to themselves, have understood. He is understood by all everywhere, even though denied. Is it because he was a contradiction? Let us not answer this immediately. Let us leave this question in suspense. . . .

Here, touching on this point, we stand very close to something which concerns us all vitally. We are approaching the enigma from behind, as it were. Let us think a moment calmly. There was Christ, the one splendid shining figure who has dominated our whole history. There was also another man—St. Francis of Assisi. He was second to Christ in every sense. He made a tremendous impression upon our world—perhaps because, like those Bodhisattvas who renounced Nirvana in order to aid humanity, he too elected to remain close to us. There were these two resplendent figures, then. Will there be a third? Can there be? If there was any man in the course of modern times who most nearly attained this summit it was D. H. Lawrence. But the tragedy of Lawrence's life, the tragedy of our time, is this—that had he been this third great figure we would never know it. The man was never fully born—because he was never squarely opposed. He is a bust perpetually bogged in a quagmire. Eventually the bust will disappear altogether. Lawrence will go down with the time which he so magnificently represented. He knew it, too. That is why the hope and the despair which he voiced are so finely equilibrated. *Consummatum est*, he cried out towards the last. Not on his death-bed, but on the cross, while alive and in full possession of his faculties. Just as Christ knew in advance what was in store for him, accepting his role, so too Lawrence knew and accepted. Each went to a different fate. Christ had already performed his work when he was led to the cross. Lawrence nailed himself to the cross because he knew that the task could not be performed—neither his own task nor the world's. Jesus was killed off. Lawrence was obliged to commit suicide. That is the difference.

Lawrence was not the first. There were others before him, all through the modern period, who had been doing themselves in. Each suicide was a challenge. Rimbaud, Nietzsche—these tragedies almost brought about a spark. Lawrence goes out and nothing happens. He sells better, that is about all.

I said a moment ago that the contradictoriness of Christ brought us very close to something vital, a fear which has us in the bowels. Lawrence made us again aware of it—though it was almost instantly dismissed. What is the essence of this enigma? To be in the world and not of it. To deepen the conception of the role of man. How is this done? By denying the world and proclaiming the inner reality? By conquering the world and destroying the inner reality? Either way there is defeat. Either way there is triumph, if you like. They are the same, defeat and victory—it is only a question of changing one's position.

There is the world of outer reality, or action, and the world of inner reality, or thought.* The fulcrum is art. After long use, after endless see-saws, the fulcrum wears itself away. Then, as though divinely appointed, there spring up lone, tragic figures, men who offer their own bare backs as fulcrum for the world. They perish under the overwhelming burden. Others spring up, more and more of them, until out of many heroic sacrifices there is built up a fulcrum of living flesh which can balance the weight of the world again. This fulcrum is art, which at first was raw flesh, which was action, which was faith, which was the sense of destiny.

Today the world of action is exhausted, and also the world of thought. There is neither an historical sense nor an inner, metaphysical reality. No one man today can get down and offer his bare back as support. The world has spread itself out so thin that

* In *Louis Lambert* Balzac uses this dichotomy in the opposite way, but the meaning is the same.

the mightiest back would not be broad enough to support it. Today it is dawning on men that if they would find salvation they must lift themselves up by their own bootstraps. They must discover for themselves a new sense of equilibrium. Each one for himself must recover the sense of destiny. In the past a figure like Christ could create an imaginary world powerful enough in its reality to make him the lever of the world. Today there are millions of sacrificial scapegoats but not enough power in the lot of them to raise a grain of sand. The world is out of whack and men individually are out of whack.

We are on the wrong track, all of us. One group, the larger one, insists on changing the external pattern—the social, political, economic configuration. Another group, very small but increasing in power, insists on discovering a new reality. There is no hope either way. The inner and outer are one. If now they are divorced it is because a new way of life is about to be ushered in. There is only one realm in which inner and outer may still be fused and that is the realm of art. Most art will reflect the death which is taking place, but only the most forward spirits can give an intimation of the life which is to come. Just as primitive peoples carry on in our midst their life of fifty or a hundred thousand years ago, so the artists.

We are facing an absolutely new condition of life. An entirely new cosmos must be created, and it must be created out of our separate, isolate, living parts. It is we, the indestructible morsels of living flesh, who make up the cosmos. The cosmos is not made up in the mind, by philosophers and metaphysicians, nor is it made by God. An economic revolution will certainly not create it. It is something we carry within us and which we build up about us: we are part of it and it is we who must bring it into being. We must realize who and what we are. We must carry through to the finish, both in creation and destruction. What we do most of the time is either to deny or to wish. Ever since the beginning of our history, our Western history, we have been *willing* the world to be something other than it is. We have been transmogrifying ourselves in order to adapt ourselves to an image which has been a mirage. This will has come to exhaustion in supreme doubt. We are paralyzed; we whirl about on the pivot of self like drunken dervishes. Nothing will liberate us but a new knowledge—not the Socratic wisdom, but *realization*, which is knowledge become active.

For, as Lawrence predicted, we are entering the era of the Holy Ghost. We are about to give up the ghost of our dead self and enter a new domain. God is dead. The Son is dead. And we are dead only as these have gone out of us. It is not death really, but a *Scheintot*. Of Proust it was said by someone that "he was the most alive of all the dead." In that sense we are still alive. But the axis has broken, the poles no longer function. It is neither night nor day. Neither is it a twilight. We are drifting with the flux.

When I talk of drift and drifting I know very well that I am only using an image. Myself I do not believe that we are going to drift forever. Some may, perhaps a great part of the world of men and women. But not all. So long as there are men and women the world itself can never become a Sargasso Sea. What creates this fearsome image is only the awareness in each of us that, despite ourselves, we are drifting, we have become one with the ceaseless flux. There is a force outside us which, because of death, seems greater than us, and that is Nature. We, as living beings, are part of Nature. But we are also part of something else, something which includes Nature. It is as this unrealized part of the universe that we have set ourselves up in opposition to the whole. And it is not our will but our destiny which has permitted such an opposition to come into existence. That force which is beyond us, greater than us, obeys its own laws. If we are wise we try to move within those laws, adapt ourselves to them. That is the real element of livingness, as Lawrence might say. When we refuse to move with the movement of that greater force we break the law of life, we drift, and in the drift Nature passes us off.

Where the great spiritual leaders have succumbed was in the conflict between these two forces, epitomized and symbolized by their own lives. Each spiritual gain has been signalized by a defeat at the hands of Nature. Each spiritual gain meant the upsetting of the equilibrium between these opposing forces. The distance between one great figure and another is only another way of estimating the time required to obtain a new and satisfactory equilibrium. The task of each new figure has been to destroy the old equilibrium. Nothing more. Nothing less.

Today it is vaguely felt that we are in a period of transition. To what? To a new equilibrium? On what fulcrum? On what are we to find a point of rest? Lawrence saw that the fulcrum itself had been smashed. He felt the tide carrying him along. He knew that a new order was establishing itself. Against this new cosmic order he set up no opposition. On the contrary, he welcomed it. But as an individual he protested. He was not fully born. Part of him was stuck in the womb of the old. Half out, alive, fully conscious, superconscious, in fact, he voiced the agony of that other half of him which was dying. It could not die quickly enough for him, even though in that partial death his own individual death was involved. He saw that the greater part of the world was dying without having been born. Death in the womb—it was that which drove him frantic.

It is no idle figure I use when I say that only the upper half of him emerged. The head and the heart. A blinding consciousness

165

he had, and a tender bleeding heart. But a potent figure of man he was not. He had only the sustaining heart—and the voice, which he used to the fullest. But he had a vision of what was to come, and in the measure that he was able to, he identified himself with the future. "Only now," he said, "are we passing over into a new era." He spoke about it over and over, cryptically, symbolically: the era of the Holy Ghost. I notice that he expressed the idea when writing to some one about the Renaissance. He had apparently just finished reading Rolland's essay on Michelangelo. "The world is going mad," says Lawrence, "as the Italian and Spanish Renaissance went mad. But where is our Reformation, where is our new life?" And then he added: "One must live quite apart, forgetting, having another world, a world as yet uncreated."

The use of the word "forgetting" is worthy of attention. Whereas Proust was able successfully to live apart, remembering, creating his own very real, fictive world, Lawrence was never able to live apart, neither to forget. Proust, by a complete break with the outer world of reality, was able to live on as if dead, to live only in the remembrance of things past. Even then it was not an absolute break. A thin, almost invisible cord connected him with the world. Often it was an inanimate object which, through his exaggerated sensory faculties, brought him with a shock to the reality which he had buried deep within himself. It was not a remembering in the usual sense. It was a magic revival of the past through means of the body. The body re-experienced the joys or the sorrows of the buried past. From a trance-like state Proust thus roused himself to a semblance of life, the powerful reality and immediacy of which was greater than in the original experience. His great work is nothing but a series of these traumatic shocks, or rather the expression of their repercussions. For him, therefore, art took on the metaphysical aspect of rediscovering what was already written in the heart. It was a return to the labyrinth, a desire to bury himself deeper and deeper in the self. And this self was for him composed of a thousand different entities all attached by experience to a mysterious seed-like Self which he refused to know. It was a path, a direction, exactly the opposite of Lawrence's. It was an effort, one might almost say, to retrace his life and, by collecting all the images of himself which he had ever glimpsed in the mirror, recompose a final seed-like image of which he had no knowledge. The use of sensation here is entirely different from Lawrence's use of it—because their conception of "body" was entirely different. Proust, having totally divorced himself from his body, except as a sensory instrument for reviving the past, gave to the human individuality thereby an entirely irreligious quality. His religion was ART—i.e., the process. For Proust the personality was fixed: it could come unglued, so to speak, be peeled off layer by layer, but the thought that lay behind this process was of something solid, already determined, imperishable, and altogether unique.

With this conception of a personal ego Lawrence had no patience. What he saw was an endless drama of the self, a whirlpool in which the individual was finally engulfed. Lawrence was interested in the development of man as a unique spiritual blossom. He deplored the fact that man, as MAN, had not yet come into his own kingdom. While emphasizing the unique quality of the individual, he placed no value on uniqueness in itself. What he stressed was the flowering of the personality. He was impressed by the fact that man is in a state of infancy, psychologically speaking. Neither the dynamic attitude of the West, anchored in the will, in idealism, nor the attitude of the East, anchored in a fatalistic quietism, seemed satisfactory to him as a way of life.

167

They were both inadequate. "Man as yet is only half-born," he said. "No sign of bud anywhere."

His first significant work, *The Crown*, is concerned primarily with an attempt to make clear the meaning of the Holy Ghost. It is his way of referring to the mysterious source of the self, the creative instinct, the individual guide and conscience. In the realization of its meaning he visualized the resolution of the god problem, an end to the vicious dichotomy of demon-angel, god-devil, an end to the alternate belittlement and aggrandizement of the personality. What he is searching for continually is the true self, that central source of power and action which is called the Holy Ghost, the mysterious, unknowable area of the self out of which the gods, as well as men, are born. His idea of a union with the cosmos meant then the restoration of man's divinity. The old cosmos, he says in *Apocalypse*, was entirely religious and godless. There was no idea of "creation" or of "separateness" or "God versus world." The cosmos was, is, and will be. It is we who have grown apart, insisted Lawrence. And it is in this growing apart that we have developed the extreme notions of the self, of the personality, and of God. The great sense of guilt which burdens man—and particularly the artist—springs from the deep realization that he is split off from the cosmos, that in a part of him he has made himself God and in another he has made himself human, all-too-human.

All this brings me to the present. We are facing an absolutely new condition of life, one that is almost unbearable, at least for a sensitive being. That such an antagonism always existed I have no doubt: the artist was always in conflict with the world, with the world in which he found himself. The fact that there are artists means that life is well-nigh insupportable. And yet, in the past there was always a thread of communication between the sensitive and the insensitive. There were forms and symbols, mythologies which served as alphabets and which enabled the uninitiated to decipher the divine script of the artist. Today the very thread, language, seems to have snapped. Powerless to communicate his vision, the artist loses his belief in himself, in his role or mission. Whereas before his escape from the pain of living was through art, today he has no escape except to deny his own validity. Today all the hierarchies have broken down: in every field of human endeavor we are faced with chaos. There is no choice, only to surrender. Surrender to the flux, to the drift towards a new and unthinkable order.

That Lawrence understood, that he revealed the trend, and that he offered a solution is what I wish to make clear. But to understand this it is necessary to recognize the peculiar nature of his temperament and the relation of such a temperament to the times. The problem of an immediate and personal solution to the all-besetting difficulties of the times may then be seen to resolve itself into a much broader and much more human problem of destiny. That we have a destiny, each and all of us, seems of more importance right now than the question of an immediate solution of life's problems. For it is in the very establishment of a relation between oneself and the cosmos that a new quality of hope will arise, and with hope faith. We must ask ourselves how it is that faced with a crushing destiny there are some of us who, instead of shrinking or cowering, leap forward to embrace destiny. There are some of us, in short, who in assuming a definite attitude towards the world seek neither to deny, nor escape, nor to alter it, but simply to live it out. Some more consciously than others. Some as though they saw it written in the stars, as though it were tattooed on their bodies.

There exist today all over the world a number of modern spirits who are anything but modern. They are thoroughly out of joint with the times, and yet they reflect the age more truly, more authentically, than those who are swimming with the current. In the very heart of the modern spirit there is a schism. The egg is breaking, the chromosomes are splitting to go forward with a new pattern of life. Something is germinating, and those of us who seem most alien, most split, most divorced from the current of life, are the ones who are going forward to create the life as yet inchoate.

This, no doubt, is mysticism—and it should remain so. We who are affected cannot make ourselves clear. We are clairvoyant because we see with other eyes. What is there to communicate when the slender thread which bound us to the world is broken? With *what*, then, can we hope to communicate? *With the pure spirit!* This is the era when the apocalyptic visions are to be fulfilled. We are on the brink of a new life, we are entering a new domain. In what language can we describe things for which as yet there are no names? And how describe *relations?* We can only divine the nature of those to whom we are attracted, the forces to which we willingly yield obedience. In short, we can only make ourselves *felt.* That we are here, that is the all-important.

When I speak of a hope and a faith I ask myself what evidences are there, what justification for such language? I think again of the Renaissance and how Lawrence was obsessed with it. I see how we ourselves stand before the future, divided between hope and fear. But at least we know that there is a future, that the moment is momentous. We stand now as we do sometimes in our own individual humdrum lives, thrilled by the thought of the morrow, the morrow which will be utterly unlike today, or yesterday. Only the rare few are privileged to regard the future with certainty, with hope and with courage. They are the ones who are already living into the future: they experience a posthumous joy. And this joy is no doubt tinged with cruelty. In bringing about the death of an old order a sort of sadistic pleasure is awakened. Another way of putting it would be to say that the *heroic* spirit is rekindled. The so-called moderns are the old and weary who see in a new collective order the gentle release of death. For them any change is welcome. It is the *end* which they are looking forward to. But there is another kind of modern who enters the conflict blindly, to establish that for which as yet there is no name. It is to this order of men that Lawrence addressed himself. The Apollonian show is over. The dance has begun. The coming men are the musicians of the new order, the seed-bearers, the *tragic* spirits.

It is of the utmost importance also to realize that the process of dissolution is quickening. Every day the difference between the few and the many becomes sharper. A great yawning fissure divides the old from the new. There is still time perhaps to make the jump, but each day the hurdle becomes more perilous. The tendency so marked in Lawrence's work—to divide the world into black and white—becomes more and more actualized. It was one of the great distinguishing features of Dante's work. It was inevitable. It marks the great split in the mind, the angel's superhuman effort, as it were, to discover the soul of the new. During this process, which is nothing short of a crisis of consciousness, the spirit flames anew. Whatever is valuable, whatever is *creative*, must now reveal the pure and flaming spirit. The poet is bound to be oracular and prophetic. As the night comes on man looks out towards the stars; he no longer identifies himself with the world of day which is crumbling, but gives himself to the silent, ordained future. Abandoning the cunning instruments of the mind with which he had vainly hoped to pierce the mystery, he now

171

stands before the veil of creation naked and awe-struck. He divines what is in store for him. Everything becomes personal in a new sense. He becomes himself a new person.

The world of Lawrence now seems to me like a strange island on which for a number of years I was stranded. Had I made my way back to the known, familiar world I should perhaps talk differently about my adventure. But this world is gone for me, and the island on which I was marooned serves as the sole remaining link, a memory which binds me to the past. This then will serve as a log of my strange adventure—if my memory does not fail me.*

* Fragment from *The World of Lawrence.*

# THE EYE OF PARIS

BRASSAÏ HAS that rare gift which so many artists despise—*normal vision*. He has no need to distort or deform, no need to lie or to preach. He would not alter the living arrangement of the world by one iota; he sees the world precisely as it is and as few men in the world see it because seldom do we encounter a human being endowed with normal vision. Everything to which his eye attaches itself acquires value and significance, a value and significance, I might say, heretofore avoided or ignored. The fragment, the defect, the commonplace—he detects in them what there is of novelty or perfection. He explores with equal patience, equal interest, a crack in the wall or the panorama of a city. Seeing becomes an end in itself. For Brassai is an eye, a living eye.

When you meet the man you see at once that he is equipped with no ordinary eyes. His eyes have that perfect, limpid sphericity, that all-embracing voracity which makes the falcon or the shark a shuddering sentinel of reality. He has the eyeball of the insect which, hypnotized by its myopic scrutiny of the world, raises its two huge orbs from their sockets in order to acquire a still greater flexibility. Eye to eye with this man you have the sensation of a razor operating on your own eyeball, a razor which moves with such delicacy and precision that you are suddenly in a ball room in which the act of undressing follows upon the wish. His gaze pierces the retina like those marvelous probes which penetrate the labyrinth of the ear in order to sound for dead bone, which tap at the base of the skull like the dull tick of a watch in moments of complete silence. I have felt the penetration of his gaze like the gleam of a searchlight invading the hidden recesses of the eye, pushing open the sliding doors of the brain. Under that keen, steady gaze I have felt the seat of my skull glowing like an asbestos grill, glowing with short, violet waves which no living matter can resist. I have felt the cool, dull tremors in every vertebra, each socket, each nodule, cushion and fiber vibrating at such a speed that the whole backbone together with my rudimentary tail is thrown into incandescent relief. My spine becomes a barometer of light registering the pressure and deflection of all the waves which escape the heavy, fluid substance of matter. I feel the feathery, jubilant weight of his eye rising from its matrix to brush the prisms of light. Not the eye of a shark, nor a horse, nor a fly, not any known flexible eye, but the eye of a coccus newborn, a coccus traveling on the wave of an epidemic, always a millimeter in advance of the crest. The eye that gloats and ravages. The eye that precedes doom. The waiting, lurking eye of the ghoul, the torpid, monstrously indifferent eye of the leper, the still, all-inclusive eye of the Buddha which never closes. *The insatiable eye.*

It is with this eye that I see him walking through the wings of the Folies-Bergère, walking across the ceiling with sticky, clinging feet, crawling on all fours over candelabras, warm breasts, crinolines, training that huge, cold searchlight on the inner organs of a Venus, on the foam of a wave of lace, on the cicatrices that are dyed with ink in the satin throat of a puppet, on the pulleys that will hoist a Babylon in paint and papier-mâché, on the empty seats which rise tier upon tier like layers of sharks' teeth. I see him walking across the proscenium with his beautiful suede gloves, see him peeling them off and tossing them to the inky squib which has swallowed the seats and the glass chandeliers, the fake marble, the brass posts, the thick velvet cords and the chipped plaster. I see the world of behind the scenes upside down, each fragment a new universe, each human body or puppet or pulley framed in its own inconceivable niche. I see the lovely Venus prone and full athwart her strange axis, her hair dipped in laudanum, her mouth bright with asphodels; she lies in the neap of the tide, taut with starry sap, her toes tinctured with light, her eyes transfixed. He does not wait for the curtain to rise; he waits for it to fall. He waits for that moment when all the conglomerations artificially produced resolve back into their natural component entities, when the nymphs and the dryads strewing themselves like flowers over the floor of the stage gaze vacantly into the mirror of the tank where a moment ago, tesselated with spotlights, they swam like goldfish.

Deprived of the miracle of color, registering everything in degrees of black and white, Brassai nevertheless seems to convey by the purity and quality of his tones all the effects of sunlight,

175

and even more impressively the effects of night light. A man of the city, he limits himself to that spectacular feast which only such a city as Paris can offer. No phase of cosmopolitan life has escaped his eye. His albums of black and white comprise a vast encyclopaedia of the city's architecture, its growth, its history, its origins. Whatever aspect of the city his eye seizes upon the result is a vast metaphor whose brilliant arc, studded with incalculable vistas backward and forward, glistens now like a drop of dew suspended in the morning light. The Cemetery Montmartre, for example, shot from the bridge at night is a phantasmagoric creation of death flowering in electricity; the intense patches of night lie upon the tombs and crosses in a crazy patchwork of steel girders which fade with the sunlight into bright green lawns and flower beds and graveled walks.

Brassai strikes at the accidental modulations, the illogical syntax, the mythical juxtaposition of things, at that anomalous, sporadic form of growth which a walk through the streets or a glance at a map or a scene in a film conveys to the sleeping portion of the brain. What is most familiar to the eye, what has become stale and commonplace, acquires through the flick of his magic lens the properties of the unique. Just as a thousand diverse types may write automatically and yet only one of them will bear the signature of André Breton, so a thousand men may photograph the Cemetery Montmartre but one of them will stand out triumphantly as Brassai's. No matter how perfect the machine, no matter how little of human guidance is involved, the mark of personality is always there. The photograph seems to carry with it the same degree of personality as any other form or expression of art. Brassai is Brassai and Man Ray is Man Ray. One man may try to interfere as little as possible with the apparatus, or the results obtained from the apparatus; the other may endeavor to subjugate it to his will, to dominate it, control it, use it like an artist. But no matter what the approach or the technique involved the thing that registers is the stamp of individuality.

Perhaps the difference which I observe between the work of Brassai and that of other photographers lies in this—that Brassai seems overwhelmed by the fullness of life. How else are we to explain that a chicken bone, under the optical alchemy of Brassai, acquires the attributes of the marvelous, whereas the most fantastic inventions of other men often leave us with a sense of unfulfillment? The man who looked at the chicken bone transferred his whole personality to it in looking at it; he transmitted to an insignificant phenomenon the fullness of his knowledge of life, the experience acquired from looking at millions of other objects and participating in the wisdom which their relationships one to another inspired. The desire which Brassai so strongly evinces, a desire not to tamper with the object but regard it as it is, was this not provoked by a profound humility, a respect and reverence for the object itself? The more the man detached from his view of life, from the objects and identities that make life, all intrusion of individual will and ego, the more readily and easily he entered into the multitudinous identities which ordinarily remain alien and closed to us. By depersonalizing himself, as it were, he was enabled to discover his personality everywhere in everything.

Perhaps this is not the method of art. Perhaps art demands the wholly personal, the catalytic power of will. *Perhaps.* All I know is that when I look at these photographs which seem to have been taken at random by a man loath to assert any values except what were inherent in the phenomena, I am impressed by their authority. I realize in looking at his photos that by looking at things aesthetically, just as much as by looking at things moralistically

177

or pragmatically, we are destroying their value, their significance. Objects do not fade away with time: *they are destroyed!* From the moment that we cease to regard them awesomely they die. They may carry on an existence for thousands of years, but as dead matter, as fossil, as archaeologic data. What once inspired an artist or a people can, after a certain moment, fail to elicit even the interest of a scientist. Objects die in proportion as the vision of things dies. The object and the vision are one. Nothing flourishes after the vital flow is broken, neither the thing seen, nor the one who sees.

It happens that the man who introduced me to Brassaï is a man who has no understanding of him at all, a sort of human cockroach living out his dream of the 18th century. He knows all the Metro stations by heart, can recite them backwards for you, line by line; he can give you the history of each *arrondissement*, can tell you precisely where and how one street intersects another, can give you the genesis of every statue and monument in Paris. But he has absolutely no feeling for the streets, no wanderlust, no curiosity, no reverence. He secretes himself in his room and lives out in imagination the hermeneutic life of the 18th century.

I mention this only as an example of the strange fatality by which two men of kindred spirit are sometimes brought together. I mention it by way of showing that even the despised cockroach serves a purpose in life. I see that the cockroach living out its dream of the 18th century can serve as a link to bind the living. It was this same cockroach, I must also confess, who revealed to me the glamor of the 13th *arrondissement*. In the very heart of it, like a spider luring me to its lair, there lived all the while this man Brassaï whom I was destined to meet. I remember vividly how, when I first came to Paris, I wandered one day to his hotel looking for a painter. The man who received me was not the man

I had expected to see. He was a petty, niggardly, querulous soul who had once painted a knife and fork and rested there. I had to return to America, come back to France once again, starve, roam the streets, listen to silly, idiotic theories of life and art, take up with this failure and that, and finally surrender to the cockroach before it was possible tௐ know the man who like myself had taken in Paris without effort of will, the man who, without my knowing it, was silently slaving away at the illustrations for my books. And when one day the door was finally thrust open I beheld to my astonishment a thousand replicas of all the scenes, all the streets, all the walls, all the fragments of that Paris wherein I died and was born again. There on his bed, in myriad pieces and arrangements, lay the cross to which I had been nailed and crucified, the cross on which I was resurrected to live again and forever in the spirit.

How then am I to describe these morsels of black and white, how refer to them as photographs or specimens of art? Here on this man's bed, drained of all blood and suffering, radiant now with only the life of the sun, I saw my own sacred body exposed, the body that I have written into every stone, every tree, every monument, park, fountain, statue, bridge, and dwelling of Paris. I see now that I am leaving behind me a record of Paris which I have written in blood—but also in peace and good will. The whole city—every arrondissement, every carrefour, every impasse, every enchanted street. Through me Paris will live again, a little more, a little brighter.

Tenderly, reverently, as if I were gathering to my breast the most sentient morsels of myself, I pick up these fragments which lie on the bed. Once again I traverse the road that led me to the present, to this high, cool plateau whence I can look about me in serenity. What a procession passes before my eyes! What a throng of men and women! What strange cities—and situations stranger still! The mendicant sitting on the public bench, thirsting for a glimmer of sun, the butcher standing in a pool of blood with knife upraised, the scows and barges dreaming in the shadows of the bridges, the pimp standing against a wall with cigarette in hand, the street cleaner with her broom of reddish twigs, her thick, gnarled fingers, her high stomach draped in black, a shroud over her womb, rinsing away the vomit of the night before so that when I pass over the cobblestones my feet will gleam with the light of morning stars. I see the old hats, the sombreros and fedoras, the velours and Panamas that I painted with a clutching fury; I see the corners of walls eroded by time and weather which I passed in the night and in passing felt the erosion going on in myself, corners of my own walls crumbling away, blown down, dispersed, reintegrated elsewhere in mysterious shape and essence. I see the old tin urinals where, standing in the dead silence of the night, I dreamed so violently that the past sprang up like a white horse and carried me out of the body.

Looking for an instant into the eyes of this man I see therein the image of myself. Two enormous eyes I see, two glowing discs which look up at the sun from the bottom of a pool; two round, wondrous orbs that have pushed back the heavy, opaque lids in order to swim up to the surface of the light and drink with unslakeable thirst. Heavy tortoise eyes that have drunk from every stratum; soft, viscous eyes that have burrowed into the mud sinks, tracked the worm and shell; hard, sclerotic gems, bead and nugget, over which the heel of man has passed and left no imprint. Eye that lurks in the primal ooze, lord and master of all it surveys; not waiting on history, not waiting on time. The cosmologic eye, persisting through wrack and doom, impervious, inchoate, seeing only what is.

Now and then, in wandering through the streets, suddenly one comes awake, perceives with a strange exultation that he is moving through an absolutely fresh slice of reality. Everything has the quality of the marvelous—the murky windows, the rain-sodden vegetables, the contours of the houses, the bill-posters, the slumping figures of men and women, the tin soldiers in the stationery shops, the colors of the walls—everything written down in an unfamiliar script. After the moment of ecstasy has passed what is one's amazement but to discover that the street through which he is walking with eyes popping is the street on which he lives. He has simply come upon it unaware, from the wrong end perhaps. Or, moving out of the confines of an unknown region, the sense of wonder and mystery prolonged itself in defiance of reality. It is as if the eye itself had been freshened, as if it had forgotten all that it had been taught. In this condition it happens that one really does see things he had never seen before—not the fantastic, harrowing, hallucinating objects of dream or drug, but the most banal, the most commonplace things, seen as it were for the first time.

Walking one night along a dark, abandoned street of Levallois-Perret suddenly across the way I notice a window lit up. As I approach the reddish glow of the room awakens something in me, some obscure memory which stirs sleepily, only to be drowned again in deeper memories. The hideous pattern of the wallpaper, which I can only vaguely decipher, seems as familiar to me as if I had lived with it all my life. The weird, infernal glow of the room throws the pattern of the wallpaper into violent relief; it leaps out from the wall like the frantic gesture of a madman. My heart is in my throat. My step quickens. I have the sensation of being about to look into the privacy of a room such as no man has seen before.

As I come abreast of the window I notice the glass bells suspended from the chandelier—three glass bells such as are manufactured by the million and which are the pride of every poverty-stricken home wherever there are progress and invention. Under this modern, universal whatnot are gathered three of the most ordinary people that could possibly be grouped together—a tintype of honest toil snapped on the threshold of Utopia. Everything in the room is familiar to me, nauseatingly familiar: the cupboard, the chairs, the table, the tablecloth, the rubber plant, the bird cage, the alarm clock, the calendar on the wall, the Sunday it registers and the saint who rules it. And yet never have I seen such a tintype as this. This is so ordinary, so familiar, so stale, so commonplace, that I have never really noticed it before.

The group is composed of two men and a woman. They are standing around the cheap, polished walnut table—the table that is not yet paid for. One man is in his shirt sleeves and wears a cap; the other man is wearing a pair of striped flannel pajamas and has a black derby tilted on the back of his head. The woman is in a dressing sack and one of her titties is falling out. A large juicy teat with a dark, mulberry nipple swimming in a deep coffee stain full of fine wrinkles. On the table is a large dishpan filled with boiling water. The man with cap and shirt sleeves has just doused something in the pan; the other man stands with his hands in his pockets and quietly puffs a cigarette, allowing the ash to fall on his pajama coat and from there to the table.

Suddenly the woman grabs the queer-looking object from the man with the cap and, holding it somewhat above her head, she commences plucking at it with lean, tenacious fingers. It is a dead chicken with black and red feathers and a bright red-toothed comb. While she holds the legs of the chicken with one hand the man with the cap holds the neck; at intervals they lower the dead chicken into the pan of boiling water. The feathers come out easily, leaving the slightly yellowish skin full of black splinters. They stand there facing each other without uttering a word. The woman's fingers move nimbly from one area of the chicken to another—until she comes to the little triangular flap over the vent when with one gleeful clutch she rips out all the tail feathers at once and flinging them on the floor drops the chicken on the table.

Strike me pink if I have ever seen anything more grotesque! Taken in combination, under that light, at that hour of the night, the three tintypes, the peculiar deadness of the chicken, the scene remains unique in my memory. Every other chicken, dressed or undressed, is scalded from my memory. Henceforth whenever I say chicken there will always come to mind two kinds—*this* chicken, whose name I do not know, and all other chickens. Chicken *prime*, let us say, so as to distinguish it from all other chicken integers that were and will be tomorrow, henceforth and forevermore.

And so it is, when I look at the photographs of Brassai, that I say to myself—chicken *prime*, table *prime*, chair *prime*, Venus *prime*, etc. That which constitutes the uniqueness of an object, the first, the original, the imperishable vision of things. When Shakespeare painted a horse, said a friend of mine once, it was a horse for all time. I must confess that I am largely unfamiliar with the horses of Shakespeare, but knowing as I do certain of his human characters, and knowing also that they have endured throughout several centuries, I am quite willing to concede that his horses too, whoever and wherever they are, will have a long and abiding life. I know that there are men and women who belong just as distinctly and inexpugnably to Rembrandt's world, or Giotto's, or Renoir's. I know that there are sleeping giants who belong to the Grimm family or to Michelangelo, and dwarfs who belong to Velasquez or Hieronymus Bosch, or to Toulouse-Lautrec. I know that there are physiognomic maps and relics of the human body which is all that we possess of buried epochs, all that is personal and understandable to us, and that these maps and relics bear the distinguished imprimatur of Dante, da Vinci, Petronius and such like. I know too that even when the human body has been disintegrated and made an inhuman part of a fragmented world—such as the one we now inhabit—I mean that when the human body, having lost its distinction and kingship, serves the painter with no more inspiration, no more reverence than a table or chair or discarded newspaper, still it is possible to recognize one sort of hocus-pocus from another, to say this is Braque, that is Picasso, the other Chirico.

We have reached the point where we do not want to know any longer whose work it is, whose seal is affixed, whose stamp is upon it; what we want, and what at last we are about to get, are individual masterpieces which triumph in such a way as to completely subordinate the accidental artists who are responsible for them. Every man today who is really an artist is trying to kill the artist in himself—and he must, if there is to be any art in the future. We are suffering from a plethora of art. We are art-ridden. Which is to say that instead of a truly personal, truly creative vision of things, we have merely an *aesthetic* view. Empty as we are, it is impossible for us to look at an object without annexing it to our collection. We have not a single chair, for example, in the sweep and memory of our retina, that does not bear a label; if, for the space of a week, a man working in absolute secrecy were to turn out chairs unique and unrecognizable, the world would go mad. And yet every chair that is brought into existence is howling for recognition as chair, as chair in its own right, unique and perdurable.

I think of chair because among all the objects which Brassaï has photographed his chair with the wire legs stands out with a majesty that is singular and disquieting. It is a chair of the lowest denomination, a chair which has been sat on by beggars and by royalty, by little trot-about whores and by queenly opera divas. It is a chair which the municipality rents daily to any and every one who wishes to pay fifty centimes for sitting down in the open air. A chair with little holes in the seat and wire legs which come to a loop at the bottom. The most unostentatious, the most inexpensive, the most ridiculous chair, if a chair can be ridiculous, which could be devised. Brassaï chose precisely this insignificant chair and, snapping it where he found it, unearthed what there was in it of dignity and veracity. THIS IS A CHAIR. Nothing more. No sentimentalism about the lovely backsides which once graced it, no romanticism about the lunatics who fabricated it, no statistics about the hours of sweat and anguish that went into the creation of it, no sarcasm about the era which produced it, no odious comparisons with chairs of other days, no humbug about the dreams of the idlers who monopolize it, no scorn for the nakedness of it, no gratitude either. Walking along a path of the Jardin des Tuileries one day he saw this chair standing on the edge of a grating. He saw at once chair, grating, tree, clouds, sun, people. He saw that the chair was as much a part of that fine spring day as the tree, the clouds, the sun, the people. He took it as it was, with its honest little holes, its slender wire legs. Perhaps the Prince of Wales once sat on it, perhaps a holy man, perhaps a leper, perhaps a murderer or an idiot. Who sat on it did not interest Brassaï in the least. It was a spring day and the foliage was greening; the earth was in a ferment, the roots convulsed with sap. On such a day, if one is alive, one can well believe that out of the dead body of the earth there will spring forth a race of men

185

immortal in their splendor. On such a day there is visible in the stalest object a promise, a hope, a possibility. Nothing is dead, except in the imagination. Animate or inanimate, all bodies under the sun give expression to their vitality. Especially on a fine day in spring!

And so on that day, in that glorious hour, the homely, inexpensive chair belonging to the municipality of Paris became the empty throne which is always beseeching the restless spirit of man to end his fear and longing and proclaim the kingdom of man.

# UTERINE HUNGER

I WAS BORN too soon. In the seventh month I ripped and clawed my way out of the womb. I fell out on the street head first, with full grown nails, cloven hoofs and a double set of teeth. They swaddled me in cotton wool and shoved me back in an incubator where under glass I enjoyed an artificial birth. It cost a dime to have a look at me, and for the same dime one could also examine the three-legged cow, the embryo with two heads and other interesting monsters. Near by was a shooting gallery. It was in Dreamland, Coney Island.

Exposed to the light too soon I developed hypertrophy of the end organs. I react to color violently. My two months in the incubator were like a prison term. By the time I was handed my birth certificate my criminal instincts were already fully developed. It was only natural that I should become a rebel, an outlaw, a desperado. I blame my parents, I blame society, I blame God. I accuse. I go through life with finger lifted accusingly. I have the prophetic itch. I curse and blaspheme. I tell the bitter truth.

From the very beginning it seems as if the world were an artificial womb, a prison, seems as though everybody and everything were conspiring to pull me back to the womb from which I broke loose too soon. I go through life raw, exposed, twisting, writhing, squirming. The light stabs me like a million needles. I dance such a violent jig inside that my articulation is thrown completely out of gear. I am always turning inside out, to protect myself with my bones. The light whistles through my bones; I glow like a skeleton under the X-ray.

And always I am hungry, voraciously hungry. I am insatiable. It is a hunger on all fronts: alimentary, sexual, spiritual. I don't eat—I attach myself, like the amoeba, to whatever morsel of food presents itself. Once I have ingested it I split—double, triple, multiple selves floating off in search of fresh morsels of food. It goes on like that ad nauseam. Women—they too seem like morsels of food. After I attach myself to them I devour them. I fuck my way through body, brain and soul, and then I split again. Parthogenic marriage. The women I have loved are only bare bones now—the armature which refused to be masticated, even though I was equipped with a double set of teeth. With ideas the same: I swallowed them boiling hot and scorched my gizzards. What remains is the pure crystalline essence, the atomic structure which refused to pass through the intestines of the brain. It's like continual fireworks going on in the upper story—an explosion that never comes off.

I suppose I am a reflection of the times, of this feverish agitation, this mad tempo, this inability to hold it in until the germ is ready to blossom. Nothing but short waves, nothing but clash, stridency, a brief meteoric flash and then extinction. Something is struggling to be born, that's evident. But the toll is frightful—the toll of stillbirths. The walls of the womb are weak, and the weak womb has a tenacious clutch. The clamor inside has the same hysterical pitch as that outside: the born and the unborn are doing the St. Vitus dance. The modern womb is like a rectum full of haemorrhoids; the child has either to be yanked out by the forceps or cut away like an ulcer. Usually the womb is turned inside out, and after that it has to be scraped and cauterized. Then a dose of alum—so that it will shrink back to normalcy. The worst is that this spawn which comes out of the womb stinks of the womb for the rest of its life. And not only that, but a continual turning and twisting, as if they were trying to turn themselves inside out.

As a matter of fact, the world is turning itself inside out. One can see the skeletal bones everywhere, like umbrella ribs lying in the gutter after a violent storm. Everything stands out nakedly—the grinning skeleton for any one who has an eye. The artist who is born of these times is the living symbol of this squirming nakedness. He is looking for meat to cover his bare bones, for a little flesh to hide the blood which was spilled at his birth. He wants to get out of the strait jacket which was slipped over him before he had the strength to raise his arms. He wants to get rid of the blinders which were put over his eyes before he had even a chance to look at the world.

Whatever the artist does now is in short wave lengths—uterine vibrations which are scarcely perceptible. He works in nascent

189

images, struggling to reveal through his colors the hidden form of things. He sees everything in terms of phylogeny and ontogeny. He is incestuous, perverted at the roots. The father is displaced, murdered by the son, because he has not asserted his power over life and death. The mother, like Osiris, searches frantically for the missing genitals.

When the body of life is wasted away there is nothing for it but to take the bare bones to our bosom and hug them and warm them. Life beats through the skeleton in some miraculous way. At the last ditch this which we imagine to be useless and an abomination gets up and walks, gets up and takes on flesh, gets up and sings. This which we carry around inside us, which took form and substance out of the irreducible elements, is the final inspiration. When we wear away to this we touch the node, the ultimate link between life and death. At that farthest extreme of life which is called death we recover the simplicity of the organic unities.

With the ebb-tide there is no consciousness of anything save atomic structure. At the last point of livingness thought spreads itself so thin that the structural element expresses itself finitely. The chemistry of the mind becomes the alchemy of the spirit. The multiverse is made a universe. Through form significance is restored.

The world is always dying and always coming back to life. Tide and pulse, and with the turn of the tide a touch of mystery. At thought's deadmost reach the miraculous seeps back and throws a glow over the wan cadaver of despair. The taut, stretched world which the mind inhabited grows smaller and smaller and more and more awe-inspiring. The feeling for life rises as the forms and symbols become illuminated. The stars gather direction in the same way that the foetus moves towards birth. The mystery is never revealed, but with birth attention is focused on creation.

Once the sacred character of the body is recognized the cosmos wheels into line. Once the cosmic accent is identified the whole edifice of life bursts into melody.

When the individual is wholly creative, one with destiny, there is neither time nor space, nor birth and death. The god-feeling becomes so intense that everything, organic and inorganic, beats with a divine rhythm. At the moment of supreme individuation, when the identity of all things is sensed and one is at the same time utterly and blissfully alone, the umbilical cord is at last cut. There is neither a longing for the womb nor a longing for the beyond. The sure feeling of eternality. Beyond this there is no evolution, only a perpetual movement from creation to creation. The personality itself becomes a creation. From symbolizing himself in his works man symbolizes himself in his being. At this stage he utters miracles and produces miracles. He speaks in a language so clear that it penetrates the densest matter. The word becomes magic, it produces a contagion. And it is through this miraculous virus that the world is poisoned and dies. It is the miracle of miracles. The world dies over and over again, but the skeleton always gets up and walks.

# SERAPHITA

It has been said that February 28, 1832, was probably the most important date in Balzac's life. It was the day that he received his first letter from Madame Hanska, the woman whom after seventeen years of courtship he was to marry, just four months before his death.

From his twenty-first to his twenty-ninth year Balzac wrote forty volumes under various pseudonyms. After the colossal failure of his publishing venture he suddenly came to himself and, resuming the role of writer, which he had thought to drop in order to gain more experience of life, he began to sign his own name to his work. Having tapped the true source of inspiration, he was so over-whelmed with ideas and literary projects that for a couple of years he was scarcely able to cope with his energies. It was a repetition of that singular state—"*congestion de lumière*," to use his own expression—which he had experienced when he was returned to his parents by the masters of the College of Vendôme in his fif-teenth year; only this time he was paralyzed by the multiplicity of outlets open to him, and not by the struggle to assimilate what he had imbibed. His whole career as a writer, indeed, was a Pro-methean drama of restitution. Balzac was not only tremendously receptive, as highly sensitized as a photographic plate, but he was also gifted with an extraordinary intuition. He read faces as easily as he read books, and in addition he possessed, as it is said, "every memory." His was a protean nature, opulent, jovial, expansive, yet also chaste, reserved and secretive. For the extraordinary endow-ments with which Nature had blessed him he was obliged to pay the penalty of submission. He looked upon himself as a spiritual "exile." It was a supreme task for him to coordinate his faculties, to establish order out of the chaos which his superabundant na-ture was constantly creating. His *physiological* flair was an expres-sion of this obsessive passion "to establish order," for then as now Europe was in the throes of dissolution. His boast to finish with the pen what Napoleon had begun with the sword signified a deep desire to reveal the significance of the true relationships existing in the world of human society. It was Cuvier rather than Napoleon whom he took as a model.

From the time of his financial set-back, from 1827 to 1836, in short, Balzac lived a life which was in many ways reminiscent of Dostoievski's lifelong bondage. Indeed, it is during this very period that, in order to stave off his creditors, Dostoievski undertook the translation of *Eugenie Grandet*. Through excessive suffering and

193

deprivation both Dostoievski and Balzac, destined to become the foremost novelists of the nineteenth century, were permitted to give us glimpses of worlds which no other novelists have yet touched upon, or even imagined. Enslaved by their own passions, chained to the earth by the strongest desires, they nevertheless revealed through their tortured creations the evidences of worlds unseen, unknown, except, as Balzac says, "to those loftier spirits open to faith who can discern Jacob's mystical stair." Both of them believed in the dawn of a new world, though frequently accused, by their contemporaries, of being morbid, cynical, pessimistic and immoral.

I am not a devotee of Balzac. For me the *Human Comedy* is of minor importance. I prefer that other comedy which has been labeled "divine," in testimony doubtless of our sublime incorrigibility. But without a knowledge of *Seraphita*, the subject of this essay—possibly also *Louis Lambert*—there can be no real understanding of Balzac's life and work. It is the cornerstone of the grand edifice. *Seraphita* is situated symbolically at the dawn of a new century. "Outside," says Balzac at the end, "the first summer of the nineteenth century was in all its glory." *Outside*, please notice. For *Seraphita* was conceived in the womb of a new day which only now, a hundred years later, is beginning to make itself clear.

It was in the midst of the most harassed period of his life, in the year 1830, that Balzac took up quarters in the Rue Cassini, "midway," as he says, "between the Carmelites and the place where they guillotine." Here were begun the truly herculean labors for which he is celebrated and which undoubtedly cut his life in half, for with anything like a normal rhythm he would have lived a hundred or more. To give some idea of his activities at this period let me state briefly that in 1830 he is credited with seventy publications, in 1831 with seventy-five. Writing to his

194

publisher, Werdet, in 1835, he says: "There is not a single other writer who has done this year what I have done . . . anyone else would have died." He cites the seven books he has just finished, as well as the political articles he wrote for the *Chronique de Paris.* The important thing to note, however, is that one of the seven books he refers to was the most unusual book of his whole career, probably one of the most unique books in all literature: *Seraphita.* How long the actual writing of it took is not known; the first installment of it appeared June 1, 1834, in the *Revue de Paris.* It appeared, together with *Louis Lambert* and *The Exiles,* in book form in December, 1835, the volume itself entitled *Le Livre Mystique.* The critics, judging it from the three installments of *Seraphita* which had appeared in the review, condemned it as "an unintelligible work." However, the first edition of the book was exhausted in ten days, and the second a month later. "Not such bad fortune for an unintelligible work," Balzac remarked.

*Seraphita* was written expressly for Madame Hanska with whom, after the receipt of her first letter, he maintained a lifelong correspondence. It was during a trip to Geneva that the book was conceived, and in December of 1833, just three months after his meeting with Madame Hanska, it was begun. It was intended, in Balzac's own words, "to be a masterpiece such as the world has never seen." And this it is, despite all its faults, despite the prophecies of the critics, despite the apparent neglect and obloquy into which it has fallen. Balzac himself never doubted its value or uniqueness, as he sometimes did in the case of his other works. Though subsequently included in *La Comédie Humaine,* it really forms part of the *Études Philosophiques.* In the dedication to Madame Hanska he speaks of it "as one of those balustrades, carved by some artist full of faith, on which the pilgrim leans to meditate on the end of man. . . ." The seven divisions of the book undoubtedly have an occult structure and significance. As narrative it is broken by disquisitions and expositions which, in a lesser work, would be fatal. Inwardly regarded, which is the only way it can be looked at, it is a model of perfection. Balzac said everything he had to say, with swiftness, precision and eloquence. To me it is the style of the last quartets of Beethoven, the will triumphant in its submission.

I accept the book implicitly as a mystical work of the highest order. I know that, if obviously it seems to have been inspired by Swedenborg's work, it was also enriched by other influences, among them Jacob Boehme, Paracelsus, Ste. Therèse, Claude Saint-Martin, and so on. As a writer, I know that a book such as this could not have been written without the aid of a higher being: the reach of it, the blinding lucidity, the wisdom, not man's certainly, the force and the eloquence of it, betray all the qualities of a work dictated if not by God then by the angels. The book is, in fact, about an angel in human guise, a being neither male nor female, or rather now one now the other, and yet always more, "not a being," as one of the characters remarks, "but a whole creation." In any case, whether Seraphita or Seraphitus, whether, as the author states, "her sex would have puzzled the most learned man to pronounce on," the subject of this book is a *being*, a being filled with light, whose behavior may baffle the blundering minds of the critics but never the earnest reader. Those who know what the book is about will share the sentiment of that young student in Vienna who is reported to have accosted Balzac in the street and begged permission to kiss the hand that wrote *Seraphita*.

The events related are almost as simple and brief as those of Christ's own life. As with that other drama, the hierarchical order of events works contrariwise to the historical, clock-time movement. The adumbration is tremendous; time is stopped, and in the awesome, all-enveloping silence which shrouds the mysterious being called Seraphita, one can actually hear the growth of those wings which will carry her aloft to that world of which Balzac was aware ever since the Angel visited him as a boy at the College of Vendôme. The story is symbolic and revelatory from beginning to end. It is not limited, as is *Louis Lambert*, to what I might call the *intellectual* aspect of occultism, but proceeds straight from the heart which Balzac knew to be the true, vital center of man's being. It is a Rosicrucian drama pure and simple. It is about Love, the triumph of Love over Desire. And who better qualified than Balzac to give us the dramatic recital of this conflict? Had he not himself confessed somewhere that if ever he should conquer over desire he would die of grief? On the highest level of creative imagination, spiritually leagues beyond *Faust*, it forms a bridge between the creative instinct, as expressed through art, and the creative intuition which will eventually liberate man from the throes of art and permit him to make of his *life* a creation. As the man of Desire incarnate, Balzac seems to have divined, in this supreme effort, that even the passion of creation must be transmuted. He recognized unerringly that the man of genius is only at the first stage of the great trine of Love, that his very desire for immortality, through immolation in the art form, is the expression of a selfish love, or love of self. It was through the world of desire, however, that Balzac, perfectly aware of his limitations as a man and reconciled to the role of artist, succeeded in giving us a vehicle which would lead us to the mysteries. Other more perfectly developed beings speak a language requiring an initiation which the great world of men and women will never experience. As the universal artist, Balzac makes clear even to the dullest mind the unlimited possibilities which are open to everyone. "The Brazen Rod belongs to all," says Seraphita. . . . "Neither the most obscure evangelists, nor the most amazing of God's prophets, have been superior to what you might become." That he himself did not pursue the high course which he realized we must all eventually take, is not a condemnation of his wisdom or sincerity: the mystery that envelops man's behavior is hidden in the laws of karma and dharma. "The supreme virtue," he says towards the close of the book, "is resignation."

In addition to Seraphita there are four other characters portrayed: David, her aged servitor, a sort of Biblical figure, a rock of faith, who seems to obey the law of inertia; Pastor Becker, an elderly man, who is the symbol of futile learning and against whom are directed the bitterest shafts; Minna, his daughter, a young girl whose love for Seraphita is really worship; and Wilfrid, a man in the prime of life, betrothed to Minna, but also devotedly in love with Seraphita. The seven divisions of the book might be dramatically summed up as follows: The High Place, or the Annunciation, the Mystic Union of Two in One as revealed through Love, the Temptation and Triumph over Desire, the Ordeal of Doubt, Renunciation, the Path of Light, the Assumption.

The scene is laid in Norway, in a village called Jarvis. The story opens with the ascent by Minna and Seraphitus of the inaccessible peaks of the Falberg. The atmosphere is magical: "they could see the stars, though it was daytime." Minna, aware of the supernatural quality of the adventure, exclaims: "We have not come here by unaided human strength." At the summit, whence they command an awesome view of the two worlds, Seraphitus plucks a saxifrage (whose etymological meaning is "stone-breaking flower") on which no human eye has yet rested and offers this unique blossom to her companion in memory of a day unique in her life, saying: "you will never again find a guide to lead you to this soeter." Seraphitus speaks as only one can speak "who has attained to the highest places on the mountains of the earth." She recounts to Minna how our knowledge of the laws of the visible world are merely a means of enabling us to conceive of the immensity of higher spheres, declaring that Man is not the final creation. . . . "Below," she says, "you have hope, the beautiful rudiment of faith; but here faith reigns, the realization of hope." And then, almost as if in Balzac's own voice, she continues: "I have no taste for the fruits of the earth. . . . I am disgusted with all things, for I have the gift of vision." By way of answering Minna's declarations of love, she exclaims, with a cry of despair: "I wanted a companion to go with me to the realm of light. . . . I am an exile far from heaven; like a monster, far from earth. . . . I am alone. I am resigned, I can wait."

Later, with Wilfrid, who sees her as a woman, Seraphita discourses on the true nature of love. "You desire me, but you do not love me," she explains. Her own love, she points out, is devoid of self-interest. "Rise to the heights," she entreats, "where men see each other truly, though tiny and crowded as the sands of the seashore." Wilfrid is baffled; he feels that whoever approaches her is engulfed in a vortex of light. He leaves her to consult Minna's father. He finds Pastor Becker in the midst of a book called *Incantations*, by Jean Weir. Throughout the narrative Pastor Becker is constantly returning to this book, as if in the hope of finding there an explanation of the mysteries which envelop him. Balzac describes him as having "the solid tenacity of happy ignorance." He is always enveloped in clouds of tobacco smoke—the fumes of learning, doubtless. In attempting to unravel the mysterious nature of Seraphita Wilfrid tells the Pastor that she is "one of those awe-inspiring spirits to whom it is given to constrain men, to coerce nature, and share the occult powers of God. She alternately kills and vivifies me!" he exclaims. In the thick clouds of smoke which enshroud the trio the saxifrage, still fresh, "gleams like another light."

In answer to Wilfrid's demand to know more about the birth and circumstances of Seraphita's life, Pastor Becker announces that it will first be necessary "to disentangle the obscurest of all Christian creeds," whereupon he proceeds to launch into a sustained and eloquent account of Swedenborg's doctrine. It appears that he has read from beginning to end the seventeen volumes of Swedenborg's work bequeathed to him by the Baron Seraphitus, deceased father of Seraphita. The subject of angels, an obsession with the author, affords Balzac the opportunity to reveal his own true religion. He describes the three stages of love—love of self, as exemplified by the human genius; love of the world at large, as exemplified by the prophets and those great men "whom the earth accepts as guides and hails as divine"; and love of heaven, which forms angelic spirits—such as Seraphita. The angelic spirits he characterizes as "the flowers of humanity." They must have either the love or the wisdom of heaven; but, he emphasizes, "they must dwell in that love before they dwell in wisdom." Thus, he concludes, "*the first transformation of man is to love*" (italics mine throughout). He then compares the superficial knowledge of the scientific man with that other wisdom which comes from the knowledge of the "correspondences," adding that science saddens man, whereas love enraptures the angel. "Science is still seeking; love has found." As if to give the clue to his own secret experience, he thereupon puts in Pastor Becker's mouth these words: "It is enough to have the smallest inkling of it to transform one forever." Here, it seems to me, lies the true secret of Balzac's greatness, for not to recognize the significance of this utterance in relation to his work is to misinterpret the man's whole life. In the next instant, almost as if to corroborate the fact, he adds, again through Pastor Becker: "The perpetual ecstasy of the angels is produced by the faculty, bestowed on them by God, of giving back to Him the joy they have in Him." Does this not explain, in the deepest sense, the record of his almost superhuman efforts? Were not his Titanic struggles to create another universe a joyous restitution for the precious moments of illumination which had been vouchsafed him as a boy? In *Louis Lambert*, which precedes *Seraphita* by two years, we have the record of his parting with his real self, the double whom he calls Louis Lambert. The description of the latter's life after leaving the College, his life with the angels, is it not a projection of Balzac's own aborted desire? And the punishment which he metes out to his double at the end, was it also not an expression of his secret fears—*the* fear, I should say, of taking the straight and narrow path? Perhaps in refusing to follow the angel in himself he displayed a discretion which was another kind of wisdom, but we know that as a result of his choice he was burdened with a guilt which assumed gigantic form in the demon of Work which drove him to a premature death. It is often said that he possessed extraordinary powers of illusion, so much so that he was able not only to create his own world, but *to live in it*. But are we to regard this ability simply as another evidence of the artist's desire to escape reality, as is said? If by reality we mean the everyday world, yes, but if we refer to that other, greater reality, then surely it was not "escape," but a desire for union. In dedicating himself to art, Balzac, who had the potentiality and equipment for leading a hundred different lives, signified his willingness to accept the cross of suffering, to acknowledge his fate and to work it out heroically, confident that in doing so he was contributing to the welfare of humanity in his own unique way; confident, too, that if not in this life, then in the next, or the next, he would free himself of his shackles. In

*Seraphita* we have a sublime expression of his desire to live in and by the Light. But it was a light, as he remarks, *"that kills the man who is not prepared to receive it."*

To resume. . . . After this eloquent disquisition on Swedenborg, Pastor Becker proceeds to inform his listeners of Seraphita's origins. The Baron Seraphitus, who was "Swedenborg's most zealous disciple," had decreed at her birth that she was not to be baptized with earthly waters since she had already been bathed in the fires of heaven. "She will always be a flower," were his words. We might add—a unique flower which does not reproduce its kind, a flower such as Seraphita herself had plucked for Minna on the mountain top, "a real miracle developed under the breath of the angels." In the midst of the discussion which ensues, David, the aged servitor, rushes in to announce that Seraphita is wrestling with the demons. The four of them set out for the Swedish castle wherein Seraphita dwells. Through the window they see her standing in prayer. Suddenly she vanishes before their eyes, to the accompaniment of celestial strains. This astonishing vision each one interprets differently: Pastor Becker felt doubt, Minna adoration, Wilfrid desire.

At this point the narrative is interrupted, seemingly to give a more detailed description of Wilfrid's character and of the genesis of his love for Seraphita. Actually, the description is a device by which Balzac permits himself to reveal the nature of his own secret struggles. After remarking that Wilfrid was in the prime of life (practically Balzac's own age at the time), that he had studied the laws of humanity, had grown pale over books ("which are human actions in death"), he describes him as a *Cain to whom hope yet remained* and who seemed to be *seeking absolution at the ends of the earth.* ("Minna suspected the slave of glory in this man.") Is this an elliptic allusion to the murder of his real self, which he describes in *Louis Lambert?* Was Balzac alluding to a

202

love which he had killed, in order to walk the path of fame and glory? At any rate, the two pages which follow are to be read like palimpsest. Here is the tenor of it. . . . "He had escaped from social life from necessity, as a criminal flies to the cloister. Remorse, the virtue of the weak, could not touch him. Remorse is impotence; it will sin again. Only repentance is strong; it can end everything. But Wilfrid, in traveling through the world, which he had made his sanctuary, nowhere found balm for his wounds; nowhere had he found a nature to which he could attach himself. Despair had dried up in him the well-spring of desire. His was one of those spirits which, having come to a conflict with passion, have proved themselves the stronger, and so have nothing left to clutch in their talons; spirits which, the opportunity failing them for putting themselves at the head of their peers to trample a whole people under their horses' hoofs, would pay the price of a dreadful martyrdom for the gift of a faith to be wrecked upon; like lofty rocks waiting for the touch of a staff which never comes, to enable them to shed springs of running water." It is difficult to imagine anything more naked and incriminating than these words which, I feel certain, Balzac meant to apply to himself. But, as if this were not sufficient, goaded by an impulse to unburden himself, he continues: "Having drained the cup of earthly love he [Wilfrid] now saw the cup of election." Speaking retrospectively, both in the narrative and in his own soul, Balzac rushes on: "He went to tell her his life, to display the greatness of his soul by the greatness of his sins, to show her the ruins in his desert." He stresses the fact that on this day when Wilfrid first saw Seraphita "the meeting wiped out all memories of his past life." (Did he not mean past lives?) At the very moment, so the narrative runs, when he is about to tell her of his life, of his great love, "a gulf opened before him in which the words of his delirium were lost, and whence a voice came up that transformed him: *he was a boy again, a boy of sixteen.*" In these all-transparent words Balzac fuses the two highest moments of écstasy which he had known; the one, when he was a boy at the College of Vendôme and most assuredly saw and spoke with the angels, the other at the moment—or perhaps just prior to the moment—when he met Madame Hanska. It was on September 26, 1833, that he met the latter for the first time, at Neufchâtel. In December of that year, as I remarked previously, he began the writing of *Seraphita*. Throughout his whole life, it is said by those competent to know, he experienced only a few weeks of real happiness. The description of Wilfrid's emotions on meeting Seraphita is undoubtedly a transcript of Balzac's own feelings on meeting Madame Hanska, a record of his joy and aspirations at that moment. In the woman whom he struggles seventeen years to attach himself to he gave human form to the cup of election whose life-giving waters he had already tasted. In her he sought the companion whom he hoped would accompany him to the realm of Light. The brief union with Madame Hanska, the intensity of the experience, revived the memory of youthful visions and ecstasies; the angel in him awoke and spake. He re-became, for a spell, the Louis Lambert whom he had parted from in his youth, whose like he was never again to find since he had chosen the earthly sanctuary in which the real self was absent. "Who has not known," he says of Wilfrid, "what it is to become young and pure again [Wilfrid is only thirty-six] after growing cold with age and foul with impurities? Wilfrid loved suddenly, *as he had never loved*; he loved in secret, with faith and awe and hidden frenzies." Madame Hanska was rather a frail, defective human vessel, as we know, but for Balzac she was *the being* who served to keep the inner flame alight. She it was, I am inclined to think, who preserved him from that sorrowful fate he had apportioned to Louis Lambert. It was

204

she who organized his madness, who kept him rooted to the earth. But under the spell of this consuming love, the artist in him, which was in danger of being snuffed out, transformed the earth into a living creature, and in the heart of this animal the earth he lived and moved and had his being.

Here, about the middle of the book, comes the fourth chapter which, like the fourth everywhere, is the crux in which the rock is metamorphosed into the waters of life. Addressed primarily to Pastor Becker, the symbol of doubt, Seraphita's words are hurled like thunderbolts. Pastor Becker *is* Europe, that Europe which, as we read subsequently, "can believe in no one but Him who will trample her under foot." As cruel and merciless to the man of genius as to the man in the street, Europe, Balzac realized, must perish. What follows is prophetic of the dawn of a new day, a day in which not only the boundaries of nationalism will be dissolved, but every barrier which separates man from man and man from God. "What does it signify," says Seraphita, "which way the worlds are moving if the Being who guides them is proved to be absurd? . . . Your scepticism permeates from above downwards . . . Your doubts include everything, the end as well as the means. . . . Everything is God. Either we are God, or God is not!" There is plenty in this chapter for the sceptic to sneer at, for the learned man to mock, for the scientific man to scorn, for the conqueror to despise, for the ideologist to crack with his sharp teeth, but how will these reply to Seraphita's challenge? "*Old Man!* this is the sum-total of your science and your long meditations." Balzac was privileged to witness the downfall of Napoleon; he was contemporaneous with Goethe, "the last man of Europe"; he was esteemed by the Apocalyptic writer of the century, Dostoievski. He saw the end of Europe, which has yet to be played out dramatically, but he had also a vision of the world to come, a world in which there would be

order, an order imposed from above where all action has its inception. The tremendous fear which now paralyzes the nations of
the world is nothing to the frenzy which will come when the
present disorder gives way to chaos. Only a man like Balzac, who
anchored himself in the very heart of chaos, could appreciate the
meaning of "order." This order he gives us, in progressive hierarchies, throughout the remainder of the book. It is an order which
is founded on faith. "There is a being," says Seraphita, "who both
believes and sees, who has knowledge and power, who loves, prays
and waits . . . he both listens and replies. In his eyes scepticism
is not impiety . . . it is a stage of transition whence a man must
go forward towards the light, or back into darkness." How better
characterize the times than by these prophetic words? "There is a
supreme science," she continues, "of which some men—too late—
get a glimpse, though they dare not own it. These men perceive
the necessity for considering all bodies, not merely from the point
of view of their mathematical properties, *but also from that of their
whole relations and occult affinities.*" What more is there to be
said? Wilfrid returns home, appalled at finding his world in ruins;
Pastor Becker returns to his *Incantations.* And Europe? Europe
then, as now, returns to her vomit, like a mad dog. "However deep
the inner revelation, however distinct the outward sign," is Balzac's
comment, "by the morrow Balaam doubts both his ass and himself." *Europe can believe in no one but Him who will trample her
under foot!*

Victory over the earth, that is Seraphita's cry. The Universe, she
says, belongs to him who will, who can, who knows how to pray.
"Sinai and Golgotha are not here nor there. *The angel is crucified
everywhere, and in every sphere.*"

At this point in the narrative it is written: "On a sudden HE sat
up to die!"

In the final chapter, rising heavenward, Balzac gives the clue to the spiritual cosmogony; "from the most vast to the smallest of the worlds, and from the smallest sphere to the minutest atom of the creation that constitutes it, *each thing was an individual, and yet all was one.*" Such is the aspect from above, whither Seraphita is led by the Guardian Angel. Minna and Wilfrid, accompanying her part of the way, through the miracle of faith, are permitted a glimpse of the higher spheres wherein they see reflected the nakedness of their own souls. So great was their joy, it is recounted, "that they felt an ardent desire to rush back into the mire of the universe, to endure trial there, so as to be able some day to utter at the sacred gate the answer spoken by the glorified Spirit." In the descent the "exiles" are privileged to look upon the rotting splendor of those who lorded it over the world—the conquerors and warriors, the learned and the rich. WHAT DO YE HERE IN MOTIONLESS RANKS? Wilfrid shouts again and again. As they open their robes to reveal the bodies which are eaten away, corrupt and falling to dust, Wilfrid exclaims wrathfully: "Ye lead the nations to death. Ye have defiled the earth, perverted the Word, prostituted justice. . . . *Do ye think there is justification in showing your wounds?* I shall warn those of my brethren who still can hear the Voice, that they may slake their thirst at the springs you have hidden."

At this the gentle Minna turns to him and says: "Let us save our strength for prayer. It is not your mission to be a prophet, nor a redeemer, nor an evangelist. We are as yet only on the margin of the lowest sphere. . . ."

Outside the first summer of the nineteenth century was in all its glory.

# BALZAC AND HIS DOUBLE

In his book on St. Francis of Assisi, Chesterton endeavors to put his finger on the weakness of that sect whose members styled themselves "the true sons of St. Francis"—the Fraticelli—and whose goal it was to carry out the complete program of St. Francis. "What was the matter with these people," writes Chesterton, "was that they were mystics; mystics and nothing else but mystics; mystics and not Christians; mystics and not men. They rotted away because, in the most exact sense, they would not listen to reason. And St. Francis, however wild and romantic his gyrations, always hung on to reason by one invisible and indestructible hair." In the

*History of Magic* by Eliphas Levi we have a similar indictment of the mystics; they are condemned and vituperated because they are extremists. In his autobiographical study called *Louis Lambert*, Balzac, who was a believer in the esoteric doctrine—too catholic a spirit to be a Catholic—gives us a picture of the conflict between the angel in man and the flesh which throws a different light upon the dangers which are supposed to attend the mystic in his unbridled desire for union with the infinite all.

Who was Louis Lambert? He was not only, as the story relates, *le copain*, the chum, the alter ego, he was Balzac's own real self, the angelic self which was killed in the struggle with the world. At that moment in Louis Lambert's life when, as Balzac says, he perceived in him "the struggle of the mind reacting on itself," he adds—"at this stage of weakness and strength, of childish grace and superhuman powers, Louis Lambert is the creature who, more than any other, gave me a poetical and truthful image of the being we call an angel." When in his fifteenth year he parts from his double at the College of Vendôme, he says: "You will live, but I shall die. If I can, I will come back to you." In the story he does come back, to find Louis mad, but in life he never came back. In taking leave of himself in this strangely prophetic manner it is interesting to note that Balzac immediately proceeds to give a physical description of his double, an exact description, including Louis' height, adding significantly: *"he grew no more!"* In the midst of his narrative, in an interlude of two short paragraphs wherein he makes a transition from the known life of his double to the subsequent and imagined life of the mystic who rotted away in the flesh, Balzac remarks that in describing Louis' boyhood he is depicting "the unknown life to which I owe the only happy hours, the only pleasant memories, of my early days. Excepting these two years I have had nothing but annoyances and weariness."

The book is an attempt on Balzac's part to justify himself not only to the world, but to himself. It is a study of the ordeal and crucifixion of a genius, a defense of the real Balzac whom the world refused to acknowledge. It is an outcry against the critics for failing to discern in the novelist the more important attributes of thinker, visionary, prophet. (Referring to Louis Lambert he says, "I think we may deplore in him a genius equal to Pascal, Lavoisier or Laplace." And elsewhere in the book: "his philosophical speculations ought undoubtedly to gain him recognition as one of the great thinkers who have appeared at wide intervals among men to reveal to them the bare skeleton of some science to come. . . .") But it was above all the failure to detect "the angel" which reduced Balzac to despair and moved him to write this harrowing study of frustration. In the story it is the angel, which, at the price of reason and sanity, is finally liberated; but in life it is the angel which is destroyed in order that the artist may triumph. What Chesterton said of St. Francis was also true of Balzac—he too had the ability to hang on to reason by that one invisible and indestructible hair. But was it worth it? If Louis Lambert may be said to succumb to madness—and even this admission is questionable, if one reads Balzac's judgment carefully—he, Balzac, the man of indomitable courage and will, certainly succumbed to a worse fate. He succumbed to fame and glory. The soaring ambitions of genius brought him nothing but trials and tribulations, brought him to the grave prematurely, at the very moment when he had hoped to sit back and reap the harvest of his tremendous labors. Even the great love, to which he struggled for seventeen years to give a solid, secure pediment, was snatched from him. He had given her in marriage the living cadaver of himself.

Just as Seraphita was written for Madame Hanska, his ideal love, so Louis Lambert was written for his "Dilecta," Madame de Berny, who had been to him not only a devoted mistress, but a mother as well, for Balzac had never known a mother's love. Da Vinci had two mothers; Goethe had the best mother a genius could possibly have; but Balzac was deprived of an affection and tenderness which he needed possibly more than either Goethe or da Vinci. His life at the College of Vendôme was a nightmare. Reserved, secretive, oversensitive, precocious, misunderstood by masters and pupils alike, he became indifferent to the world about and was forced to retire into himself—to commune with the angels. This sense of loneliness developed with the years, despite the fame and renown which he tasted early in his career. In his letters he refers frequently to a secret which no one, not even Madame Hanska, to whom he confesses this on occasion, will ever penetrate. At the very threshold of his career, in the year 1828, he writes that there are people who die without the doctor's ever being able to say what it was that carried them off. The lack of maternal tenderness, the estrangement, the hatred which was shown him by his mother, left an indelible mark upon him. His incarceration in the College of Vendôme only served to stimulate the already premature development of his spiritual nature; the man lagged behind. In fact, the man in him was never fully realized. Balzac, throughout his life, not only felt himself to be an exile and a prisoner, but deliberately made his life a prison, in order to punish himself for a crime which he had never committed. His dismal failure as a writer, throughout the years of apprenticeship when he signed false names to his work, testifies not only to the slow development common to great geniuses but points also to the powers of frustration born of his crippled affections.

In *Louis Lambert* Balzac gives us the genesis of a giant moth doomed to perish in a flame of light. To grasp the true significance of this study it should be borne in mind not only that the poet was murdered at school (where all the poets are murdered!) but that

211

the date, June-July, 1832, given for this story, represents his thirty-third year! Long before the great financial disaster, which served him as an excuse to make himself a Martyr of Work, Balzac realized that he was destined for a Purgatorial existence. In that harrowing letter which Louis Lambert writes from his miserable garret in Paris, Balzac gives the clue to his own secret hopes and disillusionment. "Compelled to live in himself alone," he writes, "having no one to share his subtle raptures, he may have hoped to solve the problem of his destiny by a life of ecstasy, adopting an almost vegetative attitude, like an anchorite of the early church, and abdicating the empire of the intellectual world." This vegetative life which he was forbidden to enjoy Balzac had tasted as a boy; it was this normal desire for natural growth, for a growth which would have altered the whole tenor of his life, which might have permitted him to become a seer rather than a novelist, it was this hunger for the opportunity to permit his real self to flower, that militated against his early development as a writer. The real Balzac is absent from the first forty volumes; it is a ghost writing. The real Balzac is still enwrapped in the chrysalis which he had spun about himself in the College of Vendôme. What a tragic, fateful moment it was when, as a boy of fourteen, Balzac was returned to his parents by the masters of the College as a walking somnambulist, an embryonic monster of thought suffering from a "*congestion de lumière.*" Even when he throws himself into life, when outwardly he seems to be fulfilling the role of a young man who is in love, who is acquiring a vocation, who is studying life, the spell in which he had wrapped himself is so strong that he has no sense of his gifts, still less of his destiny, but struggles like a worm in its cocoon in order to liberate himself from his self-imposed prison. The young man who makes his appearance in the world, who conquers by a single glance of his magnetic eye, is simply the ghost which, by

212

sheer force of will, succeeds in bursting the wrappings of a dormant soul. In *Louis Lambert* Balzac depicts himself as the dreamer who succeeds in detaching himself from his body. In seeking to violate the laws of nature his triumph is nullified, because, as he is later to know from experience, in order to overcome the world it is first necessary to accept it. As an artist he does overcome the world, by making it "transparent," but to become the artist he had first to understand the submission of the will. The submission or surrender of the artist is only the first step in the path of renunciation. That Balzac realized the nature of the conflict in himself is evident from the work which follows shortly after *Louis Lambert—Seraphita*. Between the themes of these two books there is a void which can be likened to a desert in which psychologically, or spiritually, the whole of Balzac's life is passed. Unlike the saints and mystics whom he revered, Balzac never returned from the desert. His immense production is simply a monologue, a wilderness of the soul's anguish in which the wanderer is lost.

It was only when the artist in him awakened, when he had accepted his duality, understood his role, that Balzac, by a prodigious metamorphosis, succeeded in making the world itself into a chrysalis and, from the depths of his imagination, gathers the wings which will permit him to fly beyond the world while remaining ever securely imprisoned *in* it. When he says of Louis Lambert that "the point to which most thinkers reach at last was to him the starting point whence his brain was to set out one day in search of new worlds of knowledge," did he not mean that in his stupendous vegetative slumber he had exhausted the whole world of the intellect, that though still a boy, he nevertheless stood on the frontier of a new way of life? And that as a man he was condemned to be a prisoner of the age in which he was born? What is the meaning of the words which follow on the above? "Though as yet he [Louis

213

Lambert] knew it not, he had made for himself the most exacting life possible, and the most insatiably greedy. *Merely to live,* was he not compelled to be perpetually casting nutriment into the gulf he had opened in himself?" *What gulf?* Had he already franchised the barriers of his living tomb? All his life Balzac was promising to bring forth an essay on *"les forces humaines."* All his life he struggles to deliver the secret of that imaginary document which Louis Lambert wrote at college—*Traité sur la Volonté*—and which was destroyed by the ignorant and insensitive headmaster. In *La Peau de Chagrin* (wherein we also have glimpses of his boyhood) he again gives expression to his obsession when he writes that he believed he had a great thought to express, a system to establish, a science to elucidate. Of the visions which he had at school he says that they gave to his eyes the faculty of seeing the intimate, the quintessential nature of things. Through them his heart was prepared *"pour les magies."* And then he adds, as a final tribute to the effect of these sublime visions: "they inscribed in my brain a book wherein I could read what I had to express; they gave to my lips the power of spontaneous utterance." "From the very beginning," says Ernst-Robert Curtius, "Balzac's life is dominated by a mystic star, by a ray of light emanating from the higher worlds." It is with this vision of greater things, this vision of a life as yet unknown to us, that Balzac progresses through the world, devouring everything in sight, creating a vast panorama peopled with his own figures, and yet eternally dissatisfied, because nothing the earth had to offer could compensate for that life which he was denied. The *Treatise on the Will*, which is symbolically destroyed by the ignorant headmaster, never materializes into the promised essay *"sur les forces humaines,"* unless, as one well might, we consider *La Comédie Humaine* itself as an elaborate elucidation of the subject. The embryonic Balzac, who eventually became a Colossus, was a living travesty of the Will. In *Seraphita* he reveals the true function of the Will: it is the desire to rise, to go beyond the limits of the self, to expand in the Infinite Self.

Balzac, the writer, deflected his great will in order to subjugate the world. Both the Poet and the Pythagoras in him were doomed: the Colossus was engulfed in the sands of his own creation. The whole vast edifice of his work appears, ultimately, like a Gargantuan effort to bury the secret which gnawed at his vitals. At the age of twenty-three, still inchoate, still paralyzed, though aware of the possession of a tremendous force, he writes to his "Dilecta" concerning the doctrines of Leibnitz, arrested by the thought that everything in the world, organic and inorganic, is possessed with life. He avers that even marble may be said to have ideas—"extraordinarily confused, however." He confides that he too would like to obtain "solidity, durability, immobility." It was from this crude block of marble, Curtius writes, that the gigantic edifice of *La Comédie Humaine* had to be hewn. This is tantamount to saying that it was created out of the will rather than the flame. For Balzac the Will was supreme—"*le roi des fluides*," as he put it. It was the Will which enabled him to bridge the gulf which had opened in himself and into which he flung his great work.

His whole life was a contradiction of his philosophy: it was the most stupid, aborted life that any intelligent man ever lived. What a strange tribute it is that he makes to his double in *Louis Lambert!* After making a cryptic acknowledgment of his indebtedness to his alter ego, he says: "and this is not all I have borrowed from him . . . this present volume is intended as a modest monument, a broken column, to commemorate the life of the man who bequeathed to me all he had to leave—his thoughts." In *Seraphita* he gives us his opinion of the grand edifice which he created. "Books are human actions in death," he says. From this solid, durable, unshakeable edifice, from the crude block of marble out of which his great work was fashioned, the real Balzac never emerged. Of the three great stages on the mystic path he knew only the first two, and these in reverse order—*la vie purgative et la vie illuminative. La vie unitive*, which is the grand theme pervading his works, he never knew. Like Pythagoras he knew the secret of number: like Virgil he foresaw a world to come; like Dante he proclaimed the inner doctrine, and in the book which is least known of all his work, *Seraphita*, he gave us this doctrine, and there it lies buried. His intuition was cosmic, his will was titan-like, his energy inexhaustible, his nature truly protean, and yet he was unable to emancipate himself. The study of society and the psychology of the individual, which form the material of the novel in European literature, served to create the illusory world of facts and things which dominate the neurotic life that began with the 19th century and is now reaching its end in the drama of schizophrenia. At the back of it is the Will, reducing through the powers of analysis all life to ashes. Balzac was himself aware of the disease which is killing us. It is the mind which is poisoning us, he says somewhere. "*La vie est un feu qu'il faut couvrir de cendres; penser, c'est ajouter la flamme au feu.*" Dostoievski gave expression to the conflict even more forcibly. Indeed, it is with him that the novel comes to an end, for after him there are no longer any individuals to write about, nor is there any longer a society which may be said to possess a body. Proust and Joyce epitomize the dissolution of our world in their great epics. With Lawrence the novel becomes a vehicle for the Apocalyptic visions which will occupy us for the next few hundred years, as our world fades out in blood and tears.

"Werther," says Balzac, "is a slave of desire; Louis Lambert was an enslaved soul." A tremendous admission, *shattering*, if Balzac is to be identified, as he intended, with his double. Despite the most gigantic efforts ever man made, the real Balzac did not grow an inch from the time he left his prison at Vendôme to enter the world. Adopting the Purgatorial life, after having experienced the joys and splendors of illumination, taking up his cross and nailing himself to it, he nevertheless was refused the reward of blossoming into a miraculous rose. He knew—he gave expression to it several times in his work—that the real miracle happens within, yet he persisted in looking for it without. His life was devoid of joy or hope; he is the symbol of the convict condemned to a life of hard labor. At that stage of division wherein he detects the angel in Louis Lambert he erects the tombstone over his own grave. As Louis Lambert he sinks deeper and deeper into the world of Maya; as Balzac he sinks into the morass of the world of things, the world of desire which is inappeasable. Louis Lambert gives up the struggle with the world in order to commune with the angels, but unlike Swedenborg, he forgets to leave the door open. Balzac struggles with the world in order to down the angel in himself. He rails and fumes against the world for its inability or unwillingness to understand and appreciate him, but the confusion he precipitated was of his own making. His life was as disordered, confused and chaotic as the bedeviled proofs of his manuscripts, the like of which the world has never seen, except in the work of the insane. He beclouded the real issue with a smoke screen of words; he fought like a madman to blind his own eyes to the path which he was ordained to follow. The world has been kind and at the same time cruel to him, in the very measure of duality and antagonism which he created. It has accepted him as one of the greatest of human geniuses; it has remained ignorant of the real goal which he set himself. He wanted fame, glory, recognition: he received them. He wanted riches, possessions, power over men: he obtained all of these. He wanted to create a world of his own: he did. But the true life which he secretly desired to live was denied him—because one cannot have one foot in one world and the other in another. He had not learned the lesson of Renunciation: he had renounced the world, not to abdicate, but to conquer. In his moments of illumination he perceived the truth, but he was never able to live according to his vision. For him, as he permits Seraphita to say with blinding clarity, it is true that it was a Light such as kills the man who is not prepared to receive it. Towards the end of the book he "comes back" to Louis and as he watches him with uncanny tenseness, waiting eagerly for a word to fall from his lips after the unbearable suspense of prolonged silence, what is it he puts in Louis' mouth as the first utterance? THE ANGELS ARE WHITE! The effect of this utterance, when the reader comes upon it in the natural course of the narrative, is indescribable. Even the illusion of being himself affected by these words is dissipated by the stark reality which Balzac gives them. It is like saying *truth is truth!* THE ANGELS ARE WHITE—this is the utmost Balzac can think to say in his assumed madness, after days, weeks and months of standing at the mantelpiece rubbing one leg against the other and piercing with dead eyes the veils of the Infinite. *The angels are white!* It is madder than anything Nijinsky wrote in his diary. It is pure madness, white as the light itself, and yet so thoroughly sane that it seems like a Euclidean statement of identity. It is the reduction of all his Pythagorean wisdom to an image which is hallucinating. Number, substance, weight, measure, motion—all are consumed here to give an image which is more meaningful than meaning itself.

In the limited illustrated edition of the book published by Dent, London, there is, in addition to the asinine preface by George Saintsbury, an etching of Louis inspired by this phrase. I mention it because I was astonished, after having read the story several times, to find on flipping the pages that the artist had portrayed Louis in a manner absolutely different from that which I had imagined from memory. In my own mind I always saw Louis standing at the mantelpiece in a trance, but—*looking like a horse!* On re-reading Balzac's description of him, as he appeared at this moment, I find that my image is fairly correct. But what strikes me now is that the person I really had in mind, Louis' double, as it were, is Nijinsky. And this is not really so strange as it may at first seem. For if ever there was a flesh and blood image of Balzac's extraordinary lunatic it is the dancer Nijinsky. He too left the earth while still alive, never to return again. He too became a horse equipped with chimerical wings. The horse, let us not forget, even when he has no wings, flies. So too, every genius, when he is truly inspired, mounts the winged steed to write his name in the heavens. How often, in reading Nijinsky's *Diary*, have I thought of Mademoiselle de Villenoix's words! "Louis," says this guardian angel who never deserted her lover, "must no doubt appear to be mad, but he is not, if the term mad ought only to be used in speaking of those whose brain is for some unknown cause diseased, and who can show no reason in their actions. Everything in my husband is perfectly balanced. He has succeeded in detaching himself from his body and discerns us under some other aspect—what it is, I know not. . . . To other men he seems insane; to me, living as I do in his mind, his ideas are quite lucid. I follow the road his spirit travels; and though I do not know every turning, I can reach the goal with him." Wholly aside from the question of whether Louis Lambert was mad or not, aside from the question of what constitutes madness, which will always remain a mystery, the attitude preserved throughout by this guardian angel is in itself worthy of the deepest attention. Perhaps, in depicting the devotion of this extraordinary woman, Balzac was stressing the great need for affection, understanding, sympathy and recognition which every artist demands and which Balzac more than most men stood in want of all his life. In one of his letters, I believe it is, he says that he has known neither a spring nor a summer, but that he looked forward to enjoying a ripe autumn. He looked forward above all to a consummation of his labors through love. Over and over again, in his writings, we have this announcement of a tremendous hope. Immediately he saw Mademoiselle de Villenoix Louis "discerned the angel within." "His passion," says Balzac, "became a gulf into which he threw everything." In his first letter to her, a letter doubtless very similar to the early ones which Balzac wrote Madame Hanska, Louis expressed himself thus: ". . . my life will be in your hands, for I love you; *and to me, the hope of being loved is life!*" And then, as Balzac must himself have felt when he was wooing Madame Hanska, Louis adds: "If you had rejected me, all was over for me."

Here let me give a rapid summary of the narrative, as it is given in the book. . . .

Louis Lambert is the son of a poor tanner, an only child who is adored by his parents.* The parents, being of modest means, are unable to pay the sum required to obtain a substitute for their son, as substitutes for the army at that time (the early nineteenth century) were scarce. The only means of evading conscription was to have Louis become a priest. And so, at ten years of age, Louis is sent to his maternal uncle, a parish priest in a small town on the Loire, not far from Blois. In the second paragraph of his story Balzac launches into an account of Louis' passion for books. He began, it would seem, at the age of five by reading the Old and the New Testaments . . . "and these two books, including so many

---

* This is the most singular distortion, it is interesting to notice, which Balzac makes in recounting the story of his double's boyhood.

books, had sealed his fate." During the school holidays Louis devours everything in sight, "feeding indiscriminately on religious works, history, philosophy and physics." For lack of other material he often turns to the dictionaries. "The analysis of a word, its physiognomy and history, would be to Lambert matter for long dreaming . . . What a fine book might be written of the life and adventures of a word!" Of the two words which Balzac singles out for mention, curiously, one is "true" and the other "flight." In three years Louis Lambert had assimilated the contents of all that was worth reading in his uncle's library. His memory was prodigious. "He remembered with equal exactitude the ideas he had derived from reading, and those which had occurred to him in the course of meditation or conversation. Indeed, he had every form of memory —for places, for names, for words, things and faces. He not only recalled any object at will, but he saw them in his mind, situated, lighted and colored as he had originally seen them . . . He could remember, as he said, not merely the position of a sentence in the book where he had met with it, but the frame of mind he had been in at remote dates. . . ." Louis is depicted as one who "had transferred all his activities to thinking," as one who was drawn towards the mysteries, one fascinated by the abyss. He had a "taste for the things of heaven," a predilection, Balzac remarks, which was disastrous, if Louis' life is to be measured by ordinary standards. After the Bible came the reading of Saint Theresa and Madame Guyon. "This line of study, this peculiar taste, elevated his heart, purified, ennobled it, gave him an appetite for the divine nature, and suggested to him the almost womanly refinement of feeling which is instinctive in great men. . . ." At fourteen Louis leaves his uncle to enter the College of the Oratorians at Vendôme, where he was maintained at the expense of Madame de Staël who, forbidden to come within forty leagues of Paris, was in the habit of spending several months of her banishment on an estate near Vendôme. Impressed by the boy's unusual powers of mind Madame de Staël hoped to save Louis from the necessity of serving either the Emperor or the Church. During the three years he spent at the College, however, Louis never heard a word from his benefactress. Madame de Staël, in fact, dies on the very day that Louis, who had set out on foot from Blois to see her, arrived in Paris.

The life at the College is like a miniature description of Hell. "The punishments originally invented by the Society of Jesus," says Balzac, "as alarming to the moral as to the physical man, were still in force in all the integrity of the original code." Visits by the parents were extremely infrequent, holidays away from the school were forbidden; once a pupil entered his prison he never left it until his studies were terminated. The lack of physical comforts, the bad sanitation, the meager prison diet, the frequent beatings, the refined tortures inflicted by masters and pupils alike, the stupidity and bigotry of the life, the isolation, all tended to demoralize and devitalize any one with promise, and particularly a sensitive being, such as Louis Lambert. Balzac describes himself as then being twelve years of age. What the effect of such a life must have been, for his sensitive soul, can best be understood by the description of his emotions upon hearing the announcement of Louis' arrival at the College. "I can compare it with nothing but my first reading of *Robinson Crusoe*," he says. From the first he felt sympathy (sic!) with the boy whose temperament had some points of likeness to his own. "At last I was to have a companion in daydreams and meditations!" In this naked description of the split in his psyche Balzac reveals to us the true nature of his liberation. *At last!* Like a cry of desperation.*

* Later, when describing Louis' feverish anticipation of a union with the woman he loves, Balzac gives us another rupture with the world, this time the final one.

222

The physical description of Louis Lambert which Balzac gives at this point is remarkable for the resemblance to his own self. He speaks glowingly of "the prophetic brow," of the extraordinary eyes which bespoke the existence of a soul. Though he had not the ordinary strength which permitted him to rival the others in sports, Louis was possessed of a mysterious power of will which he could summon on occasion and which was capable of defying the united strength of his comrades. He speaks of the wealth of ideas, the poetry, that lay hidden in Louis' brain and heart, commenting on it in strangely revelatory fashion. "It was not till I was thirty years of age, till my experience was matured and condensed, till the flash of an intense illumination had thrown a fresh light upon it, that I was capable of understanding all the bearings of the phenomena which I witnessed at that early time." The description of Louis' struggle to preserve a semblance of order, to respond to the petty routine of the institution, to show interest in his studies, or even fear or respect when threatened with punishment, is a remarkable transcription of Balzac's own struggle with chaos, discipline and convention. It is a description of the innate maladaptation of the man of genius, of his blindness and deafness to everything except what he intuitively knows will nourish him. It is a picture of the anarchist who is later to become a martyr, or a tyrant, a portrait of the Will pure and naked. Even that irritating reproach which he puts in the mouth of the headmaster, the phrase which is forever startling Louis from his reveries, is significant since it is the tacit reproach which the world in its hatred and envy of the man of genius always makes: "You are doing nothing!" Balzac takes pains to make it clear that whenever Louis was accused of doing nothing he was probably most active in his own right way. It was from these seeming spells of inertia that Balzac's brilliant and devastating ideas were born. Subsequently, in expanding on Louis' philosophical speculations, he elucidates this cogently. There are two beings in us, he says—the Inner one, the Being of Action, and the External one, the Being of Reaction. The whole philosophy of duality enunciated through Louis Lambert is an effort on the part of Balzac, the artist, to establish a totality or acceptance of life. It is Balzac's own dynamic, positive interpretation of what we know as Tao. It runs counter to the whole European trend of metaphysics, which is purely intellectual and idealistic, and ends in a cul de sac.

At any rate, it was the "Poet-and-Pythagoras," as he styles his twin self, who was crushed by the educational routine, "as gold is crushed into round coin under the press." They were an idle and incorrigible pair who could neither play ball, nor run races, nor walk on stilts. "Aliens from the pleasures enjoyed by the others, we were outcasts, sitting forlorn under a tree in the playing-ground." "The eagle that needed the world to feed him," he adds, "was shut up between four narrow dirty walls. And thus Louis Lambert's life became 'an *ideal* life' in the strictest meaning of the words."

At eighteen, having lost his parents, Louis leaves college. He makes his home with his uncle who, having been turned out of his benefice, had come to settle at Blois. There Louis lives for some time, but consumed by a desire to complete his studies, he goes to Paris "to drink of science at its highest fount." The few thousand francs which he had inherited vanish during his three years in Paris. At the age of twenty-three he returns to Blois, driven out "by sufferings to which the impecunious are exposed there." In a long letter to his uncle, written at intervals during his sojourn in Paris, Louis pours out his impressions and experiences. It is no doubt a transcript of Balzac's own experiences upon first coming to Paris. Back in Blois, at the first house to which he is introduced by his uncle, Louis meets a Mademoiselle Pauline de Villenoix, a young and beautiful Jewess, the richest heiress in Blois. Louis falls madly in love with her at first sight. Three years after Louis' return to Blois Balzac encounters the aged uncle in the diligence, while on his way to that town, and through him learns that Louis, on the eve of his announced wedding to Mademoiselle de Villenoix, had gone mad. The uncle, who had taken Louis to Paris to be examined by the eminent physicians of that city, was informed that the malady was incurable. The physicians had advised that Louis "be left in perfect solitude, and that he should always live in a cool room with a subdued light." His fiancée insists on devoting herself to him nevertheless. She removes him to her château at Villenoix, where Balzac, two years later, arrives to visit them. Louis does not recognize his old chum, and after a prolonged effort to get him to break the silence, the only words he utters are—"the angels are white." Before leaving, Balzac obtains from Louis' devoted companion a few fragments of his thoughts (given as an appendix) which she had written down. Louis Lambert dies at the age of twenty-eight in his true love's arms.

The cornerstone of Louis Lambert's philosophy, by which he explained everything, was his theory of the angels. This theory, which Balzac borrowed from Swedenborg, is worth giving in its entirety, for it is this view of man which Balzac later raises to apotheosis in *Seraphita*. It is the highest expression of the duality which he sensed in his own nature and which he transmuted through art. . . .

"In each of us there are two distinct beings. According to Swedenborg, the angel is an individual in whom the inner being conquers the external being. If a man desires to earn his call to be an angel, as soon as his mind reveals to him his twofold existence, he must strive to foster the delicate angelic essence that exists within him. If, for lack of a lucid apprehension of his destiny, he allows bodily action to predominate, instead of confirming his intellectual being, all his powers will be absorbed in the use of his external senses, and the angel will slowly perish by the materialization of both natures. [Which is precisely what happened to Balzac!] In the contrary case, if he nourishes his inner being with the aliment needful to it, the soul triumphs over matter and strives to get free. [In this Louis Lambert failed, but Seraphita succeeded!]

"When they separate by the act of what we call death, the angel, strong enough then to cast off its wrappings, survives and begins its real life. The infinite variety which differentiates individual men can only be explained by this twofold existence which, again, is proved and made intelligible by that variety.

"In point of fact, the wide distance between a man whose torpid intelligence condemns him to evident stupidity, and one who, by the exercise of his inner life, has acquired the gift of some power, allows us to suppose that there is as great a difference between men of genius and other beings as there is between the blind and those who see. This hypothesis, since it extends creation beyond all limits, gives us, as it were, the clue to heaven. The beings who, here on earth, are apparently mingled without distinction, are there distributed, according to their inner perfection, in distinct spheres whose speech and manners have nothing in common. In the invisible world, as in the real world, if some native of the lower spheres comes, all unworthy, into a higher sphere, not only can he never understand the customs and language there, but his mere presence paralyzes the voice and hearts of those who dwell therein."

Here, embedded in the midst of a work which was only too obviously destined to be neglected by the great majority of his admirers, Balzac, like one of those medieval masons at work on a cathedral, leaves the visible evidence of his secret initiation into the mysteries. In the very next breath, as though to give the clue to the high importance of this passage, he mentions Dante's *Divine Comedy*, which is the mystic cathedral of words that enshrines the great Rosicrucian mystery of the Middle Ages. But why he should have said that "Dante had perhaps some *slight* intuition of those spheres which begin in the world of torment and rise, circle on circle, to the highest heaven," baffles me. Why "slight" intuition? Was he appalled by Dante's audacity? Had he too recently fallen under the dominion of the "Buddha of the North," as he styles Swedenborg? He was no doubt highly familiar with Dante's work. In *The Exiles*, the last of the three studies which make up *Le Livre Mystique*, he records an episode in Dante's life which occurred during his stay in Paris whilst attending the lectures given at the old School of the Four Nations by the celebrated Sigier, "the most noted doctor of Mystical Theology of the University of Paris." But possibly the real clue to this apparent "slight" is given in what follows upon the theory of the angels, viz., *the role of love*. To Lambert, says Balzac, "pure love—love as we dream of it in youth—was the coalescence of two angelic natures. Nothing could exceed the fervency with which he longed to meet a woman angel. And who better than he could inspire or feel love?" Strangely enough, though Louis Lambert is destined to meet and to be loved by precisely the angelic creature he sought in his dreams, the union is tragically aborted and Louis is robbed of the fruits of his yearning. The interval which marks the short separation in time between the appearance of *Louis Lambert* and *Seraphita* is not the merely natural one attributed to artistic ripening, but rather it seems to me, a time difference (of infinite duration or brevity) as between one incarnation and another. As a human being, Louis Lambert had not earned the right to be wedded to an angel in the flesh. His madness, which breaks out on the eve of the wedding, seems at first more like the voluntary assumption of a Purgatorial role, in preparation for the higher union which is to take place when Louis, reincarnated as Seraphita-Seraphitus, elects to espouse Heaven. "The fortuitous separation of our two natures," which is one of the phrases Balzac employs in describing Louis' pathologic condition, is an occurrence familiar to Hindus and Tibetans, and the causes ascribed by them differ considerably from the scientific explanations offered us by the psychopathologist. The cataleptic states which signalled Louis' sudden swerve from "pure idealism to the most intense sensualism" were as familiar to Balzac as the epileptic attacks described by Dostoievski. "The excitement to which he had been wound up by the anticipation of acute physical enjoyment, enhanced by a chaste life and a highly-strung soul, had no doubt led to these attacks, of which the results are as little known as the cause," says Balzac. "What was really extraordinary," he comments significantly, "is that Louis should not have had several previous attacks, since his habits of rapt thought and the character of his mind would predispose him to them." This, of course, Balzac is able to say without fear of refutation because he is speaking from intimate experience. The walking somnambulist who was returned to his parents at the age of fourteen was well qualified to speak on the relation between ecstasy and catalepsy. Says Louis Lambert: "Deep meditation and rapt ecstasy are perhaps the undeveloped germs of catalepsy." This in the course of a discussion of their favorite subject, for as Balzac writes, the two of them "went crazy over catalepsy."

However, what *is* truly extraordinary, in my opinion, is that Balzac himself did not succumb to madness. The study of Louis Lambert's morbid degeneration is really the story of Balzac's own narrow escape. Endowed with extraordinary vitality, he succeeded somehow in holding on to reason by that one invisible, indestructible hair. But by all the logic of fate and circumstance he should have perished like his double. It is the classic fate of the genius in modern times. Deprived of the maternal affection which a sensitive, precocious child demands, incarcerated like a leper in the educational penitentiary of the College of Vendôme, his unusual gifts unrecognized by his educators, condemned to the tower for long periods, like a convict, having no one to commune with but his imaginary double, experiencing all the terrors of schizophrenia, the miracle is that Balzac survived the ordeal even as well as he did. The story has a triple significance. In the ordinary child the result would be insanity, or psychosis; in the budding genius the result is a transmutation of suffering permitting us a work of art (I refer to his complete works) which is typical only of the art of the Western world, that is to say, an art which is at once a tribute to the imperishable angel in man and a prophecy of the fate which lies in store for a people whose culture is founded on the persecution and suppression of the highest types. With Louis Lambert there perished a seer; only the artist survived, in the person of Balzac. But the loss is irreparable. Not even the discovery of a companion, another angelic creature like himself, could preserve the better half of Balzac from dying. Towards the end of the book, when he is discussing Louis' case with the aged uncle, he chooses his words most carefully. Was not Louis' malady, he asks, perhaps the result of possessing a too highly organized nature? "If," he says, "he is really a victim of the malady as yet unstudied in all its aspects, which is known simply as madness, I am inclined to attribute it to his passion. His studies and his mode of life had strung his powers and faculties to a degree of energy beyond which the least further strain was too much for nature; Love was enough to crack them, or to raise them to a new form of expression which we are maligning perhaps, by ticketing it without due knowledge. In fact, he may perhaps have regarded the joys of marriage as an obstacle to the perfection of his inner man and his flight towards spiritual spheres."

Knowing Balzac's life as we do, are we not to infer that this desire for perfection, coupled with an uncontrollable passion, prevented him from realizing the joys of marriage? The truth is that it was desire at war with itself which frustrated Balzac. Louis, though chaste, succumbs to his sensual nature. Balzac, also capable of great chastity, succumbs to his inordinate passion for power and recognition. Whereas Louis Lambert succumbs to the devil, as it were, by ignoring the physical part of his being, Seraphita, who, as I hinted before, might be regarded as the subsequent incarnation of this strange being, triumphs over the demons in every Shape and Species! Seraphita knows evil; Louis is ignorant of it. Louis Lambert evinces neither lust nor hatred—at the most, an indignant, silent scorn for his persecutors. With Dante, to take a familiar example, we traverse every region of Hell, are confronted with every form of evil. It is the audacious and sane solution later propounded through the poetic genius of Blake. It is acceptance, total acceptance, of every phase of life. Only thus is there, or can there be, any spiral evolution, involution, or devolution possible. The path is the same for God as for man, the same for the vegetable as for the star. Balzac never fully accepted life; he struggled, as we know from the endless stories about him, first against sleep, the restorative agency, second against death, the mystery which he longed to embrace. Crucified by passion and desire, he represents, like Beethoven, the very incarnation of a restless, tortured spirit. In his living he denied his own philosophy: he split and foundered on the antagonism of his own being. Of Louis

Lambert he says that the latter had even reached the point of "preparing to perform on himself the operation to which Origen believed he owed his talents." It is only when Balzac perceives the deep meaning of castration, when he realizes the real nature of his conflict, that he is able to conceive of a creature more evolved, a being burned by the fires of temptation, the one he calls Seraphita, in whom the male and female halves of our being are truly wedded, one in whom good and evil are so balanced that the real transition into a higher state of being is made possible. In this lofty conception of the essential nature of man Balzac leaps forward to a realization which it may yet require thousands of years to justify but which is undeniably true and inevitable. Like Dostoievski, Balzac discerned the coming of a dawn in which the very essence of man's nature would be profoundly altered; Lawrence had a similar vision when he proclaimed the advent of the era of the Holy Ghost. It is an idea which astrologers associate with the Aquarian Age which, according to some, we entered about the time of Balzac's birth, which again is coincident with the time in which the story of *Seraphita* is laid. "*Outside,*" he says, at the conclusion of that book, "the first summer of the new century was in all its glory." But *inside* the seed was blossoming into life—the seed of that future which now seems so black, but wherein man will find salvation through his own efforts. The whole emphasis, with Lawrence, Dostoievski and Balzac, is on the creative powers of man. In them, in their vision of the world to come, the Christ spirit is seen to be triumphant. The Saviour is dead, they seem to cry, *long live the Saviours!* And the saviour of man, as every creative spirit knows, is man.

It is worth noting here the comparison which Spengler makes between Dostoievski and Tolstoi. "Dostoievski is a saint," says he, "Tolstoi only a revolutionary. To Dostoievski's Christianity the next thousand years will belong. . . . Tolstoi is the former Russia, Dostoievski the coming Russia. He [Dostoievski] has passed beyond both Petrinism and revolution, and from *his* future he looks back over them as from afar. His soul is apocalyptic, yearning, desperate, but of his future *certain*. . . . 'Conservative' and 'revolutionary' were terms of the West that left him indifferent. Such a soul as his can look beyond everything that we call social, for the things of this world seem to it so unimportant as not to be worth improving. No genuine religion aims at improving the world of facts, and Dostoievski, like every primitive Russian, is fundamentally unaware of that world and lives in a second, metaphysical world beyond."

What is the final expression of humanity, according to Balzac? In *Seraphita* he expresses it thus: "The union of a spirit of love with a spirit of wisdom lifts the creature into the divine state in which the soul is woman and the body man." This is the final expression of humanity, "in which the spirit is supreme over the form."

In the case of Louis Lambert the spring of passion is muddied at the source. The conflict in his nature, repressed for so long, bursts out at the most unexpected moment, when, as I have said, he is about to ally himself to the angelic creature of his choice. Did we not know the events of Balzac's own life the tragedy would seem less convincing. When I express the opinion that Balzac was miraculously spared the fate of his double, I am only saying what Balzac himself implies throughout and what he seems to attest in dedicating his *Seraphita* to Madame Hanska. At the very threshold of maturity he had found a mother and a mistress in the person of Madame de Berny; he had other loves too, but in none, as he admits, could he find the companionship, the sympathy and the understanding which he demanded of a woman. He was not to find it in Madame Hanska either, for that matter, but because of his great passion for her he was given to find the solution within himself, a solution, be it said, sufficient to carry on, to plunge himself in work, to adapt himself to the world by creating his own world. The *partial* solution of the artist! Balzac was aware that it was only a partial solution, and reconciled himself to it. Never able to reach the center of his being, he at any rate succeeded in situating himself at a point whence he glimpsed the angle of creation. In *Louis Lambert* this parallax, or angle of displacement, becomes enormous, because Louis is moved nearer to the point of fixation. Louis' whole desire is fixed on the beyond— obstinately fixed, one might almost say. Louis' desire to commune with the angels, perhaps just because it is inflexible and unswerving, entrains a dénouement which is in perfect accordance with the law of consequence: Louis remains fixed and his wings are burned in the blinding light that invades him. Louis' madness *is*, like Nijinsky's, of an exceptional character. If he be a lunatic, he is an extraordinary lunatic! Balzac, be it noted, took pains to portray him as a higher type of man whose motives are pure, whose intelligence is vast. But it is wisdom which Louis lacks, the wisdom of life, which comes from experience. In the *Book of the Golden Precepts* it is written: "Learn above all to separate Head-learning from Soul-wisdom, the Eye from the Heart doctrine. Yea, ignorance is like unto a closed airless vessel; the soul a bird shut up within. It warbles not, nor can it stir a feather; but the songster mute and torpid sits, and of exhaustion dies." Louis' malady was diagnosed and minutely described thousands of years ago; today it is the universal malady. Despite the frenzied activity of the nations of the earth, *the songster mute and torpid sits and of exhaustion dies!*

Nobody knew better than Balzac that it is the wisdom of the

heart which must prevail. He says it over and over again, in brilliant fashion. It is the heart of man which will rule in the ages to come, of that he is certain. But the heart must first be purified! and Louis Lambert, who had never *lived*, was inevitably destroyed by the very anticipation of a passionate release. "The selfish devotee lives to no purpose. The man who does not go through his appointed work in life has lived in vain. . . . In separation thou becomest the playground of Samvritti, origin of all the world's delusions." * The condition which Balzac is loath to call "madness" is really the demonic state of the world, which now horrifies us, and which is really the product of idealism. No century in history can boast of so many madmen, among its superior types, as the one following upon Balzac's time. The virulence of this widespread disease, which we now recognize as schizophrenia, or to use a vulgar, literal expression—"soul-splitting"— is by no means a new phenomenon in the evolution of man's psychic being. It was known to the ancients also; it has been described again and again in occult lore; it is familiar to the saint and to the mystic. It might even be regarded as a beneficent punishment, inflicted upon the highest types among us, in order to encourage a wider and deeper exploration of reality. Nothing more vividly resembles what we call "death" than the condition of neurosis. "He who isolates himself," says Eliphas Levi, "is given over to death thereby, and an eternity of isolation would be eternal death." No man, however, can give himself over to eternal death! But there is a living death, of which all occultists speak and of which even the most ordinary man has an understanding. In the highest sense, this is not a state to fear or avoid; it is a transitional state, containing promise or doom, according to the way we regard it. It is the moment, brief as a lightning flash or prolonged for a

* (*Book of the Golden Precepts*)

lifetime, in which, confronted by the necessity of a break with the past, we are paralyzed. It is the moment of arrest at the frontier of a new and greater realm of being. The majority of men, unable to seize the import of this new state or condition of mind, relapse, sink, founder and are carried off by the time current. The forward spirits accept the challenge and, even though they perish, remain with us in spirit to fecundate the new form of life.

In the person of Louis Lambert Balzac gives expression to the great paralyzing fear which beset him when confronted with the sublime duty which his nature had prepared him to obey. His vision, temporarily deflected, shed a fantastic brilliance on the dream world in which he was imprisoned. Louis is made to gaze steadfastly upon the beyond, but with dead orbs. His sight is turned inward. He remains fixed in the hallucinatory state of dream. As the writer, Balzac liberated himself to swim in the ocean of the universal imagination. Only by a miracle was he saved. But he lost his soul! In this realm of the universal imagination, to quote again from Eliphas Levi, we have "the source of all apparitions, all extraordinary visions, and all the intuitive phenomena peculiar to madness or ecstasy. . . . Our brain is a book printed within and without, and with the smallest degree of excitement, the writing becomes blurred, as occurs continually in cases of intoxication and madness. *Dream then triumphs over real life and plunges reason in a sleep which knows no waking. . . .*"

In the esoteric doctrine there is no "place" which corresponds to our conception of Hell; "*Avitchi*," the Buddhist equivalent to our Hell, is a state or condition, not a locality. And, according to this doctrine, the greatest of all Hells is *Myalba*, our earth. It is from a firsthand knowledge of this Hell that Balzac wrote his books. When he parts company with Louis at school he is parting company with the angel he had endeavored to nourish. He sees

235

nothing more of Louis, nor does he hear of him again, until the accidental meeting with Louis' uncle on his way to Blois. The account of his struggles, his deceptions and disillusionment, as he gives it to us in the long letter from Paris, is a description of the torments of Hell. From this ordeal of fire Balzac emerged only partially purified: he never fully accepted the wisdom of the supreme test. His colossal activity as a man of letters is only the reverse of the mute torpor in which his double sits, or stands, without stirring a feather. Torpor and activity are the two faces of the same malady: action proceeds only from a being whose center is at rest. For Balzac, as for the whole modern world, dream triumphed over reason; the dreamer dies of exhaustion in his feverish sleep of meaningless activity. He wrote in a world of the imagination, but he lived in a world of things, amidst a nightmare of bric-a-brac.

When, in *Seraphita*, rhapsodizing on Swedenborg's theory of the angels, Balzac appears to be struck by the expression "there are *solitary* angels," one feels that he has given this phrase his own special emphasis. This is further enhanced when, shortly afterwards, he remarks: "According to Swedenborg, God did not create angels independently; there are none but those who have been human beings on earth. Thus the earth is the nursery ground for heaven. The angels are not angels by original nature; they are transformed into angels by an intimate union with God which God never refuses, the very essence of God being never negative, but always active." One knows, that towards his thirtieth year Balzac finally caught a glimpse of the meaning of suffering, that as a writer he chose a path of renunciation which, though partial, enabled him to accept that Hell which a life on earth is for a man of genius. The ways of the earth had not changed, but Balzac himself had changed since that period of youth which he describes in *Louis Lambert*. By accepting the role of writer, bitter as it was, he was able to work out a partial solution of his lot. When, in the narrative, he comes back to Louis, as he promised he would one day, he finds the angelic being lost to the world. The single self which he had molded into an artist looks back upon the divided self which he formerly was. The angelic youth is swallowed up in dream and illusion; the warrior who battled the world and triumphed, after his fashion, discerns in his counterpart only the husk of his adolescent self. The man who would remain pure and undefiled is turned to clay; he is returned to the earth, to Hell, as it were, robbed of the light and splendor of the living soul. Rodin, in wrestling with the problem of immortalizing this conflict in stone, has given eloquent form and expression to the antagonism which lodged in Balzac with sphinx-like tenacity. In that rough-hewn mold of heavy earth, in which Balzac's soul was imprisoned, the Buddhist drama of Desire was played out in a manner such as we have never witnessed in another European.

The man to whom Balzac was tremendously indebted for an understanding of the World of Desire was Louis Claude Saint-Martin, "*le philosophe inconnu*" whose ideas, according to Curtius, he took over bodily. Balzac was this "*Homme de Désir*" of whom Saint-Martin wrote. Saint-Martin's system of philosophy, derived from Martinez Pasquales' law of numbers, the revelations of Swedenborg and the visions of Jacob Boehme, is based essentially on the idea that man can always find his unity in himself. The following brief commentaries on his doctrine may serve to give an idea of the relation of Balzac's theories to Saint-Martin's philosophy. . . .

"For Saint-Martin man turned to another light than that for which he was destined to be the supreme manifestation, and matter was born out of the Fall; for God created matter to arrest man's precipitation into the abyss, and to give him a world where he would have a chance to redeem himself. In the actual state of things, man holds deep within him the vestiges of his first destiny and the obscure reminiscence of the Golden Age, the primitive paradise. If he comes to listen to the interior signs which are given him, and to descend within himself until he is able, by a spiritual magic, to grasp the germs which brood in his soul, he will achieve his own reintegration in God; but, at the same time, he will restore the entire Creation to its primordial Unity. Man alone, artisan of the Fall, can be the workman for reconciliation, the saviour of Nature. He is a 'being charged to continue God, there where God no longer is known by Himself alone. . . . He continues it in the series of manifestations and emanations, because *there* God is to be known by images and representatives.' If the man of desire craves for harmony and unity, it is because he holds in himself the vestiges, for one cannot crave what one has not first previously known. '*Everything tends to the unity from which it issued.*' The principal agent for this reintegration is the word, which holds the analogy with the Word which created the world; and that is why the act of the poet is sacred and literally creative. Music, in her turn, can contribute to this redeeming magic, since its principle, number, is the reflection of the numbers which rule the courses of the stars, the centuries and the whole of Nature." *

"The human soul, says Saint-Martin, is an extract of the 'universal divine.'" However, he makes it consist of one sole faculty, the will, which in turn he confounds in his mind with desire. But desire, for him, is the basis, the root of our being. It is through desire that "God first entered into us, and it is through desire that we have the power of returning to Him; for desire, being the re-

* From *"L'Ame Romantique et le Rêve"*—Albert Béguin.

sult of the separation of the two existences which, because of the similarity of their natures, experience the need to be united, is necessarily in God as in man. The desire of man, as long as he is not corrupted, is the development of the divine properties that are in us, and the desire of God is the communication of his properties, is the infiltration of this marvellous sap without which man falls back on himself dry and withered. . . . This is why Saint-Martin defines man as the desire of God, and shows us, as the highest dignity to which we may aspire, that of *l'homme de désir*." *

Before proceeding to the "letter" which Louis Lambert pens to his uncle, and which is dated 1819, it may be worth while to observe that in a letter to Madame Hanska (1846) Balzac explains that he had never had a mother, that by the time he was eighteen his mother had rendered his life so miserable that he was obliged to leave home and install himself in a garret, in Paris (Rue Lesdiguières), where he led the life described in *La Peau de Chagrin*. It should also be borne in mind that when he announced his intention to abandon the law for literature his parents accorded him just one year in which to prove his ability as a writer. In this letter to Madame Hanska, wherein he speaks of his mother's hatred for himself and his sister, he says: "Laurence she killed, but I, I am alive." It is this period in Paris which, as he says in *Louis Lambert*, was to "close this portentous childhood and unappreciated youth." This letter, he says, "betrays the struggle of Louis' soul at the time when youth was ending and the terrible power of production was coming into being." And, as though to close the poignant cry of distress which is still fresh in his memory, he concludes: "Are there not some lofty souls who endeavor to concentrate their powers by long silence, so as to emerge fully capable of governing the world by word or by deed?"

* *"Le Mysticisme Français du 18ᵉ Siècle"*—Adolphe Franck.

The spectacle of "Parisian civilization" which presented itself to Louis Lambert's eyes is the picture of a world in decay. The death and disintegration which Balzac sensed over a century ago has now seemingly reached its maximum. Today every great world-city stinks to high heaven, and it is from this death of the world that the artist is obliged to draw his inspiration. I give the gist of Louis' lamentation in telegraphic style. . . .

"I find no one here who likes what I like . . . or is amazed at what amazes me. Thrown back on myself, I eat my heart out in misery. . . . Here, money is the mainspring of everything, even for going without money. . . . I am not frightened at poverty. If it were not that beggars are imprisoned, branded, scorned, I would beg, to enable me to solve at my leisure the problems that haunt me. . . . Everything here checks the flight of a spirit that strives towards the future. I should not be afraid of myself in a desert cave; I am afraid of myself here. . . . Here man has a thousand wants which drag him down. You go out walking, absorbed in dreams; the voice of the beggar asking an alms brings you back to this world of hunger and thirst. You need money only to take a walk. . . . Your organs of sense, perpetually wearied by trifles, never get any rest. The poet's sensitive nerves are perpetually shocked, and what ought to be his glory becomes his torment; his imagination is his cruellest enemy . . . Even vice and crime here find a refuge and charity, but the world is merciless to the inventor, to the man who thinks. Here everything must show an immediate and practical result. . . . The State might pay talent as it pays the bayonet; but it is afraid of being taken in by mere cleverness, as if genius could be counterfeited for any length of time. . . . At the Museum a professor argues to prove that another in the Rue St. Jacques talks nonsense. . . . A professor of philosophy may make a name by explaining how Plato is Platonic. . . . Professors are appointed to produce simpletons—how else can we account for a scheme devoid of method or any notion of the future? . . . This vagueness and uncertainty prevails in politics as well as in science. . . . Politics, at the present time, place human forces in antagonism to neutralize each other, instead of combining them to promote their action to some definite end. . . . I see no fixed purpose in politics; its constant agitation has led to no progress. . . . The arts, which are the direct outcome of the individual, the products of genius or of handicraft, have not advanced much. . . . Man is still the same: might is still his only law, and success his only wisdom. . . . No political theory has ever lasted. Governments pass away, as men do, without handing down any lesson, and no system gives birth to a system better than that which preceded it. . . . Means are lacking both for attack and for resistance. If we should be invaded, the people must be crushed; it has lost its mainspring —its leaders. The man who should foresee two centuries ahead would die on the place of execution. . . ."

And now let us contrast these bitter reflections on the state of France in the early 19th century with another picture of decay and corruption such as it presented itself to the eyes of a man in the so-called New World. The citation is from Walt Whitman's *Democratic Vistas* (1870), written shortly after the victory of the North in the Civil War. . . .

"Never was there, perhaps, more hollowness at heart than at present, and here in the United States. Genuine belief seems to have left us. The underlying principles of the United States are not honestly believed in . . . nor is humanity itself believed in. . . . The spectacle is appalling. We live in an atmosphere of hypocrisy throughout. . . . The depravity of the business classes of our country is not less than has been supposed, but infinitely greater. The official services of America, national, state and municipal, in all their branches and departments, except the judiciary, are saturated in corruption, bribery, falsehood, mal-administration; and the judiciary is tainted. The great cities reek with respectable as much as non-respectable robbery and scoundrelism. . . . The magician's serpent in the fable ate up all the other serpents; and money-making is our magician's serpent, remaining today sole master of the field. . . . I say that our New World democracy, however great a success in uplifting the masses out of their sloughs, in materialistic development, products, and in a certain highly-deceptive superficial popular intellectuality, is, so far, an almost complete failure in its social aspects, and in really grand religious, moral, literary and aesthetic results. . . . In vain have we annexed Texas, California, Alaska, and reach north for Canada and south for Cuba. It is as if we were somehow being endowed with a vast and more and more thoroughly appointed body, and then left with little or no soul. . . . Coming down to what is of the only real importance, Personalities, and examining minutely, we question, we ask, Are there, indeed, men here worthy the name? . . . Are there arts worthy of freedom and a rich people? Is there a grand moral and religious civilization—the only justification of a great material one? Confess that to severe eyes, using the moral microscope upon humanity, a sort of dry and flat Sahara appears, these cities, crowded with petty grotesques, malformations, phantoms, playing meaningless antics. Confess that everywhere, in shop, street, church, theatre, bar room, official chair, are pervading flippancy and vulgarity, low cunning, infidelity—everywhere the youth puny, impudent, foppish, prematurely ripe—everywhere an abnormal libidinousness, unhealthy forms, male, female, painted, padded, dyed, chignoned, muddy complexions, bad blood, the capacity for good motherhood decreasing or deceased, shallow notions of

242

beauty, with a range of manners, or rather lack of manners (considering the advantages enjoyed), probably the meanest to be seen in the world."

Here are two diagnoses of modern society by men of vision and integrity. Both of them were vilified by the critics of the day; both of them waged an unholy struggle for recognition, Whitman even going so far as to peddle his book from door to door. Since their day the struggle of the creative individual has become increasingly difficult: it is a deadlock, between the man of genius and the mob. Practically all the governments of the world, since their time, have fallen; manners have not improved, nor art either, and as for faith and religiousness, it is even more absent than ever.

"Sooner or later," says Whitman, "we come down to one single, solitary soul. . . . In the future of these States must arise poets immenser far, *and make great poems of death*. The poems of life are great, but there must be the poems of the purport of life, not only in itself, but beyond itself. . . . Surely this universal ennui, this coward fear, this shuddering at death, these low, degrading views, are not always to rule the spirit pervading future society, as it has the past, and does the present. . . ." (Italics mine.)

And what is Balzac's conclusion, as we receive it through the utterances of Louis Lambert? After asking himself why he had come to Paris, why he was given such vast faculties without being permitted to use them, asking what meaning to give his sufferings if he is to suffer unknown, he says: "Just as that blossom vainly sheds its fragrance to the solitude, so do I, here in a garret, give birth to ideas that no one can grasp. . . . My point is to ascertain the real relation that may exist between God and man. Is not this a need of the age? . . . If man is bound up with everything, is there not something above him with which he again is bound up? If he is the end-all of the unexplained transmutations that lead up to him, must he not be also the link between the visible and invisible creations? The activity of the universe is not absurd; it must tend to an end, and that end is surely not a social body constituted as ours is! . . . It seems to me that we are on the eve of a great human struggle; the forces are there, only I do not see the General. . . . I feel in myself a life so luminous that it might enlighten a world, and yet I am shut up in a sort of mineral. . . . I should need to embrace the whole world, to clasp and recreate it; but those who have done this, who have embraced and remoulded it, began—did they not?—by being a wheel in the machine. *I can only be crushed.*" (Italics mine.)

The core of Louis Lambert's philosophy may be said to be the idea of unity in duality. Balzac's whole life and work, as Curtius well says, represent a veritable "search for the absolute." The sustained antagonism in the very heart and core of life is the key-note; it is the same passionate quest, the same struggle to wrest from life the secret of creation, which influenced D. H. Lawrence in writing *The Crown.* "For Balzac," to quote Curtius again, "unity is a mystic principle, the mark, the seal of the Absolute." In the book called *The Search for the Absolute* this secret of the philosopher's stone is discovered by the hero only when he is dying.

Louis Lambert's views may be briefly summarized thus. . . . All life reflects the antagonism between inner and outer, will and thought, spirit and feeling. Man is a dual being, expressing the rhythm of the universe in action and reaction. At the basis of all life is one etheric substance, manifestation of a primal energy, assuming infinite forms of manifestation and evidencing itself to our senses as matter. In man this primordial substance is transformed into psychic energy, or will. The special attribute of this will is thought, whose organs are the five senses which, in reality, are but differentiations of one sense, *vision.* Vision expresses itself through

244

the mysterious phenomenon of the Word. Everything in the universe is indicative of an hierarchical order. Over and above the three realms of nature is the world of ideas. Ideas are living creatures, active and activating, like flowers. This world of ideas may be divided into three spheres: instinct, abstraction and specialism. The majority of men are prisoners of instinct; a small number attain to the level of abstraction, with the emergence of which society may be said to begin. It is from this level that laws, the arts and all social creations emerge. Specialism is the gift of intuition which permits man to see the inner as well as the outer in all its ramifications. (The perfection of the inner eye gives rise to the gift of Specialism.) The human genius is a type functioning in a realm between abstraction and intuition. Intuition, consequently, is the most satisfactory and adequate form, the highest form of knowing. To know is to see. There is at bottom only one science, and all the imperfect forms of knowledge are nothing but a confused vision! This "superior science," which Louis Lambert proclaims, is what Balzac styles *"le magisme,"* a term not to be confused with magic or Magianism. (Already, in 1847, Balzac was dreaming of the establishment by the Sorbonne of a new school of "occult philosophy," under the name of Anthropology. This dream was subsequently to be realized, under the name of Anthroposophy, by Rudolf Steiner.)

In the fragments of Louis Lambert's "system," recorded by his faithful companion, Mademoiselle de Villenoix, which come as a sort of appendix to the story, these ideas are put down in the form of aphoristic notes. In apologizing for the cryptic, fragmentary quality of these speculations, Balzac says: "I ought perhaps to have made a separate book of these fragments of thought, intelligible only to certain spirits who have been accustomed to lean over the edge of abysses in the hope of seeing to the bottom. The life of that mighty brain, which split up on every side, like a too vast empire, would have been set forth in the narrative of this man s visions—a being incomplete for lack of force or of weakness; but I preferred to give an account of my own impressions rather than to compose a more or less poetical romance." As a matter of fact, earlier in the book, Balzac gives us the clue to the terminology employed in the Aphorisms. "New ideas," he says, "require new words, or a new and expanded use of old words, extended and defined in their meaning." Thus Lambert, to set forth the basis of his system, had adopted certain common words that answered to his notions. The word *Will* he used to connote the medium in which the mind moves, or to use a less abstract expression, the mass of power by which man can reproduce, outside himself, the actions constituting his external life. *Volition*—a word due to Locke—expressed the act by which a man exerts his will. The word *Mind*, or *Thought*, which he regarded as the quintessential product of the Will, also represented the medium in which the ideas originate and to which thought gives substance. The *Idea*, a name common to every creation of the brain, constituted the act by which man uses his mind. Thus the Will and the Mind were two generating forces; the Volition and the Idea were the two products. . . . According to him, the Mind and Ideas are the motion and the outcome of our inner organization, just as the Will and Volition are of our external activity. He gave the Will precedence over the Mind. *You must will before you can think, he said.*

To Louis Lambert, *Will* and *Thought* were living forces, as Balzac says. "The elements of Will and Mind," says Louis Lambert, "may perhaps be found; but there will always remain beyond apprehension the x against which I once used to struggle. That x is the Word, the Logos. . . . From your bed to the frontiers of the universe there are but two steps: Will and Faith. . . . Facts are nothing; they do not subsist; all that lives of us is the Idea." He points out that Jesus possessed the gift of Specialism. "He saw each fact in its root and in its results, in the past whence it had its rise, and in the future where it would grow and spread. . . ."

According to Balzac, Louis Lambert had too much good sense to dwell among the clouds of theories. "He had sought for proofs of his theories in the history of great men, whose lives, as set forth by their biographers, supply very curious particulars as to the operation of the understanding." The description of Louis which he gives at the time of their parting is altogether that of a man preparing to lead the life of an initiate. "He ate little and drank water only; either by instinct or by choice he was averse to any exertion that made a demand on his strength; his movements were few and simple, like those of Orientals or of savages, with whom gravity seems a condition of nature. Though naturally religious, Louis did not accept the minute practices of the Roman ritual; his ideas were more intimately in sympathy with Saint Theresa and Fénelon, and several Fathers and certain Saints who, in our day, would be regarded as heresiarchs or atheists. . . . To him Jesus Christ was the most perfect type of his system. *Et Verbum caro factum est* seemed a sublime statement intended to express the traditional formula of the Will, the Word and the Act made visible. Christ's consciousness of His Death—having so perfected His inner Being by divine works, that one day the invisible form of it appeared to His disciples—and the other Mysteries of the Gospels, the magnetic cures wrought by Christ, and the gift of tongues, all to him confirmed his doctrine. . . . He discerned the strongest evidence of his theory in most of the martyrdoms endured during the first century of our era, which he spoke of as the great era of the *Mind*."

There is one more passage, in this connection, which seems to me worthy of attention. After referring to Louis Lambert's study of the laws of Mind and Will, and their correlations, Balzac says:

"Louis Lambert had accounted for a multitude of phenomena which, till then, had been regarded with reason as incomprehensible. Thus wizards, men possessed, those gifted with second sight, and demoniacs of every degree—the victims of the Middle Ages—became the subject of explanations so natural, that their very simplicity often seemed to me the seal of their truth. The marvellous gifts which the Church of Rome, jealous of all mysteries, punished with the stake, were, in Louis' opinion, the result of certain affinities between the constituent elements of matter and those of mind, which proceed from the same source."

The triumph of energy, will and faith in man, the existence of magic and the evidences of the miraculous, the relation of God to man through Desire, the notion of hierarchies in every realm of life, as well as the belief in transmutation, all these manifestations of the spiritual attributes of man, Balzac has summed up in the story of his own life, or rather of the most important years of his life, the period of germination. The period, in other words, when *the terrible powers of production were coming into being.*

In the Rue Cassini, where he wrote so many of his great works, Balzac is reported to have said to George Sand: "Literature! but my dear lady, literature doesn't exist! There is life, of which politics and art are part. I am a man who's alive, that's all . . . a man living his life, nothing more." Whereupon he proceeded to forfeit his life through the bondage of work. He wanted to be great ("man must be great or not be at all," are his words), and he was great, but he died a failure. Perhaps the best justification of his failure is the one he makes himself somewhere. "The man of genius," he said, "is one who can invariably convert his thoughts into deeds. But the truly outstanding genius does not unremittingly allow this evolution to take place; if he did, he would be the equal of God."

At the best, it is a poor excuse. Balzac, like Beethoven, seemingly gave the maximum that a man can give, but it was not enough, not for a Balzac! I am not thinking of the forty books he is said to have left unfinished at his death, but of the life he left unlived, of the vision he failed to live by. His life, which is the very symbol of Work, epitomizes the futility of Western life, with its emphasis on doing rather than being; it epitomizes the sterility of even the highest efforts when characterized, as they are in our world, by the divorce between action and belief.

If Louis Lambert's life may be regarded as a typical example of the crucifixion of genius by the society in which he was born, Balzac's own life may be regarded as a typical example of the immolation exacted of our superior types through a limited conception of, and a slavish devotion to, art. The criticism of the social structure which Balzac makes, not only in this book but in all his books, is absolutely just. But it is only half the picture. There is a duty which devolves upon every individual, regardless of the state of society into which he is born. Art is only the stepping-stone to another, larger way of life. If the artist himself is not converted by the Word, what hope can there be for the masses who read him? It is not enough to lead the life of an inspired drudge; will and faith, activated by desire, should carry a man beyond such a mode of life. I have no respect for Balzac's herculean labors, nor for his colossal output, nor for his genius, when I realize that his life sputtered out ingloriously. If a man cannot find salvation in himself all his words are futile. The real Balzac died in the mythical person of Louis Lambert whose very name he tells us he disliked.

If the foregoing seems like a contradiction to all that I have written hitherto in this essay I am willing to let it remain a contradiction, for it is this contradiction which must be resolved, and especially by the artist. I cannot conclude without expressing my deep appreciation of Ernst-Robert Curtius' book, *Balzac*, from

249

which I have liberally drawn both inspiration and material. This book, which is the most penetrating and comprehensive study of Balzac that I know of, has not enjoyed a great success in France. As in Balzac's own day, it seems probable that his greatest admirers continue to be foreigners. The canonization and immortalization of the dead, which seems to be the chief characteristic of French culture, has not, despite all the museum work, succeeded in revealing the full measure of Balzac's genius. The qualities of his mind which were most important the French still pretend to ignore, if not to deprecate and depreciate. The dead are still more honored than the living, and even the dead sometimes fail to receive their due. Nothing is changed since Louis Lambert's day. Perhaps no other people in the world, occupying the high cultural position which the French do, have mistreated and ignored their men of genius so persistently—unless it be the Greeks whom the French pretend to emulate. The mummification of ideas goes on as before, the forward spirits are crushed, the people, when they have a leader, are delivered over to death. Realism has taken the place of reality, and the true leaders are only discovered after their death.